Down Trodden Maryland.

THIRD EDITION REVISED.

1.

Down-trodden, despised see brave Maryland lie,
  The noblest of all States;
Up and to ransom her let each one try,
  To hasten the plans of the Fates.
Her land is of the greatest beauty
  That e'er the eye gazed on;
Fearless she roused her to her duty,
  Nor paused she 'till 'twas done.

2.

Her press is bound with iron chains,
  For truth no loop-hole left,
In God her only hope remains,
  Or she's of all bereft!
Shackled are bravest and her best,
  Who lifting for the free,
Or now they in a dungeon rest,
  Refusing to bend the knee.

3.

From Her, the Old Line has departed
  Wise leaders true and brave,
She . . . of the . . . hearted
  Why should she be a slave?
She . . . long with moaning deep,
  . . . .
. . . . leap,
. . . .

4.

You owe her now a mighty debt,
  An awful debt and great;
She's looking anxious for you yet,
  Her righteous rage to sate.
You must not keep her waiting long
  With wrongs that cry to heaven,
But come with your own mighty throng,
  Let all her bonds be riven.

5.

She's borne their foul oppression
  Yet has not recreant proved,
Though their myriads took possession
  Of the land the Old Line loved;
She's waited sad in hoping still,
  She would but cannot dare,
However much she loves the will
  To seize the despot's lair.

6.

But yet she hopes for better things,
  When Gideon's . . . commands,
That . . . . brave . . .
  With peace to our southern lands,
And when the South is free once more
  'Twill be her proud . . .
That South she . . . her men did pour
  To crush the invading host.

The South — Washington City. N. G. R.

Baltimore, March 4, 1862.

Our Left.

DEDICATED TO THE

Maryland Hero, Gen. Arnold Elzey, C. S. A.

From dawn to dark they stood,
  That long midsummer's day;
    While fierce, and fast,
    The battle's blast,
  Swept rank and rank away!

From dawn to dark they fought,
  With legions swept and cleft;
    While black and wide,
    The battle's tide,
  Passed ever on "Our Left."

They closed each ghastly gap,
  They dressed each shattered rank;
    They knew how well,
    That Freedom fell,
  With that exhausted flank!

"Oh! for a thousand men,
  Like those who melt away!"
    And down they came,
    With steel and flame,
  Four thousand to the fray!

They left the laggard train,
  The panting steam might say;
    And down they came,
    With steel and flame,
  Head-foremost to the fray!

Right through the blackest cloud,
  Their lightning path they cleft;
    Freedom and Fame,
    With Triumph came,
  To "Our immortal Left!"

Ye of your living sure,
  Ye of your dead bereft;
    Honor the brave,
    Who died to save,
  Your all upon "Our Left!"

"Ole Secesh."

Baltimore, Oct. 20, 1861.

We'll be free in Maryland

AIR — "GIDEON'S BAND."

Composed by Robert E. Holtz, Jan. 30, 1862.

The boys down South in Dixie's land,
The boys down South in Dixie's land,
The boys down South in Dixie's land
Will come and rescue Maryland.

Chorus: If you will join the Dixie band,
Here's my heart and here's my hand,
If you will join the Dixie band,
We're fighting for a home.

The Northern foe have tied us down,
The Northern foe have tied us down,
The Northern foe have tied us down,
But we will rise with true renown.

Chorus: If you will join the Dixie band, &c.

The tyrants they sought to enslave,
The tyrants they must bow'r . . .
The . . . tyrant . . .
From . . . to . . . in Baltimore.

Chorus: If you will join the Dixie band, &c.

These Northmen they no more stand,
These Northmen they'll no more stand,
These . . . stand,
Where'er they . . . the Southern land.

Chorus: If you will join the Dixie band, &c.

Old Abe has got into a trap,
Old Abe has got into a trap,
Old Abe has got into a trap,
And . . . .

Chorus: . . . Dixie band, &c.

. . . . . .
. . . . . .
. . . . . .
. . . .

Chorus: . . . Dixie band, &c.

. . . . . .
. . . . . .
. . . . . .
. . . .

UNITED WE STAND!

SPIRIT OF '76.

The Debt of Maryland.

Remember,—men of Maryland,
  You have a debt to pay,
A debt which years of patience
  Will never wear away;
Which must be paid, at last,—although
  Our dearest blood it cost—
A debt which *shall* be paid unto
  The very uttermost.

We owe for confidence betrayed,
  By those we trusted best;
The sword we gave them, to defend,
  They turned against our breast!
For spies that noted down our words,
  The while they shared our bread,
For *hounds* that even dared disturb,
  The quiet of the dead!

We owe for all the love they lied,
  The wolfish hate they showed,
For all these glittering bayonets
  That meet us on the road;
For black suspicion, deadlier far
  Than flash of Northern swords,
For treason threatened at our hearths,
  And poison at our boards.

For many a deed of darkness done
  Beneath their "Stripes and Stars,"
For women outraged in their homes,
  And fired on in the cars;
For those black tiers of cannon trained,
  To bear on Baltimore—
We owe for friends in prison kept,
  And Davis in his gore!

Wrongs such as these,—aye,—more than these,
  Make up our fearful debt,
And many a gallant heart has sworn,
  It shall be settled yet!
Each moment near and nearer brings
  That solemn reckoning day;
And when it comes—*as come it must*
  Remember—and repay!

A BAND OF BROTHERS

Photographic Epilogue
to
Marylanders in the Confederacy

by
Daniel D. Hartzler

HERITAGE BOOKS
2008

HERITAGE BOOKS
AN IMPRINT OF HERITAGE BOOKS, INC.

Books, CDs, and more—Worldwide

For our listing of thousands of titles see our website
at
www.HeritageBooks.com

Published 2008 by
HERITAGE BOOKS, INC.
Publishing Division
100 Railroad Ave. #104
Westminster, Maryland 21157

Copyright © 1992 Daniel D. Hartzler

Other books by the author:
Carroll County, Maryland Baseball: Men's Amateur and Semi-Pro Baseball, 1850-1999
Marylanders in the Confederacy
Medical Doctors of Maryland in the C.S.A.

All rights reserved. No part of this book may be reproduced or transmitted in any form or by any means, electronic or mechanical, including photocopying, recording or by any information storage and retrieval system without written permission from the author, except for the inclusion of brief quotations in a review.

International Standard Book Numbers
Paperbound: 978-0-7884-3151-7
Clothbound: 978-0-7884-7349-4

Dedication

This volume of *A Band Of Brothers* is dedicated to

GEORGE B. CROUSE

one who shares the same vaules, principles and interests.
If one could choose, I would like to call him brother.

Table of Contents

Chapter		Page
	PREFACE	vii
	FORWARD	xi
1	PHOTOGRAPHY	1
2	SENIOR GRADE AND FLAG RANKED OFFICERS	9
3	MILITIA	13
4	ARTILLERY	35
5	CAVALRY	43
6	INFANTRY	67
7	NAVY	85
8	MARINES	93
9	PHYSICIANS	97
10	CLERGY	103
11	FLAGS	109
12	UNIFORMS	135
13	WEAPONS	171
14	ACCOUTREMENTS	195
15	DEVASTATIONS OF WAR	217
16	VETERANS	221
	INDEX	227

PREFACE

A *Band of Brothers* is a supplement to *Marylanders in the Confederacy* through the eyes of the camera. For the complete story of Maryland's true sons who served the Southland, these two volumes should be referred to simultaneously.

The uncivil war for some in the Baltimore and Frederick militia companies the hostilities began when they went to Harpers Ferry to put down the John Brown insurrection. There were some Maryland volunteers and more than 500 enlisted men known as the Baltimore Secessionists in Charleston Harbor when the first blow was struck. It was, however, on the streets of Baltimore on April 19, 1861, that the first Federal blood was drawn and the first Southerners killed were Marylanders. Every Maryland boy had many thrilling stories from adventures in running the blockade to achievements in battle. This volume attempts to shed some light on some of these exciting tales, as they reached the edge of glory, by using brief biographies.

Those who remained loyal were not a happy lot; division was present in many Union families. General William Hickey, who was secretary of the U.S. Senate, had two sons, Edmond P. and John F., who opposed him in Confederate service. Major General George Vickers, of the Eastern Shore, had a son, Benjamin Clothier Vickers, who was mortally wounded at Shiloh in defense of the South. The grandson of General Edward Shriver of Frederick, Charles S. Shriver, was killed while serving in Mosby's Rangers.

The true patriots, who buckled on the implements of war in defense of the South, were bound together by their interpretation of our forefathers' constitution. Some were slave holders, while others did not believe in slavery but lived in an era of regard for truth and justice and toleration of a difference of opinion. Whether they were raised in the lap of luxury and had all of the wealth and culture that this could provide or were apprentices and sharecroppers, they were tied together by the Federal seizure of their state. These brethren were all volunteers and there was no separation by class. They were linked in their willingness to sacrifice all in the cause for liberty, as they believed it to be. This brotherhood went beyond bloodlines, yet there were many brothers who went to Dixie. Surprisingly, many did not serve in the same command.

The Confederate Marylanders embodied the faith and pride of generations. Men of Maryland descent were scattered over all the Confederacy and scarcely was there a company that did not contain Maryland blood. Bradley T. Johnson, who commanded the Maryland Line, rode at the head of 72 kinsmen, descendants of soldiers in the Revolution, his own flesh and blood. There was not a historic family which was not represented in the Maryland Line. Five grandsons of John Eager Howard of Cowpens carried a musket in the 1st Maryland Infantry. A grandson of Charles Carroll of Carrollton rode as a private in K Company, 1st Virginia Cavalry. Tench Tilghman, whose grandfather of the same name was a personal secretary to General George Washington, was a West Pointer who became a militia major general of the 2nd Division on the Eastern Shore. He was the founder of the Maryland Military Academy in 1849 at Oxford. Three of his four sons, Tench F., John Leeds and Oswald, served in the C.S.A. In May of 1861 Stanley Byers and his sons, William, Robert, Charles and Stanley, left Cambridge to join the Confederacy. The Valliant family of Talbot County was composed of three girls and five boys. Edwin S., William, Thomas and George all became soldiers, but the youngest was not old enough. The Griffith brothers of Edgehill, near Olney, went South and Thomas II, David and Frank rode in Company A, 1st Maryland Cavalry, while Festus served in the 8th Virginia Infantry, Company F. There were six Gilmor brothers. The eldest, Robert III, and the youngest, Arthur, were held in a Federal prison while Howard, Meredith and Richard served under their brother, Harry, in the 2nd Maryland Cavalry.

Even in predominantly Union areas there were brothers who stayed united in the Confederate Army. On the Mason-Dixon Line from Emmitsburg were the three Cretin brothers,

Andrew, Hillary and John T., who all served in Company G, 2nd Maryland Infantry, while brothers Alfred and Joseph Riddlemoser served in Company H. In the 2nd Maryland Artillery were twins Daniel and David Hammett from St. Mary's County. Joseph L. and Richard C. Wagner of Libertytown were both wounded and captured on Culp's Hill at Gettysburg. Joseph was wounded in the abdomen and his brother succumbed to his chest wounds. The two sons of Captain George Kephart of Carrollton Manor became fatalities. Charles was killed at Bull Run and George A. at Chancellorsville. Joseph and James Henry Thomas, from Frederick County, were members of Company C, 18th Louisiana Infantry. Both were killed at Shiloh.

Let's take a look at the amazing statistics from two companies that indicate the often high numbers of brothers serving together. Company D, 1st Maryland Cavalry was organized at Winchester on November 25, 1862, and was composed of Carroll and Frederick Countians.

Libertytown:	Captain Warner G. Welsh
	2nd Lt. Milton Welsh
	Pvt. Luther Welsh
Libertytown:	Pvt. Charles H. Geasey
	Pvt. James W. Geasey
Westminster:	Pvt. Francis W. Neal
	Pvt. Harry S. Neal
Frederick:	Pvt. John M. Delashmutt
	Pvt. William G. Delashmutt
Frederick:	Pvt. George Tyler
	Pvt. John E. Tyler
	Pvt. Samuel Albert Tyler
New Market:	Pvt. Denton Hammond
	Pvt. Oliver B. Hammond
New Market:	Pvt. Henry Hall Bromwell
	Pvt. Josiah R. Bromwell
	Pvt. Thomas C.S. Bromwell
Unionville:	Pvt. Aubrey Pearre
	Pvt. Oliver Hazzard Pearre

Company B, 35th Virginia Calvary, was organized in June of 1862 in Montgomery County, while the state was under Federal martial law. Composed of Frederick and Montgomery Countians, they rode as a unit to Frederick on September 10 where they joined Colonel E.V. White.

Adamstown:	Pvt. Frederick N. Crown
	Pvt. John R. Crown
	Lt. Joshua R. Crown
Buck Lodge:	Pvt. Lee M. Dade
	Cpl. Robert L. Dade
Darnestown:	Pvt. George W. Dove
	Pvt. Joseph Dove
Carrollton Manor:	Pvt. Thomas Hardwood
	Pvt. William Hardwood

Carrollton Manor:	Pvt. Joseph H. Trundle
	Pvt. Samuel Trundle
Old Medleys:	Pvt. Charles Martin Butler Jr.
	Pvt. George William Butler
Old Medleys:	Pvt. Benjamin Franklin Pyles
	Pvt. M. Thomas Pyles
Old Medleys:	Sgt. Samuel C. White
	Pvt. Thomas Henry White
Old Medleys:	Pvt. Elijah Viers
	Pvt. Henry Bollingbroke Viers
	Pvt. William Seneca Viers
Monocacy:	Sgt. Charles E. Scholl
	Pvt. John H. Scholl
Park Mills:	Pvt. Charles Williams Eader
	Lewis A. Eader
Poolesville:	Pvt. Charles W. Matthews
	Pvt. James Monroe Matthews
Poolesville:	Pvt. Charles W. Smith
	Pvt. Jesse Rice Smith
Point of Rocks:	Pvt. Edmond Thomas
	Pvt. Jacob N. Thomas
	Pvt. Levin Thomas

A Band of Brothers is not the sole work of the author but a gathering of pictures shared by fellow brethren. A special thanks to **Les Jensen** for opening doors; to **Howie Madaus** for providing direction; to **Bryce Workman** for being my sounding board; to **Ross Kimmel** for laying the ground work; to **Fred Schroyer** for critiquing; to **Jack Dissinger** for layout; to the **Baltimore Ladies of the U.D.C.** and the **Maryland Historical Society** for providing many resources. The following are just a few to whom I am indebted:

Chris Allen
John R. Bangs
Hugh Benet Jr.
Nancy M. Bramucci
Sandra H. Brothers
William L. Brown III
Ronald Byrnes
Earl Catlett
Roger Catlett
Tom Clemens
Janet R. Colburn
Erick Davis

Paul M. Dean
Frederick S. De Main
Jack R. Dissinger
Ralph W. Donnelly
Diane Evans
Butch Fravel
Frederick C. Gaede
Jennifer F. Goldsborough
Thomas S. Gordon Jr.
Jay Graybeal
Richard Grim
Stan Grim

Catharine O. Hartzler	Carroll County Historical Society
Margaret G. Hering	
Leslie D. Jensen	Confederate Memorial Hall
Hugh C. Keen	
Lon W. Keim	Harry W. Gilmor Camp Sons of
Ross J. Kelbaugh	Confederate Veterans #1388
Ross M. Kimmel	
H. Micheal Madaus	Maryland Division United Daughters
Dave Mark	of the Confederacy
Karen Miles	
Michael Musick	Maryland Historical Society Museum
Cy Nelson	and Library of Maryland History
R. J. Rockefeller	
Frederick Schroyer	Maryland State Archives Hall of Records
Timothy L. Shipley	
Clyde Smith	Museum of the Confederacy
Fonda G. Thompsen	
Mary Ringgold Trippe	Smithsonian Institution
Raymond W. Watkins	
Warner G. Welsh	Textile Preservation Association, Inc.
R. Bryce Workman	
Malinda Wyatt	Virginia Historical Society

FOREWORD

During the Southern States war for their independence, Maryland found itself in a unique position. Although culturally more aligned to the South, she found herself coerced into remaining in the Union. With its capital on Maryland's southern border, the Federal Government could ill afford to allow the state even a resemblance of separation. Even though the majority of the state's populace were sympathetic to the Southern cause, most could not bring themselves to rend asunder the Union they had been born under and defended through many wars. However, those Marylanders that did follow the dictates of their conscience and "went South" were among the best and bravest the Confederacy had to offer.

Many of these Marylanders made a name for themselves fighting for Southern independence. They came from well-known families whose names are familiar to every Civil War scholar, like Richard Snowden Andrews, Bradley T. Johnson, Harry Gilmor, Arnold Elzey, George H. Steuart Jr., William Worthington Goldsborough and James R. Herbert, to name a few.

But for every one of these, there were many more unknown, faceless, but thankfully not nameless, individuals whose ideals were no less lofty. In some cases there was brother against brother, father against son, cousin against cousin, each defending what he believed to be right. Many of these brave men would inherit only an unknown grave in a land far distant from their beloved home.

The written word is the voice of the past, but photographs give this voice dimension. *A Band of Brothers* adds just this dimension and is the perfect compliment to the author's previous book on this subject, *Marylanders in the Confederacy*. These volumes are a must for any student on Maryland's role in the Civil War, especially those studying its contribution to the Confederacy.

R. Bryce Workman

New Windsor, Maryland

Chapter 1

PHOTOGRAPHY

In the past, military images were recorded by an artist through drawings or paintings, the standard procedure of the time for depicting a portrait. For publication there were line engravings, an arranging of a pattern of dots and lines that created tones on a metal plate that produced a picture when pressed upon ink. By 1860 photographic galleries had spread across America, the French process of reproducing an image had been in existence just 22 years when the War Between the States would solidly establish this new business. Many young rural lads in their new uniforms with bright, shiny buttons and buckles were elaborately clad as they had never been before. By sitting for the photographer they could easily impress the homefolks and loved ones who were anxious for a likeness of the patriots defending their country's liberties. The figures produced by the lens would capture the moment and is one of the reasons this period of our history is so exciting. Even those who had too much pride to sit before the camera realized that in answering the call to arms a visual image might be a lasting memory for their families, especially if they fell in battle. T. Douglas Mercer, on February 16, 1863, wrote his mother, thanking her for sending a package. "The likeness Doc brought over was splendid. I have supplied the two blank spaces in my album with a picture of you and one of Mary. Mary's is the most beautiful picture I ever saw. I should like very much to get a large collection including the whole family to carry with me. If I go to Richmond I will have another likeness taken and send home."

OIL PAINTING of John W. Albaugh (/1864) - He was born in Howard County and reared in Frederick County. He joined his brother, Ira H. Albaugh, in Company K, 1st Virginia Cavalry as a private, and was killed shortly thereafter at Bunker Hill on August 13, 1864. His body was wrapped in a blanket, covered with a flag and returned to his family for burial.

CASED PHOTO PAINTED OVER WITH WATER COLORS of Ira H. Albaugh (1839/   ) He left his Frederick County home and enlisted on May 14, 1861, in Company M, 1st Virginia Cavalry. He rode with the Maryland troops, and soon after the company designation became K, rose to 3rd sergeant. Captured at Gettysburg on July 3, 1863, he was imprisoned for 14 months before being exchanged. Albaugh returned to his company, which had been reassigned to the 1st Maryland Cavalry, and was paroled on April 23, 1865, at Martinsburg, West Virginia.

2 - Photography

ENGRAVING of Osmun Latrobe - Latrobe was reared in Baltimore and educated at St. James College. Abandoning his civil pursuit in September of 1861, he made his way through the Federal lines. Osmun was a volunteer aide on the staff of General D.R. Jones. Soon he was made an aide-de-camp, and after the Antietam Campaign, was assigned as assisant inspector general on the staff of James Longstreet. Going to the Army of the West with his commander in the summer of 1864, he was promoted to lieutenant colonel and became chief of staff. Because of wounds received during the Wilderness Campaign, he was disabled for six weeks. He was unable to participate in the fighting at Spotsylvania and Cold Harbor, but did participate in all the other action seen by his commander. He remained with the Army of Northern Virginia and surrendered with them on April 9, 1865. Mourning the loss of the cause, Osmun went to Europe and remained abroad for 15 years before returning to Baltimore. He was a member of the Franklin Buchanan and Isaac R. Trimble United Confederate Veterans Camps.

DAGUERREOTYPE of John Calhoun Clemson (1841/) - After leaving his home at Bladensburg, he enlisted in the 1st Battalion, South Carolina Artillery, Company H. He was appointed a 2nd lieutenant on January 24, 1862, to rank from December 16, 1861. The unit designation was changed to the 1st South Carolina Artillery. On May 27, 1863, he resigned to accept a position in the Nitre and Mining Bureau. As a 1st lieutenant Clemson saw service with the Army of the West, was captured at Boliver, Mississippi, on September 9, 1863, and was sent to Johnson's Island. After the war, prisoners were released according to their rank and he received his on June 11, 1865, after taking the oath of allegiance.

The first photographs were produced by fixing an image upon a light sensitive metal plate with a polished silver surface and were known as daguerreotypes. In 1854 the ambrotype was developed by an American and reduced exposure time and cost. The ambrotype produced a negative on glass which, when backed with a dark substance, gave the appearance of a positive image. Two years later, also invented in this country, was the process of japaning, which used a metal surface instead of glass. Using the readily available substance of tin made an even less costly process which produced an image called a tintype. Just prior to the war, images were also printed on paper. The most popular was a small card called a cartes de viste, or visiting card. Larger images on heavier cardboard would become most popular just after the war and often contained war-period images. An albumin photograph is a contact print produced from a negative on albumanized paper that could be made any size. Further enlargement was done on thin paper and was termed a paper enlargement.

Many studios employed a colorist to hand color glass for any type of photograph. Some are well done by fine artists in watercolors or pastels. Many times they highlighted the cheeks, buttons and braids but the entire uniform was sometimes hand colored.

AMBROTYPE of Emory Fiske Best (1840/1912) - by Bendann Brothers in October of 1862 while a prisoner of war in Baltimore. Born the son of a Methodist clergyman in Bladensburg, he moved to Georgia in 1858 and was one of three brothers to serve in the C.S.A. While practicing law in Rome, he helped organize the 23rd Georgia Infantry and was elected major. The unit was sent to the Army of Northern Virginia and, on August 16, 1862, he became lieutenant colonel. After the Battle of Antietam Best was captured, and was paroled on October 2, 1862, being exchanged for a Federal officer of equal rank. After his release, he returned to his regiment and in early May of 1863 participated in the Confederate victory at Chancellorsville. His conduct during the battle was questioned due to his command being surrounded and captured at the railway cut, after its left flank gave way. Lt. Col. Best contended the orders from General James J. Archer to fall back arrived too late. He was court martialed and cashiered on December 23, 1863. After the war he made his home in Baltimore and was an attorney for the Interior Department in Washington.

NUMBERED AMBROTYPE BY REES STUDIO. It was made by Charles R. Rees, Richmond, Virginia, from a negative which is numbered in the righthand corner as 2189. Assistant Surgeons Richard Emory (right) (1839/1895) from Taylor in Baltimore County, and Bodisco Williams (left), of Washington, D.C., were photographed in 1863 while they served together in Winder Hospital at Richmond. They appear in regulation medical corps physician attire.

4 - Photography

TINTYPE of Samuel Woodward Anderson (left) (1839/1863) and Richard T. Anderson (right) (1842/   ) - These brothers left their father's farm in Prince George's County and enlisted on August 30, 1862, in Company C of the 2nd Maryland Infantry. Both enlisted for three years or the war, and were later ill with chronic dysentery at Strasburg when captured on December 21. They were exchanged the same day and paroled. On Culp's Hill at Gettysburg, Samuel was wounded in the arm and entered Howard Grove Hospital in Richmond on July 20. He again developed chronic dysentery and died on September 17, 1863. Richard continued with the command until August 12, 1864, when, while occupying the trenches, he was wounded in the left leg, breaking both the tibia and fibula. He was sent to the Receiving and Wayside Hospital in Richmond. He August 14 and was paroled on April 24, 1865.

TINTYPE of James C. Kane (left) John K. Kane (rigth)- sons of George Proctor Kane who was the chief of police in Baltimore. Colonel Kane was arrested on June 27, 1861 and held as a political prisoner until the latter part of 1862. He went south becoming the inspector of the Maryland Line and recruited for the 1st. Maryland Cavalry, 2nd. Maryland Cavalry and the 35th. Virginia Cavalry in equal protions. James C., after being in the ranks of the 1st. Maryland Infantry joined his younger brother John K., who had been in Stuart's Horse Artillery, in the 2nd. Maryland Cavalry. Both reenlisted on October 11th., 1864 in Mosby's Rangers. They rode with Company D, 43rd. Virginia Cavalry and James was captured at Charlottesville on March 4, 1865 and sent to Point Lookout. After the war Colonel Kane and his two sons returned to Baltimore.

Some images are marked with the studio, which served as a means of advertisement. Many, however, carry no logo at all and the maker remains unknown. Rees of Richmond numbered their negatives in the emulsion in the lower righthand corner. There is no known criteria for why some images bear the photographers name while others do not. By studying the props and backdrops some photographs can be attributed to a specific maker. Many Confederate photographs did not use backdrops, just a plain wall with less props.

Images were often enclosed in a frame in a leatherette case. These were made by compressing cardboard which bore a design and that was covered by a thin layer of leather or cloth. Gutta percha had been invented by Goodyear, and cases of this material wee produced by pouring the liquid rubber into molds to produce very elaborate case designs. The two Southern pre-war gutta percha cases most desired to enshrine martial photographs bear the likeness of the Washington Monument in Richmond, and Francis Marion, the Swamp Fox. During and after the war images of heroic soldiers were so highly regarded that they were remounted in better cases. Thus, it is obvious that some cases are not the originals.

There are people today who have inscribed spurious names on unknown photographs. The most common means of writing was ink, and it can be detected in many cases. As photo prices have increased, fakery has been done on all forms of photography. Old plates with a modern image can be housed in an original matte or case on paper prints. The real imprint is soaked off and mounting of the impostor on the original card. Individual script signatures of autographs should be closely scrutinized.

Isaac Briggs was an itinerant daguerreotypist who, in 1848, had learned the process from Henry Pollock, perhaps Baltimore's leading pioneer photographer. Briggs worked in numerous towns in Maryland: Union Bridge, New Windsor, Sandy Springs and Rockville. During the war he became a photographer in Virginia.

CARTE DE VISTE of Henry Gordon (/1863) - From Anne Arundel County, he enlisted for the war on November 24, 1861, at Richmond in the 3rd Maryland Artillery. The unit was sent to the Army of the West and Gordon was assigned detached service at Sunflower. During the battle of Jackson, Mississippi, the 3rd Maryland was entrenched west of town on the Vicksburg Road at an angle in the line. On the evening of the second day of battle, July 11, 1863, he was in Ritters section, and was killed during an artillery duel while firing "Black Bess."

CABINET CARD by David J. Wilkes of Baltimore of William H.B. Dorsey (1841/1879) - Born and raised near Mt. Airy, Dorsey enlisted as a private in the Company A, 1st Maryland Infantry, on May 21, 1861, at Harpers Ferry. By September 1, he was appointed sergeant. With his 12-month enlistment expiring, he re-enlisted in the Company D, 1st Maryland Cavalry, on September 20, 1862, and was chosen 1st lieutenant. On May 27, 1864, his bay horse was killed in action at Hanover Courthouse. In the summer of 1864 he came into Maryland and drove a herd of cattle back to Southern lines. That fall he served several months on detached service under General L.L. Lomax. This command was not paroled with Lee's Army of Northern Virginia, but was paroled individually. On September 18, 1865, he signed the oath of allegiance at Frederick and then proceeded to his home. He was soon arrested and conveyed to the Frederick Jail. While a prisoner in jail, he was visited by a young lady who later became his wife.

Daniel and David Bendann were born in Richmond and became photographers in Baltimore. Daniel, at the age of 16, had learned under the employment of Jesse Whitehurst of Richmond. In 1854 Daniel went to Baltimore to run Whitehurst Studio there. After becoming proficient in the art of photography, he returned to Richmond in 1856 and opened his own business. In that same year he and his brother David, whom he had introduced into the business, left Virginia and established themselves in Baltimore. Jesse Whitehurst himself, would eventually become a Baltimore resident. The Bendann brothers became the leading purveyors of photographic art in Baltimore and were known as one of the foremost galleries in all the South. With the onset of hosilities, the Bendanns were quick to take advantage of the public's thirst for images of prominent persons of the day. They

6 - Photography

LEATHER CASED AMBROTYPE of Daniel L. Thomas Jr. (1843/) - He left Baltimore and enlisted for one year as a private at Richmond in C Company, 1st Maryland Infantry. On December 1, 1861, he was sent to the General Hospital No. 18 at Richmond because of an illness. He re-enlisted June 10, 1862, for two years at Richmond, in K Company, 1st Virginia Cavalry. At the termination of this period he enlisted a third time in the 43rd Virginia Cavalry, Company F. He rode as a private with Mosby's Partisan Rangers until being paroled at Winchester, on April 22, 1865. Returning to Baltimore, he was a member of the Society of the Army and Navy of the Confederate States in the State of Maryland, and the John S. Mosby United Confederate Veterans Camp No. 821 of Baltimore.

began publishing a series of carte de visite portraits of southern military and political leaders from negatives they had made in Richmond. David was arrested in 1862 after an altercation with a union naval officer and was incarcerated in Fort McHenry, Fort Lafayette and Fort Hamilton. He was finally released from prison after four months by signing the oath of allegiance. Daniel also got into trouble and was detained by military authorities in 1865 when we was accused of disloyal language and reproducing images of rebel generals.

Cyrus Creedle was born in North Carolina and established himself as a photographer at Easton, on Maryland's eastern shore.

Richard Walzl was a Baltimore photographer who was held in Old Capitol Prison. On January 6, 1862, he wrote William H. Seward "Left Baltimore August 18, 1861, ran the blockade to Richmond taking with me $1000 worth of photographic material. Worked in Richmond for several months,

GUTTA PERCHA WALL FRAME AMBROTYPE of Henry Ford (1845/) - Henry was born and raised in Leonardtown and attended Georgetown University, class of 1861. Receiving word that students were to be drafted into Federal service, and unable to restrain his southern feelings, he and several other students crossed the Potomac in a rowboat in August of 1862 to enlist in the Southern Army. On April 27 he became a member of Company B, 2nd Maryland Infantry, where he served for the war as a private. He was wounded on Culp's Hill at Gettysburg, during the action of the second day, after 300 Marylanders and 18 North Carolinians were ordered to charge the strong position defended by three brigades of the enemy. Returning among the casualties, he was placed in Chimborazo Hospital in Richmond until August 25, 1863. Because of the scanty army diet, he again became ill and was admitted to Stuart Hospital in Richmond on June 10, 1864. After returning to his unit, Ford became one of only nine men left in Company B when the 2nd Maryland reached Appomattox Courthouse. He was paroled on April 9, 1865

decided to return to Maryland, arrested at Charlestown, (West) Virginia." He was later released and established a photographic business in Baltimore.

A. J. Riddle, a native Marylander, practiced as a daguerreotypist in Baltimore in the 1850's. He moved to Macon, Georgia, where he continued his trade. He entered the Confederate service as a 2nd lieutenant in the Georgia State Troops on August 29, 1861, and resigned on April 8, 1862. He ran the blockade to obtain photographic materials, and after being captured on June 4, 1863, was sent to Old Capitol Prison. His prison statement says, "In the last 8 months I was doing business in Richmond as a photographic artist, last November 1862, I was arrested in Charles County, Maryland with 2 trunks of photographic equipment and was brought to Washington City where my goods were confiscated and I was fined $100. I returned home (Maryland) and borrowed more money, purchased stock at enormous prices. I tried my luck again by the underground railroad, my second offense. I arrived at New York alright and purchased more stock and started for home." He was released on January 18, 1864. On April 7 of that year he was detailed by the Confederate government as official photographer for the Army of the West. He was most remembered for his photographs of Andersonville Prison. He used numerous backmarks. His most interesting were "A. J. Riddle, Chief Photographer, Division of the West" and "A. J. Riddle, Chief Photographer, Army of Tennessee."

8 - Photography

John P. Blessing was born October 11, 1835, near Jefferson in Frederick County, Maryland. At the age of 20, he migrated to Texas where he learned the daguerreotype process. He worked in Houston, and later in Galveston. In 1861 he served in a Galveston militia company until stricken with typhoid pneumonia when he was then assigned to the provost marshal. Upon recovering he joined the Confederate navy. After the war he practiced his art in the Galveston area until he returned to Baltimore in 1879, and opened a gallery at 46 North Charles Street. In 1880 the firm became known as Blessing & Kuhn Photographic and Portrait Gallery. Blessing retired in 1890 and returned to Western Maryland near Brownsville.

James Taylor, a well-known Union artist, was a friend of James J. Williamson and painted uniforms on civilians for illustrations of veterans to be used in Williamson's book Mosby's Rangers.

CARTE DE VISTE WITH HANDPAINTED CONFEDERATE UNIFORM painted by an artist over the civilian clothes of James J. Williamson - Born and raised in Baltimore, Williamson was employed at the Government Printing Office in Washington until he read about the invasion of his native state by Federal troops. He immediately proceeded to Baltimore and then to Richmond where he was employed by Ritchie and Dunnavant's Printers for the Confederate Government. Williamson was soon joined by his wife and two children. He decided to run the blockade in August of 1862 and returned his family to their home in Washington. On January 31, 1863, he was arrested and imprisoned in the Old Capitol Prison until exchanged on March 29, at Upperville. He enlisted in Mosby's Partisan Rangers, Company A, 43rd Virginia Cavalry on April 25, and was later slightly wounded in the ribs while doing picket duty at Myer's Ford on the Shenandoah. After the surrender, he resided in Jersey City, New Jersey, becoming a member of the District of Columbia United Confederate Veterans and the Confederate Veterans Camp of New York City.

Captain Fred M. Colston, who was an ordnance officer of Alexander's Virginia artillery, was an early collector of Civil War martial photographs and was a major contributor to Miller's Photographic History of the War.

The superb renditions of photographs that are left to us through the labors of the early photographers, instead of an artist's subjective impression, provide an insight to this period not previously available. Whether field, camp or portrait photographer, they have left us a sense of true feeling for posterity.

Chapter 2

SENIOR GRADE AND FLAG RANKED OFFICERS

Maryland would give 17 officers to the Confederacy who would obtain the rank of general or admiral. Six of these flag ranked men would not survive the war. A complete biography of each can be found in <u>Marylanders in the Confederacy</u>. To the federal government 12 men from Maryland would become senior officers but only five of these were actually born in the Free State.

Brig. Gen. James Jay Archer
1817-1864

Admiral Franklin Buchanan
1800-1874

Brig. Gen. Joseph Lancaster Brent
1826-1905

Maj. Gen. Arnold Elzey
1816-1870

Commodore George Nicholas Hollins Sr.
1799-1878

10 - Senior Grade & Flag Ranked Officers

Brig. Gen. Bradley Tyler Johnson
1829-1903

Brig. Gen. Lewis Henry Little
1817-1862

Maj. Gen. Mansfield Lovell
1822-1884

Brig. Gen. William Whann Mackall
1816-1891

Rear Admiral Raphael Semmes
1809-1877

Brig. Gen. George Hume Steuart Jr.
1828-1903

Senior Grade & Flag Ranked Officers - 11

Brig. Gen. Allen E. Thomas
1830-1907

Brig. Gen. Lloyd Tilghman Sr.
1816-1863

Maj. Gen. Isaac Ridgeway Trimble
1802-1888

Brig. Gen. Robert Charles Tyler
1833-1865

Brig. Gen. Charles Sidney Winder
1829-1862

Brig. Gen. John Henry Winder
1800-1865

Chapter 3

MILITIA

In the 1840s, most of Maryland's counties had a number of militia units. They went from a high of 15 in Baltimore County to a low of 6 in Frederick County. In the decade following the Mexican War, there was a gradual decline in the number of these organizations. In October of 1859 however, when some of the state militia units returned from Harpers Ferry where they had assisted in subduing the adherents of John Brown, the excitement and fervor gave rise to an immediate increase in the number of new units being raised. Amidst the perplexities of the times, the questions causing sectional diversity were well evidenced by the members of the volunteer military organizations as the young men sought out units with their same political views. The legislature, in 1860, appropriated $70,000 to arm the state's militia. At that time the military division of the Monumental City was under the command of Major General George H. Steuart Sr., with Brigadier Generals John Wesley Watkins and Charles C. Egerton commanding the 1st and 2nd brigades, respectively.

The confrontation between resisting unarmed citizens and the 6th Massachusetts, as that regiment passed through Baltimore on their way to Washington on April 19, 1861, represented the first fatalities in the War Between the States. The Baltimore City Militia were ordered to assemble with their uniforms, arms and accoutrements the next day under orders from Major General Steuart and Brigadier General Egerton. With the aggression and physical attack of Northern soldiers upon Southern civilians, the militiamen of the Monumental City flew to muster and were anxious to repulse the Yankee invaders.

The assembled Baltimore militia units were formed into four regiments: 1st Rifle Regiment, Colonel George Peters, commanding; 1st Artillery and Cavalry Regiment, Colonel Joseph P. Warner, commanding; 5th Infantry Regiment, Colonel Augustus P. Shutt, commanding. All were local men with Southern sympathies. The fourth unit, the 53rd Infantry Regiment, was assigned to Colonel Benjamin Huger, a South Carolinian who had just resigned from the Army. Prior to his resignation Colonel Huger had been commandant of the Pikesville Arsenal. Huger was appointed in place of J. Alden Weston, who was already serving with the Confederate Army.

BALTIMORE CITY MILITIA

1ST RIFLE REGIMENT MM

uniformed, rifles and sabre bayonets
Colonel George Peters
Major Epaphroditus Swinney
Adjutant John H. Weber

Company A Wells & McComas Riflemen MM

Captain George W. Bowers
1st Lt. Charles Ford
2nd Lt. Robert Miller

Company B Wells & McComas Riflemen MM

Captain William D. Melville
1st Lt. William H. Stagmer

Company C East Baltimore Rifles MM

72 men   Captain George Hoffman

Company D Baltimore City Rifles MM

50 men   Captain Charles W. Hiltz
1st Lt. William H. Watson
2nd Lt. Daniel Verlanders
3rd Lt. George T. Rice

14 - Militia

Company E Baltimore City Riflemen MM

    54 men   Captain J.H. Webber
                   1st Lt. Ludwig

Company F Franklin Guards MM

    53 men   Captain J.B.J. Onion
                   1st Lt. N.B. Talbot
                   2nd Lt. J.M. Bouchelt

Company G Shields Guards MM

            Captain E.J. Christy
            1st Lt. Robert H. Walker
            2nd Lt. Philip Graham
            Ensign Thomas H. Crosby

East Baltimore Military Band MM

            Captain B.H. Charles

1ST REGIMENT ARTILLERY AND CAVALRY MM

            uniformed and armed
            Colonel Joseph P. Warner
            Major Lloyd B. Parks
            Adjutant A. Smith Falconer

Company A Eagle Artillery MM

    40 men 7 brass 6 pound cannon
    driven by two horses each
            Captain John M. Bruce

Company B Baltimore City Guard MM

            Captain Emerson L. Matthews
            1st Lt. J.S. Mubbell
            2nd Lt. Jacob C. Brown

Company C Baltimore City Guard MM

            Captain David E. Woodburn
            1st Lt. Edward R. Dorsey

Company D Baltimore City Guard MM

            Captain Grafton D. Spurrier

Company E Baltimore City Guard MM

            Captain John G. Johannes

            1st Lt. Andrew W. Dennison

Company F Baltimore City Guard MM

            Captain George Walters

Company G Taylor Light Dragoons MM

            Captain Jacob Dahl
            1st Lt. Frederick Theile
            2nd Lt. Michael Smith
            Ensign Henry Stine

Company H Lafayette Light Dragoons MM

            Captain Augustus Ballauf
            1st Lt. George Younger
            2nd Lt. William Schaeffer
            Ensign Louis Lindner

5TH INFANTRY REGIMENT MM

            uniformed and armed
            Colonel Augustus P. Shutt
            Lt. Colonel Hiram E. Fox
            Major Hugh D. Gelston
            Adjutant George W. Talbott

Company A Independent Blues and Full Band MM

            Captain Professor A.H. Holland

Company B Law Greys MM

    30 men   Captain Thomas Bowers
                   1st Lt. Robert G. King
                   armory - Metropolitan Hall

Company C Law Greys Zouaves MM

    60 men   Captain Robert H. Walker

Company D Law Greys Cornet Band and Drum MM

            Captain Schreiber

Company E Jackson Guards MM

    45 men   Captain Anton Heidrick
                   1st Lt. Martin Wurst
                   2nd Lt. George Pestel
                   Ensign Gottleth Wurst

Company F Maryland State Guard MM

65 men   Captain Edward W. Salmon

Company G Governor's Guards MM

50 men   Captain William H. Taylor
                  1st Lt. J.J. Poker
                  2nd Lt. Andrew B. Braner
                  armory - Green and Raborg Streets

Company H Monumental Guard MM

30 men   Captain William Hunter Griffin

Company I Irish American Volunteers MM

85 men   Captain John E. Toole
                  1st Lt. Henry McCowan

Company J Winans Guard MM

70 men   Captain C. Ferrandia
                  1st Lt. C. Camper
                  2nd Lt. Alexander Cross
                  3rd Lt. Francis A. Tormey

Company K Jillard Guard MM

64 men   Captain W.H. Jillard
                  1st Lt. Joseph W. Sachse
                  2nd Lt. Thomas W. Goodrich
                  3rd Lt. William H. Cowan

53RD INFANTRY REGIMENT MM

uniformed and armed
Colonel Benjamin Huger
Lt. Colonel Samuel S. Mills
Major Charles G. Kerr
Quartermaster William Kellinger
490 men
armory - Carroll Hall

Company A Independent Greys MM

Captain J. Lyle Clarke
1st Lt. Benjamin J. Simpson
2nd Lt. F. William Kerchner
Ensign Henry Shuck

Company B Maryland Guard MM

Captain Henry D. Loney
1st Lt. Edward R. Dorsey

Company C Maryland Guard MM

Captain Harry D.G. Carroll Jr.
Lt. D. C. Trimble

Company D Maryland Guard MM

Captain William H. Murray
2nd Lt. James F. Pearson

Company E Maryland Guard MM

Captain Richard H. Conway
1st Lt. Alexander Ridge Murdock
2nd Lt. Edward F. Pontier

Company F Maryland Guard MM

Captain William Woodville Jr.
1st Lt. Richard C. Hoffman

Company G Maryland Guard MM

Captain William C. Pennington
Lt. Samuel Knox George Jr.

Company H Independent Greys MM

Captain Benjamin Simpson

Company I Independent Greys MM

Captain Thomas B. Allard

Maryland Guard Band and Drum Corps MM

25 musicians   Drum Major Charles M. Chad
10 drummers

16 - Militia

The only company refusing to muster was the Turners Guard. This unit, commanded by Captain T. Odenwald, consisted mainly of people of German extraction. Many of these people retained their allegiance to the Union. As a consequence, their armory was looted and they were taunted by the general public.

The Baltimore militia units were exquisitely clad in elaborately decorated, close fitting and stylish uniforms. The colorful uniforms of the Maryland Guard Battalion were typical of many of these pre-war militia units. The Guard was organized in December of 1859 with a compliment of 226 names on the original roster. Published uniform regulations for 1861 show four uniform combinations for the battalion:

Class A	Class B	Class C	Class D
Full Chasseur uniform without overcoat	Fatigue jacket	Fatique Jacket	Fatique Jacket
White belts	Chasseur pants	Chasseur pants	Dark pants
Knapsack	Overcoat without cape	Overcoat with cape	Black belts
	Knapsack		
	White belts		

MARYLAND GUARD BATTALION CLASS A DRESS ZOUAVE UNIFORMS - Watercolored albumin photograph signed by Bendann Brothers - The uniforms are dark blue close fitting coats, embroidered in yellow, light blue shirt with a close row of small buttons, dark blue baggy pantaloons trimmed in yellow gathered below the knee, and white drab gaiters. Pictured left to right are Samuel J. Hough, sergeant in the Maryland Guard who later enlisted in Company A, 1st Maryland Cavalry; Capt. William Henry Murray, 1839-1864, elected captain of the 3rd Company in 1860, commander Company H, 1st Maryland Infantry; and Clapham Murray, private in the Maryland Guard and who later enlisted in his brother's command.

MARYLAND GUARD BATTALION CLASS D FATIGUE UNIFORM of John Minge Bolling (1835/) - The 1st Company uniform is dark blue, trimmed in yellow with a nine-button front as shown in this Bendann photo. He enlisted in Weston's Maryland Guard Company and was transferred to the 1st Maryland Infantry, Coompany H. He re-enlisted in D Company, 43rd Virginia Cavalry and, on February 20, 1864, he and his brother Bartlett were captured by Cole's Maryland Federal Cavalry while foraging for corn and bacon in Loudoun County.

MARYLAND GUARD BATTALION WINTER DRESS - Charles R. Thompson (1845/1865) of the 4th Company wearing an overcoat without a cape, kepi with an oil cloth covering, and a black belt as photographed by Stephen Israel. He was a farm lad from Charles County who had come to Baltimore for school. He enlisted in Winder's Cavalry on October 30, 1862. During the retreat of the 1st Maryland Cavalry from Gettysburg, his horse was wounded and abandoned at Hagerstown. He was captured at Moorefield on August 7, 1864, and was sent to Camp Chase. Thompson became ill with encephalitis and died on January 23, 1865, and was buried near there.

MARYLAND GUARD BATTALION HALF FATIGUE UNIFORM - McHenry Howard, a corporal in the 3rd Company, wearing a uniform as stated and shown in his book, Recollections of a Maryland Confederate Soldier and Staff Officer. The rug reveals it was taken in Stephen Isral's Baltimore studio. In July of 1862, two federal enrollment officers from the 3rd district in Baltimore County came to his mother's house. They said, "Madam, we are enrollment officers and have come to get the names of the male members of your family. Have you a husband and sons capable of bearing arms?" She answered, "Yes, a husband and six sons." "Your husband, what is his name and where is he?" "Charles Howard, he is a prisoner in Fort Warren." "Your eldest son?" "Frank E. Howard, he is also a prisoner

with his father." "Your next son?" "John Eager Howard, he is a captain in the Confederate Army." "And the next?" "Charles Howard, he is a major in the Confederate Army." "And the next?" "James Howard, he is a lieutenant colonel in the Confederate Army." "And the next?" "Edward Lloyd, he is a surgeon in the Confederate Army." During this time the men became more and more flustered. "And your youngest son, McHenry Howard?" "He is also with the southern army with Stonewall Jackson and I expect he will be here soon."

18 - Militia

These various outfits were often mixed and matched depending upon the type of event in which they were participating.

Early Saturday morning the mayor issued a notice for citizens who were armed and willing to enroll themselves for the defense of the city, to report to a recruiting office at city hall. From these recruits, Isaac R. Trimble formed three regiments of citizen militia: the Maryland Line, George W. Hughes, commanding; Southern Guerrilla Home Guard Regiment, John R. Johnson, commanding; and Trimble's Un-uniformed Volunteer Regiment. Over 15,000 volunteers were enrolled and began drilling. The sound of fifes and drums were heard in every section of the city. The new companies, consisting of 40 or more men, were to elect their own officers and be assigned to one of the new regiments. Regimental headquarters were to be in various armories in the city.

MARYLAND LINE

armed with personal shotguns and rifles
Colonel George Hughes
Major Samuel T. Walker
armory - Gay and Fayette Steets

Naval Harbor Marines

75 men   Captain J.P. Levy
4 gunboats
Engineer
          Captain W.H. Jackson

1st Battalion

Company A
41 men   Captain D. Blanford
Company B
55 men   Captain J. Mulkin

2nd Battalion

Company A
62 men   Captain Charles C. Edelin
          1st Lt. G. Morrill
          2nd Lt. G.E. Shaw
Company B
47 men   Captain W.H. Frazier

3rd Battalion

Company A
42 men   Captain William L. Gage
Company B
55 men   Captain E.W. Stockman

4th Battalion

Company A
40 men   Captain George P. Kraft
          1st Lt. J.G.W. Manicott

Company B
75 men   Captain James Martin
          1st Lt. Thomas Horkiner
          2nd Lt. Adam Shaeffer

5th Battalion

Company A Byrne's Guard
45 men   Captain J. Holmes Taylor
          1st Lt. L.E. Ballard
          2nd Lt. J.B. Bragdon
          Ensign W.O. Linthicum
Company B
          Captain William B. Redgrave
          2nd Lt. W.H. Vernum

6th Battalion

Company A
71 men   Captain James O'Brien
          1st Lt. John L. Roach
          2nd Lt. Benjamin M. Height
          Ensign Samuel Harlan
Company B
          Captain Roberts

7th Battalion

Company A
          Captain H. O'Brien
Company B
          Captain Fields

8th Battalion

Company A
          Captain Huckman
Company B
          Captain Frank S. Price

9th Battalion

Company A
45 men   Captain Thomas Smith Rhett
                 1st Lt. J.B. Roberts
                 2nd Lt. B. Watkins
                 Ensign James Selby

Company B
79 men   Captain Samuel R. Dunnock
                 1st Lt. William Fithrstone
                 2nd Lt. Frank Landsdale
                 Ensign J.C. Holstine

SOUTHERN GUERILLA HOME GUARD REGIMENT

armed with rifles, shotguns and pistols
Colonel John R. Johnston
Lt. Colonel Leonard Grover
armory - South and Second Streets

1st Battalion

113 men   Major Quinton William Radcliff

Company A
                 Captain Richard S. DeFord
                 1st Lt. L.B. Hall
                 2nd Lt. James M. Blanche

Company B
                 Captain John Hughes
                 1st Lt. Thomas R. Walsh
                 2nd Lt. Henry Gleason

Company C
                 Captain Robert Grover
                 1st Lt. Jacob Wisong
                 2nd Lt. W.E. Sinn

Company D
                 Captain William C. Whittington
                 1st Lt. George Spurrier
                 2nd Lt. Victor Larogue

2nd Battalion

                 Major William Hamilton Smith

Trimble's Un-Uniformed Volunteer Regiment

2/3 armed with personal weapons
Colonel Isaac R. Trimble
Lt. Colonel William H. Hayward
Major James H. Millikin

Jeff Davis Rifles No. 1
131 men   Captain William H. Quincy
                 1st Lt. James H. King
                 2nd Lt. A.J. Kone
                 3rd Lt. Henry Clay Hack
armory - 11 South Street

Jeff Davis Rifles No. 2
57 men   Captain E.W. Albaugh
                 1st Lt. C.D. French
                 2nd Lt. G.C. Griest
                 3rd Lt. William H. Rundle

Eutaw Gaurds
74 men   Captain Charles McDonald
                 1st Lt. Joseph H. Amey
                 2nd Lt. John Cooke
                 3rd Lt. Thomas G. Tibbles

Central Avenue Guards
60 men   Captain Krine

Canton Light Infantry
56 men   Captain Phillip Hensel
                 1st Lt. James E. Campbell
                 2nd Lt. K.J. Kervick

Trimble Guards No. 1
95 men   Captain William Wesserly
                 1st Lt. Louis Sherzer
                 2nd Lt. John Timerel
                 3rd Lt. John Reese

Trimble Guards No. 2
61 men   Captain William F. Bragg
                 1st Lt. James Farrell
                 2nd Lt. John W. Hamilton
                 3rd Lt. John W. Neidhammer

Maryland Rifles No. 1
60 men   Captain Thomas H. Holbrook
                 1st Lt. J.B. Connolly
                 2nd Lt. J.R. Wright
                 3rd Lt. William Wood
armory - Basen, Jackson Hall, French Sts.

Maryland Rifles No. 2
35 men   Captain A.B. Coulter
                 1st Lt. Edward Small
                 2nd Lt. R.C. Hardesty

Carroll Guards
43 men   Captain E.J. Chaisty Jr.
                 1st Lt. F.P. Fitzpatrick
                 2nd Lt. T.J. Keener
                 3rd Lt. J.F. Dempsey

20 - Militia

MARYLAND BLUE SECESSION COCKADE which was purchased by Bradley T. Johnson when he brought the Frederick Volunteers to Baltimore to resist the Northern invasion. It appeared in the relic room of the Maryland Line Confederate Soldier's Home and was then conveyed to the Richmond Confederate Museum. The body of the cockade is blue silk made into a rosette with a center Maryland state seal button which tops two streamers.

BALTIMORE CIVILIAN VOLUNTEER MILITIAMAN. This unidentified militiaman is holding a musket and wearing a belt, traditional cap box and a civilian hunting pouch. He is clothed in a military-type frock coat with two Maryland blue cockades.

Eastern Home Guard
119 men   Captain John E. Harvey
          1st Lt. Thomas J. Coates
          2nd Lt. John H. Suter
          3rd Lt. William W. Chaffinch

Mason Rifles
65 men   Captain F. Hugh Gifford
          1st Lt. Nicholas Lynch
          2nd Lt. John A. Brown
          3rd Lt. J. Edward Kirby

Baltimore Home Guard
63 men   Captain John H. Waggoner
          1st Lt. James Beachan
          2nd Lt. William Hunt
          3rd Lt. Thomas N. Spencer
armory - Eastern Avenue

Spurrier Guard
57 men   Captain George A. Freeberger
          1st Lt. Jacob H. Hines
          2nd Lt. William Ferry
          3rd Lt. Martin P. Shimp

Bush Rangers
44 men   Captain William DeRough
          1st Lt. Homestead Samuel Henderson
          2nd Lt. P. Garvy

Dumfries Riflemen
64 men   Captain John W. Darley
          1st Lt. Robert C. Bell
          2nd Lt. John P. Galloway

Howard Guards
50 men   Captain Edward Foxton
armory - Patapsco engine house
St. Paul Street

Liberty Guards
61 men   Captain William Lee Stiles
          1st Lt. John Miller

　　　　　　　　　　2nd Lt. John C. Bunting
　　　　　　　　　　3rd Lt. J.F. Stumry
　　armory - Clark's Hall
Watson Rifles
　　93 men　　　　Captain James Mullen
　　　　　　　　　　1st Lt. John Sullivan
　　　　　　　　　　2nd Lt. Lewis Apron
　　　　　　　　　　3rd Lt. E.H. Harrison
City Hall Guards
　　80 men　　　　Captain John J. Graves
　　　　　　　　　　1st Lt. J. Barney Williams
　　　　　　　　　　2nd Lt. R.H. Johns
　　　　　　　　　　3rd Lt. John Brachamp
　　　　　　　　　　3rd Lt. John Brown
Ward Home Guard
　　82 men　　　　Captain Thomas S. Sumwalt
　　　　　　　　　　1st Lt. George R. Berry
　　　　　　　　　　2nd Lt. George Needham
　　　　　　　　　　3rd Lt. John Fitzpatrick
State Rights Guards
　　54 men　　　　Captain D.K. Kimbell
　　　　　　　　　　1st Lt. John F.C. Offutt
　　　　　　　　　　2nd Lt. A.B. Chiveler
　　　　　　　　　　3rd Lt. James F. Simpson

Madison Rifles
　　46 men　　　　Captain George W. Myers
　　　　　　　　　　1st Lt. Aid Pindle
　　　　　　　　　　2nd Lt. Zack Bilson
Scott Rifles
　　　　　　　　　　Captain James W. Thompson
　　　　　　　　　　1st Lt. John Goldsborough
　　　　　　　　　　2nd Lt. James K. Bordiey

Independent Volunteers
　　　　　　　　　　Captain Mortimer Carroll
　　armory - Monument and Constitution Streets
Maryland Duckers
　　70 men　　　　Captain William McDonald
　　　　　　　　　　1st Lt. Thomas Sheppard
　　　　　　　　　　2nd Lt. William Cordery
　　　　　　　　　　3rd Lt. James Turner
　　armory - Newton University
Artillery Company
　　76 men　　　　Captain Robert E. Haslett
　　　　　　　　　　1st Lt. George Washington Goodrich
　　　　　　　　　　2nd Lt. Robert Wilson
　　　　　　　　　　3rd Lt. John F. Slater
Independent Light Dragoons
　　　　　　　　　　Colonel Sam Houston
　　　　　　　　　　Colonel G.H. Zimmerson
Maryland Chasseurs
　　　　　　　　　　Captain Edmund Law Rogers
　　armory - Bank Lane and St. Paul Street
Southern Liberators
　　43 men　　　　Captain James H. Barney
　　　　　　　　　　1st Lt. Thomas H. Belt
　　　　　　　　　　2nd Lt. E.W. Blanchard
　　armory - North Central Railroad Station
Institute Guard
　　60 men　　　　Captain J. Crawford Neillison
　　　　　　　　　　1st Lt. G.M. Conradt
Maryland Scouts
　　28 men　　　　Captain John W. Loane
　　　　　　　　　　1st Lt. William G. Frank
　　　　　　　　　　2nd Lt. Henry E. Loane
Baker's Company
　　26 men　　　　Captain Baker

　　The majority of Marylanders were sympathetic to the Southern cause but opposed the thought of their state entering into the question of secession as a remedy or relief. But the pervailing spirit within the volunteer military organizations was very different. Many men of the old liberty loving state, who cherished military pomp and circumstance, were convinced of the rightness of the Southern struggle for independence and now, after forceful encroachment of their domiciles, they were ready to resist. Others, who could not stand to think of their muskets being used against those who marched behind Old Glory, resigned.

　　Officers were quickly changed to reflect the unimpaired feeling of their own unit while some county companies were so diverse in sentiment they disbanded immediately.

　　New companies instantly sprang up throughout the counties as bellwethers of the Confederate view, and cried that the state had been cursed by conservatism but now the threat of the heroes of coercion was genuine. The time to fight had come, and they were organizing to stand shoulder to shoulder under their interpretation of the Constitution in the struggle against those who would change

22 - Militia

the Bill of Rights. The leaders of the new loyalist companies, on the other hand, preached the importance of Maryland's fidelity to the government and the far reaching influence and effect they would have upon the struggle for national unity. The civilian volunteer units formed in April of 1861 were issued whatever old arms were available within their local areas. The two companies of Maryland Rifles were issued old Hall breechloading carbines that had been housed in a Baltimore armory. These had been manufactured on the Potomac and were considered to be inferior weapons. Most, however, used personal weapons which they brought into the ranks. Recorded accounts reveal revolvers, single shot pistols, double barrel pistols, Kentucky style longrifles, half stock rifles and shotguns. The Maryland Duckers decided "the uniform adopted is a drab shirt and pants and slouch hat bearing the coat of arms of Maryland. The arms will be large double barrelled fowling pieces, revolvers and Bowie knives." The uniforms of the Maryland Line were gray Garibaldi shirts, black pants and a glaze fatigue cap. They were armed with 150 minnie rifles, 250 muskets and 2,000 Ross Winans pikes. The medical-surgical militia staff officers had a silk hat badge which was made to display on their stovepipe top hats. It read surgical staff with the state seal displayed between the two words. Trimble's Un-uniformed Corps formed at Calvert Street, numbered 2,265 and was displayed with the following gear: "number of arms delivered or on hand, 586; number of uniforms with shirts, 200; number without arms, 1,604."

STATE SEAL HAT EMBLEM. It is cast in brass from a chin scale shako plate. Unlike the stamped chin scale shako plate and the shako buckle this hat emblem is gilded in gold.

The county militia organizations are aligned according to the chronology of their formation or last reorganization. Some of the units in the spring of 1861 were of short duration accounting for scanty information. The Union and Confederate flags signify the composition of the political loyalties of the majority of the company. When there is no flag assigned it signifies that either the company was divided, no roster has been found, or no accounts of their loyalties have been uncovered.

Northern

Loyal Marylanders

Southern

True Marylanders

Militia - 23

ALLEGANY COUNTY

Cumberland Continentals - 50th Reg. MM - Cumberland

September 5, 1860   Captain Alexander King
issued 50 minnie   1st Lt. Samuel T. Little
muskets and acct   2nd Lt. Samuel Luman
   2nd Lt. Horace Resley
   was Captain by
   April 16, 1861

ANNE ARUNDEL COUNTY

Union Guards - 3rd Regiment MM

July 14, 1860   Captain James A. Iglehart
issued 50 sabers,   1st Lt. Fayette Ball
pistols and acct   2nd Lt. John B. Stewart

West River Guards - 3rd Reigment MM - West River

July 18, 1860   Captain George B. Stewart
issued 50 sabers,   1st Lt. John C. Rogers
pistols and acct   2nd Lt. Fenwick Hall
   3rd Lt. Sprigg Harwood

Patapsco Light Dragoons - 3rd Regiment MM

February 20, 1861   Captain E. G. Hinkle
issued 40 sabers,   1st Lt. Regin Harman
pistols and acct   2nd Lt. Henry H. Thomas

Chesapeake Home Guard - 2nd Regiment MM

August 9, 1861   Captain James T. Nutwell
issued 40 rifle   1st Lt. Thomas T. Norris
muskets and acct   2nd Lt. George Nutwell

Governor's Guard - Annapolis

September 3, 1861   Company A
issued 70 rifle   Captain John R. Magruder
muskets and acct   1st Lt. Tuck
   Company B
   Captain Gassaway

United Rifles

issued 36 rifle   Captain Frank A. Bond
muskets and acct   1st Lt. William B. Bond

Severn Guards - Severn

issued 40 swords,   Captain George Clayton
pistols and acct   1st Lt. Edward Walton
   2nd Lt. Charles Waters

Southern Guards

issued 40 sabers,   Captain Thomas Hall
pistols and acct   1st Lt. Alvin Wilson

State Rights Guard

 Captain Duvall

Magothy Home Guard

April 1861   Captain W.F. Dunbar
50 men

South River Guard

Captain Iglehart

Home Guard

Captain Boyle

Guerilla Company

BALTIMORE COUNTY

Towson Guards - 46th Regiment MM - Towson

September 1859, org.   Captain Charles R. Chew
June 29, 1860 issued   1st Lt. Edward Rider
50 minnie muskets   2nd Lt. William Bryson
& acct, 60 men in April 1861

24 - Militia

Reisterstown Riflemen - 1st Rifle Reg. MM - Reisterstown

October 1859, org.   Captain
November 24, 1860   Richard L. Worthington
issued 40 rifle muskets   1st Lt. Jacob T. Forney
& acct   2nd Lt. Amos A. Carryman

Baltimore County Horse Guard - 6th Reg. MM - Towson

February 2, 1861   Captain Charles Ridgley
issued 50 sabers,   1st Lt. John Merryman
pistols and acct   2nd Lt. George H. Carman
    2nd Lt. Richard Grason

Garrison Forrest Rangers - 45th Reg. MM - Pikesville

February, org.   Captain Wilson C. Nicholas
March 28, 1861   1st Lt. Samuel B. Mettam
issued 48 rifle   2nd Lt. Amos A. Carryman
muskets & acct   2nd Lt. Charles M. Shipley

Warren Rifles - Warren Factory

March 1861   Captain John W. Wilson
    1st Lt. Robert Smith
    2nd Lt. Isaac Wilson
    2nd Lt. James H. Wilson

Orangeville Horse Guard - 12th District

April 21, 1861   Captain Nicholas Gatch
    1st Lt. S.T. McComas
    2nd Lt. Nathaniel Melcher

Border Guard - Pikesville

1861

Reisterstown Horse Troop - Reisterstown

1861

Morgan Riflemen - Huntington

March 1861   Captain Jacob Pelch
    1st Lt. George W. Ritter
    2nd Lt. Augustus F. Dames
    2nd Lt. T.S. Bonsal

Lake Guards - Mt. Washington

1861   Captain William E. Hobleitzell
65 men   1st Lt. Jacob Hobleitzell
    2nd Lt. William H. Kemp

Maryland Mounted Guard - Catonsville

March 1861   Captain T.S. Taylor

CALVERT COUNTY

Calvert Cadets MM

40 muskets and acct   Captain Dr. Magruder
50 men   1st Lt. Basil D. Bond
    was Captain in April 1861
    Lts: Mills, Williams, Sedwick

Southern Guards

1861   Captain George Lyles
50 men

CAROLINE COUNTY

Caroline Guard - 19th Regiment MM

October 2, 1861   Captain William M. McMahon
issued 40 rifle   1st Lt. James F. Douglas
muskets and acct   2nd Lt. William H. Stafford

CARROLL COUNTY

Manchester Blues Infantry - Manchester

formed a company and 40 men took
possession of arms at Irving College
June 11, 1855   Captain Dr. Jacob Shower

Carroll County Border Rangers - 15th Regiment MM

1859   Captain J. A. Campbell
    1st Lt. William J. Houck
    2nd Lt. Charles E. Cocks

Militia - 25

Smallwood Infantry - 12th Regiment MM - Westminster

July 10, 1860   Captain W. Scott Roberts
issued 50 minnie   1st Lt. Edwin H. O'Brien
muskets and acct   2nd Lt. John C. Frizell
  Ensign P. Liffendall

Carroll Guards - 15th Regiment MM - Westminster

August 7, 1860   Captain George E. Wampler
issued 45 minnie   1st Lt. Thomas B. Gist
muskets and acct   2nd Lt. Ruben W. Stein

Morgan's Company

Captain Morgan

Freedom Troop of Horse - Sykesville

CECIL COUNTY

Union Rifles - 30th Regiment MM - Port Deposit

January 26, 1861   Captain John W. Taylor
issued 50 rifle   1st Lt. George Smith
muskets and acct   2nd Lt. Wesley Wiley

Cecil Guards - 49th Regiment MM

January 28, 1861   Captain John A. J. Creswell
issued 50 rifle   1st Lt. John B. Rowan
muskets and acct   2nd Lt. Nicholas P. Manley
  3rd Lt. Arthur W. Mitchell

CHARLES COUNTY

Smallwood Riflemen - 1st Regiment MM - Port Tabacco

June 14, 1860   Captain Elijah Wells
issued 50 minnie   1st Lt. William Boswell
rifles and acct   2nd Lt. Philip Muschett

Charles County Mounted Volunteers Co. 1 MM

  1st Lt. William F. Dement
  2nd Lt. Barnes Compton
  3rd Lt. Jeremiah Dyer

Charles County Mounted Volunteers Co. 2 MM

Issued 60 swords,   Captain Samuel Cox
pistols and acct,   1st Lt. Frederick Stone
Allen pistols,   2nd Lt. John W. Michell
carbines and sabers

DORCHESTER COUNTY

Dorchester Guards MM - Cambridge

December 11, 1860   Captain James Wallace
issued 50 minnie   1st Lt. John S. White
muskets and acct   2nd Lt. William Grason

Taylor Greys - 48th Regiment MM

January 12, 1861   Captain Joseph L. Bryan
issued 50 rifle   1st Lt. William W. Caton
muskets and acct   was Captain by April 1861
2nd Lt. Thomas H. Travers

FREDERICK COUNTY

United Guards MM - Frederick

March 31, 1858   Captain John T. Sim
45 men   1st Lt. B. Henry Schley
  2nd Lt. William Rogers

Manor Mounted Guards MM - Carrollton Manor

1859 issued 42   Captain Joseph N. Chiswell
swords, pistols   1st Lt. Jacob M. Buckey
and acct   2nd Lt. Richard Thomas
  3rd Lt. William Richard

Independent Riflemen - 16th Regiment MM

1859   Captain Ulysses Hobbs
  1st Lt. Walter Saunders
  2nd Lt. Henry T. Mahler

26 - Militia

Union Riflemen - 16th Regiment MM

1859	Captain Cornelius A. Staley
	1st Lt. Albert W. Burkhart
	2nd Lt. John W. Zimmerman

Junior Defenders - 16th Regiment MM - Frederick

1859	Captain J. Ritchie
	2nd Lt. Anthony Z. Kimmel

Liberty Riflemen - 20th Regiment MM - Libertytown

September 14, 1860	Captain Alfred Schley
issued 39 minnie	1st Lt. Albert Jones
muskets and acct	2nd Lt. Augustine A. Sappington
	was Captain by April 1861
	3rd Lt. John C. Hines

Frederick Mounted Dragoons MM - Frederick Volunteers

December 29, 1860	Captain Bradley T. Johnson
60 men	1st Lt. George K. Shellman
	2nd Lt. Young
	2nd Lt. Lally

Linganore Mounted Guard MM - New Market

Issued 40 swords,	Captain Thomas Jones
pistols and acct	1st Lt. Charles Beavans
	was Captain in April 1861
	2nd Lt. O. P. Harding

Union Guards MM

January 10, 1861	Captain G. Beckley

Maryland Defenders - 13th Regiment MM

February 9, 1861	Captain Joseph Wood
issued 50 rifle	1st Lt. William Downey
muskets and acct	2nd Lt. Lebben Griffith

Minute Men - Adamstown

1861	Captain Dr. Robert H.E. Boteler
	1st Lt. Dr. Jacob G. Thomas
	2nd Lt. William H. Beary
	2nd Lt. Dr. James Thomas Johnson Jr.

Catoctin Home Guard - Jefferson

April 1861

General Edward Shrive Cavalry

April 1861
10 men

Brengle Horse Guard - Frederick

April 27, 1861	Major Dr. Richard Potts
160 men	Captain Alfred F. Brengle
	1st Lt. J. McPherson
	2nd Lt. James Cooper

Middletown Home Guards - Middletown

May 1861	Captain Hanson T. Rudy
	1st Lt. Samuel Ausherman
	2nd Lt. John Castle

Liberty Home Guard - Libertytown

May 1861	Captain Henry Baker
	1st Lt. Thomas Carr
	2nd Lt. Lewis Peters

Zouave Cadets

Captain Charles Baugher

HARFORD COUNTY

Sasputie Mounted Rangers - 7th Regiment MM

July 6, 1860	Captain Robert H. Archer
issued 50 sabers,	1st Lt. William Evans
pistols and acct	2nd Lt. B. H. Keene

Harford Riflemen - 40th Regiment MM

September 1860	Captain Herman Stump
issued 50 rifled	1st Lt. William J. Dallam
muskets and acct	2nd Lt. George G. Finney

Chesapeake Riflemen - 40th Regiment MM

January 13, 1861	Captain John L. Bradberry
issued 50 muskets	1st Lt. John H. O'Neill
and acct	2nd Lt. John R. Thompson

Militia - 27

Harford Light Dragoons - 7th Regiment MM

January 31, 1861 Captain Archer H. Jarrett
issued 40 revolvers 1st Lt. William Bepell
sabers and acct 2nd Lt. James Moore

National Guards - 40th Regiment MM

February 6, 1861 Captain Robert L. Rogers
issued 50 rifle 1st Lt. Joseph M. Simmons
muskets and acct

HOWARD COUNTY

Border Guards - 32th Regiment MM

December 28, 1860 Captain Edward A. Talbott
issued 50 stands 1st Lt. David B. McLaughlin
minnie rifle 2nd Lt. Robert H. Thompson
muskets 3rd Lt. George Bond

Howard County Dragoons Company A

Howard County Dragoons Company B

40 men Captain George R. Gaither
 1st Lt. Milton Warfield
2nd Lt. John R. Clarke

Archer Home Guard - Ellicott City

1861 Captain Henry L. Hozelhurst

KENT COUNTY

Reed Rifle Corps - 21st Regiment MM - Chestertown

1857, org. Captain Eben F. Perkins
June 28, 1860 1st Lt. Simon Wickes
equipped with 50 2nd Lt. David A. Benjamin
minnie rifles & acct 3rd Lt. James Aurthur

Marion Blues - 8th Regiment MM

February 6, 1861 Captain Richard C. Johnson
issued 40 sabers, 1st Lt. R. B. Mapey
pistols and acct 2nd Lt. Samuel Hurlock

Chester Blues - 21st Regiment MM - Chestertown

March 30, 1861 Captain William W. Volks
issued 50 rifle 1st Lt. Jesse K. Hines
muskets and acct 2nd Lt. J.N. Aselton

Union Guards - 33rd Regiment MM

May 3, 1861 Captain Elijah Mapey
issued 39 rifle 1st Lt. Thomas C. Ringgold
muskets and acct 2nd Lt. John Duling

Columbian Hussars - 8th Regiment MM

July 16, 1861 Captain John T. Skirven
issued 40 sabers, 1st Lt. Arthur Wallis
pistols and acct 2nd Lt. G.C.M. Brooks

Battle Swamp Rangers

42 men Captain T.O.G. Kidd

MONTGOMERY COUNTY

Montgomery Mounted Guard - 3rd Regiment MM

June 26, 1860 Captain Edward W. Owing
issued 40 swords, 1st Lt. B. Walters
pistols and acct 2nd Lt. Z. Walters
2nd Lt. O.P. Watkins

Poolesville Guard - 3rd Regiment MM - Poolesville

February 2, 1861 Captain Samuel C. White
issued 40 rifle 1st Lt. Joseph Piles
muskets and acct 2nd Lt. John T. Fletchall
was Captain by April 1861
2nd Lt. Alexander Dade

Poolesville Light Dragoons MM - Poolesville

Issued 40 swords, Captain George W. Spates
pistols and acct 1st Lt. Benjamin S. White
was Captain by 1861
2nd Lt. R.W. Williams

Rockville Riflemen - 3rd Regiment MM - Rockville

February 16, 1861 Captain William Veirs Bouic
issued 50 rifle 1st Lt. John A. Spates
muskets and acct 2nd Lt. John William

28 - Militia

Barnesville Guards - Barnesville

      Captain William O. Sellman

Dufier's Company - Darnestown

      Captain John Dufier

PRINCE GEORGE'S COUNTY

Planter's Guard MM - Marlboro

Issued 50 swords, pistols and acct	Captain John Contee 1st Lt. Samuel H. Barry 2nd Lt. J. Thomas Sasser 3rd Lt. Thomas Fielder Bowie Jr.

Vansville Rangers MM - Beltsville

Issued 40 swords, pistols and acct	Captain Edward Herbert 1st Lt. Nicholas Snowden was Captain by 1861 2nd Lt. Theodore Robert Jenkins Jr. 2nd Lt. Fielder C. Duvall

Piscataway Rifles - 1st Regiment MM - Piscataway

June 18, 1860 issued 50 rifle muskets and acct	Captain George R.W. Marshall 1st Lt. E. Pliny Bryan 2nd Lt. Joseph B. Edelen

Mounted Rifles - Upper Marlboro

1861	Captain Oden Bowie 1st Lt. Charles C. Hill 2nd Lt. Joseph K. Roberts Jr. 2nd Lt. John B. Magruder

Independent Guards - Nottingham

      Captain John K. Pumphrey

Patuxent Rifles - Nottingham

      Captain John H. Skinner
      1st Lt. W.A.K. Braden

Potomac Riflemen

QUEEN ANNE'S COUNTY

Scott Rifles - 38th Regiment MM - Centreville

June 18, 1860 issued 50 rifle muskets and acct	Captain John Palmer 1st Lt. Robert Goldsborough 2nd Lt. John B. Brown 2nd Lt. John Wilkinson was Captain by spring of 1861

Chesapeake Riflemen - 38th Regiment MM - Kent Island

January 16, 1861 issued 50 rifle muskets and acct was	Captain A.S. Barnes 1st Lt. Broderick W. Earrickson Captain by April 1861 2nd Lt. W.K. Goodhans

Washington Blues - 9th Regiment MM - Church Hill

March 30, 1861 issued 38 sabers, pistols and acct	Captain Solomon Betts 1st Lt. Joshua S. Casden 2nd Lt. William H. Beck

Colonel Samuel T. Harrison Cavalry Company

 April 1861

Bryan-Town Company - Bryantown

 April 1861

Company B - Stevensville Company - Stevensville

 April 1861

Company E - Kent Island Company - Kent Island

  April 1861

Sudlersville Company - Sudlersville

  April 1861   Captain Edward Sudler

Centreville Company - Centreville

  April 1861   Captain William H. Jacobs
            1st Lt. James Tilghman of John

2nd Lt. E. Bourke Wright
3rd Lt. R.E. Feddeman

Mounted Rifles - Spaniard's Neck

April 1861 — Captain John R. Emory

Centreville Infantry - Centreville

April 1861 — Captain R. Goldsborough

Queenstown Infantry - Queenstown

April 1861 — Captain S. Ogle Tilghman

Ruthsburg Infantry - Ruthsburg

April 1861 — Captain Lemuel Wright

Piney Neck Infantry - Piney Neck

April 1861 — Captain James Grason

Wye Island Artillery - Wye Island

April 1861 — Captain William B. Paca

Centreville Guards Infantry - Centreville

April 1861
Major J.W. Thompson
Captain John Goldsborough
1st Lt. J.H. Thompson
2nd Lt. J.K. Bordley
3rd Lt. J.O. Rasin

Maryland Zuoaves - Centreville

April 1861
90 men
Captain T. Cook Hughey
1st Lt. Joseph H. Goldsborough
2nd Lt. J. Lockerman Goldsborough

ST. MARY'S COUNTY

Riley Rifles - 12th Regiment MM

June 24, 1860
issued 50 rifle muskets and acct

Captain James S. Raley
1st Lt. R. Ford
2nd Lt. James S. Downs
2nd Lt. William A. Token

St. Mary's Dragoons - 4th Regiment MM - Leonardtown

March 1859, org.
October 5, 1860 issued 40 sabers, pistols and acct

Captain Randolph Jones
1st Lt. George A. Toker
2nd Lt. Edward S. Abell

Charlotte Hall Light Infantry - St. Mary's Light Infantry - Charlotte Hall

Company A

Captain Richard Thomas
1st Lt. William T. Blakistone

Factory Riflemen - Clifton Factory

February 1860

Captain Reeves
Captain J. Parran Crane
1st Lt. Thomas Dent
2nd Lt. C.B. Wise
3rd Lt. E.A. Wilson

Home Guard - Leonardtown

December 1860

Captain Dr. A. McWilliams
1st Lt. James T. Blakistone
2nd Lt. James F. Abell

Smallwood Vigilante - Patuxent District

February 9, 1861

Captain James H. Heard
1st Lt. James G. Spalding
2nd Lt. A.M. Garner

St. Mary's Guards

Captain Robert Neale

Clifton Guards - Clifton Factory

Captain J. Edwin Coad
1st Lt. Henry I. Carroll

Oakley Rifles - Beslam Neck

May 1861

Captain Walter Dent
1st Lt. John V. Posey
2nd Lt. Robert Alvey
3rd Lt. J.H. Mattingly

St. Mary's Rangers

Captain Joseph Forrest

SOMERSET COUNTY

Lyaskin Guards - 25th Regiment MM

July 24, 1860   Captain John W. Moore
issued 50 minnie   1st Lt. George H. Riall
muskets and acct   2nd Lt. George White

Somerset Guard - 25th Regiment MM

January 31, 1861   Captain John W. Polk
issued 50 rifle   1st Lt. Hampden H. Dashiell
muskets and acct   2nd Lt. William T. Polk

Somerset Life Guard Dragoons - 9th Regiment MM

February 5, 1861   Captain Andrew Crawford
issued 40 sabers,   1st Lt. Henry Crawford
pistols and acct   2nd Lt. Levin Bounds

TALBOT COUNTY

Home Guard - 4th Regiment MM - Easton

July 2, 1860   Colonel Henry J. Standberg
issued 50 minnie   Major N.E. Nichols
muskets and acct   Captain Samuel T. Hopkins

Talbot Blues - 4th Regiment MM

July 5, 1860   Captain A. G. Hennisee
issued 40 minnie   1st Lt. James C. Mullikin
muskets and acct   2nd Lt. Robert W. Ross
   was Captain by April 1861

Talbot County Horse Guard - 9th Regiment MM

February 4, 1861   Captain M.T. Goldsborough
issued 40 sabers,   1st Lt. Charles King
pistols and acct   2nd Lt. S.N. Ambleton

Easton Horse Guard - Easton

 1861   Captain Aaron Bascom Hardcastle
   1st Lt. Charles Key
   2nd Lt. William Powell

Bay Hundred Home Guard

May 1861   Captain William H. Dawson
   1st Lt. Samuel S. Ridgeway
   2nd Lt. John W. Baker
   3rd Lt. Thomas S. Daw

Oxford Guards - Oxford

Captain Donovan

Easton Zouaves - Easton

May 1861

Easton Band - Easton

Captain Robinson

WASHINGTON COUNTY

Sharpsburg Riflemen 1st Co. - 54th Regiment. MM - Sharpsburg

    Captain Edward G.W. Herr
   1st Lt. John H. Hallman
   2nd Lt. Samuel Hollenberger
   3rd Lt. John R. Wilson

Sharpsburg Riflemen 2nd Co. - 10th Regiment MM - Sharpsburg

 August 11, 1860   Captain R. Ellsworth Cook
issued 42 minnie   1st Lt. Jacob Hewitt
muskets and acct   2nd Lt. William M. Cronise

Boonsboro Guards - 10th Regiment MM - Boonsboro

February 4, 1861   Captain John C. Brining
issued 50 rifle   1st Lt. J.W. Shank
muskets and acct   2nd Lt. George R. Strause

WORCHESTER COUNTY

Worchester Sentinals - 9th Regiment MM

March 30, 1861   Captain James M. Moore
issued 40 rifle   1st Lt. G.M. Upshua
muskets and acct   2nd Lt. John R. Purnell

MANOR MOUNTED GUARD UNIFORM. Joseph H. Trundle enlisted at the formation of the unit in 1859 at Carrollton Manor. Upon disbanding at Buckeystown, he and his brother Samuel went south and joined the 35th Virginia Cavalry, Company B. He is wearing a high collar coat with epaulettes and a plumed shako hat. After the war he was commander of the Alexander Young Post, United Confederate Veterans of Frederick County.

The Manor Mounted Guard voted as a unit to volunteer to serve the Southern cause. There was an objection by two of the married men which led the company to individually volunteer. None joined the Union effort. The testimony in Ridgely vs. Grayson of 1865 reveals that, out of 60 members of the Towson Guards, two went south and the remainder joined Maryland Union regiments.

The organized uniformed Maryland Militia companies, designated MM, received state arms and accoutrements by a bond of trust, usually signed by the individual company captain.

In early June, the state arms of the MM units were repossessed by order of Governor Hicks. Some of the militia commanders were unable to comply with this order due to the weapons having been carried home by their troops. Visits were made to the houses of the rank and file and they were threatened with arrest if the weapon was not turned over. Many militiamen sought out hiding places so that they could not be used by loyal forces and a number were taken to Dixie by true Marylanders where they were used in the fight for Southern independence.

The first seal of Maryland was made of silver and was stolen in 1644. In 1648, Lord Baltimore sent a new seal to the colony which was used as the great seal. The seal shield was Lord Baltimore's hereditary coat of arms. The first and fourth quarters represented the arms of the Calvert family and the second and third quarters showed the arms of the Crossland family. Above the shield was an earl's coronet, a helmet and two pennons. The supporters were a plowman and fisherman standing over the motto "Fatti maschi parole femine" (manly deeds, womandly words). The other side contained a completely armored equestrian bearing a drawn sword.

1648 SEAL sent to the province by Cecilius Lord Baltimore which incorporates his family arms.

32 - Militia

The Governor's Council wrote on March 31, 1777 "the Great Seal of Maryland, heretofore used, the Great Seal of this State, and as such to be used in future until a new one can be devised and executed, which cannot be done for immediate service." Not until February 5, 1794, was the new seal adopted. It shows lady liberty holding aloft the scales of justice in her left hand and an olive branch in her right while standing above another olive branch and facines. The reverse depicts an upright hogshead of tobacco topped with bundles of corn, two sheaves of wheat, a ship, and a cornucopia.

1794 SEAL of Lady Liberty with indigenous symbols.

On March 14, 1817, the council ordered the seal changed to the device of the coat of arms of the United States. It features a shield in front of an American eagle with its wings spread upward while clutching arrows and olive branches and 13 stars surrounded by a border ornamented with 13 points.

1817 SEAL with the device of the United States coat of arms.

The state legislature, feeling that the seal device had no significant relation to the state's history, recommended an act restoring the old great seal. The only change incorporated the familiar figure of the American eagle with outstretched wings replacing the coronet, helmet and pennons. On May 1, 1854, the former seal was broken and the old revised seal was adopted.

1854 SEAL which is the resurrection of the heraldic arms with an eagle.

During the legislative session of 1874 the ancient arms of the coronet, helmet and pennons were restored. It was not until February 27, 1879, that it was finally used. Thus ended the cycle of the return to the historic great seal which is still in use today.

1876 SEAL which has the restoration of the ancient arms.

VANSVILLE RANGERS MILITIA FLAG. This silk flag bears the 1794 state seal of Lady Liberty with a scale of justice in her left hand and in her right a sword of war and olive branch of peace. On a ribbon is the motto "INDUSTRY THE MEANS & PLENTY THE RESULT." It is 54" on the fly and 36" on the staff and the means of attachment is five pairs of silk ties. The flag is signed by the artist, Thomas R. Jeffreys, and is dated 1860. The reverse side has 30 hand-painted gold stars and there are 7 red and 6 white stripes. The flag was taken south by Nicholas Snowden (1828/1862) and some of the Vansville Rangers. He enlisted in Company D, 1st Maryland Infantry, was elected a lieutenant and killed during the Battle of Harrisonburg. In 1887, on the anniversary of the death of Snowden, this flag was returned by Bradley T. Johnson to Snowden's wife, four daughters and one son, Francis, through which it was handed down.

Chapter 4

ARTILLERY

The first volunteers for Confederate service from Maryland were 500 men referred to as the Baltimore Secessionists, recruited in the Monumental City by officers from South Carolina. They were sent to Charleston during three different periods in the early spring of 1861. They were formed into three companies: J.J. Lucas' South Carolina Battalion of Heavy Artillery, Rhett's 1st South Carolina Regular Heavy Artillery, and Company G, 1st South Carolina Infantry. They served under General "States Rights" Gist and Roswell Sabine Ripley, both officers with Maryland affiliations. General Gist was of Maryland parentage and a descendent of Mordecai Gist of Revolutionary War fame. General Ripley had resigned from the army prior to the war and went into business in Baltimore. He was elected captain of the Independent Greys on July 8, 1853, which commanded for two years before moving to Charleston. These three units served as articifers at various installations, in and around Charleston Harbor, manning artillery defenses at Castle Pinckney, Fort Ripley, Fort Sumter, James Island, Sullivan Island and Fort Moultrie. They became proficient with huge columbiads, dahlgrens, Brooke's naval shell-guns and mortars. The Baltimore Secessionists attained a high degree of excellence whether working in a casemate or on the ramparts.

Baltimorean Richard Snowden Andrews, later to make medical history, opened a recruiting office in Richmond for fellow orphans. His cousin, Charles Snowden Contee, also opened a branch in Fredericksburg. In June of 1861 they enlisted 143 men into the Maryland Flying Artillery, later to be redesignated the 1st Maryland Light Artillery. No Confederate artillerymen were to achieve more distinction during the war than this battery.

On September 17, 1861, the Baltimore Light Artillery, after being mustered into service, proceeded to a camp near Centerville, Virginia, subsequently becoming the 2nd Maryland Artillery on December 19. The battery was detached from the Maryland Line to General J.E.B. Stuart during his foray at Yellow Tavern. Stuart lost his life while leading a charge to recapture two of the battery's guns.

Henry B. Latrobe, eldest son of Baltimore businessman John H.B. Latrobe, was one of three brothers who fought under the Southern cross. Henry was authorized to organize an artillery company on September 9, 1861. Recruited in Ashland, they subsequently were named the 3rd Maryland Artillery upon being mustered in and assigned to the Army of the West.

In March of 1862, Webster H. Sothorn organized a light artillery battery which went into Virginia service.

Forrest Company, a unit of Free Staters, was formed as infantry but became the second company of David Gregg McIntosh's Artillery Battalion instead. The Chesapeake Battery was sent to Camp Lee for instruction and was designated the 4th Maryland Light Artillery.

Dea's Maryland Light Artillery was organized under Captain J. Norris Montgomery in May of 1862. They became Battery 8 in the Richmond defense and later Company C, 19th Virginia Heavy Artillery.

Captain Charles C. Edelin's Company B, 1st Maryland Infantry, re-enlisted in January of 1862. After receiving a furlough, they were ordered from Gordonsville to Goldsboro, North Carolina. With the scarcity of infantry arms, they served as heavy artillerists and were known as Edelin's Maryland Battalion of Heavy Artillery. By the summer of 1864 they were in Winder's Legion in the defense of Richmond.

Holbrook's Independent Light Artillery was formed from a number of men discharged from the 1st Maryland Infantry, then sent to the Army of the West. After serving in the 13th Virginia Infantry, Robert Marion Chambers II was commissioned a lieutenant colonel to organize an independent artillery battalion. It was to consist of four companies, A,B, C and D, commanded by his father and namesake, Robert Marion Chambers, Charles E. Tarr, Robert H. Goldsborough and John Williams, respectively. Chambers' Independent Artillery Battalion proceeded to Sharpsburg where they suffered severe losses and, with the capture of their leader, were absorbed into other artillery units.

Lee's Baltimore Light Artillery was organized under Captain John Donnell Smith in October of 1864 and served with Alexander's Artillery Battalion.

Stuart's Horse Artillery contained many Marylanders. This unit grew out of Newton's Virginia Battery at Centerville in November of 1861 and was attached to the cavalry. Dr. James Breathed was serving as a private in the ranks when General J.E.B. Stuart suggested that he and John Pelham form a mobile artillery battery. The horse artillery differed from foot and mounted field batteries in that the cannoneers were all mounted, enabling them to maneuver at a gallop and change positions frequently. Each gun was pulled by six horses and had a driver on each left-hand horse. There was a caisson for each gun, also pulled by six horses. As the original officers were promoted, additional Marylanders moved up into command positions. Philip Preston Johnson succeeded Breathed and when he became major, Daniel Shanks became commander. There were 10 commissioned officers and over 100 enlisted men from Maryland in Stuart's Horse Artillery.

RICHARD SNOWDEN ANDREWS (1830/1903) - Carte de Viste - In April of 1861 he volunteered for the Baltimore Militia and proceeded to the Pikesville arsenal, then in possession of the Garrison Forest Rangers. Before proceeding to Virginia to become a captain of artillery, Andrews obtained the inspection reports and drawings of the new light 12-pound Napoleon gun. In Richmond, he enlisted 146 fellow expatriots into the Maryland Flying Artillery, in which he was elected captain. Early in the Seven Days fighting at the Battle of Mechanicsville, he was wounded in the leg but did not leave the field. He was promoted to major for gallantry. The battery's old guns were returned to the government after they captured a set of superior U.S. guns at Frazier's Farm. At Cedar Mountain, Andrews fell with a terrible abdominal wound. Left on the field, surgeons saw his protruding abdominal viscera, and not expecting him to survive, refused to administer to him. Finally his wound was sewn up with a silver plate 12 inches square added to his abdomen. In October of 1862, he reported for duty and was placed in charge of the Ordnance Bureau. In April of 1863 he returned to the field where, at Winchester, he was wounded in the arm. In December of 1863 he was appointed by the president of the board, in Richmond, and was sent to Europe to procure cannon. He proceeded on his mission in February of 1864. Returning to the United States, he learned of Lee's surrender and went to Bermuda, Havana, and then to Mexico where he worked for two years in the construction of the Imperial Railroad between Vera Cruz and the capital. In 1867 he returned to Baltimore and re-established himself as an architect and builder. He was appointed a brigadier general of artillery in the Maryland National Guard by Governor Carroll in 1877 and held this rank for three administrations, participating in the great Baltimore & Ohio Railroad riots, along with many other Confederate officers such as John Donnell Smith, William Wirt Robertson, Carvel Hall and John Gale of his old battalion.

EUGENE WORTHINGTON SR. (1842/1914) - Oil Painting - Born at Summer Hill, Anne Arundel County, he was an art student at the Maryland Institute in Baltimore and his enthusiasm for the military enabled him to become a private in Company B, Maryland Guard Militia. When hostilities broke upon the land he walked to Harpers Ferry and then travelled to Richmond where he mustered into the Maryland Flying Artillery at Brook's Station on September 8, 1861. He had a defect in his sight known at the time as moon blindness and at night could not see distinctly. Many nights while on the march he came to a comrade, James W. Owens, and asked to take his arm and they would then march together like Siamese twins. With the 1st Maryland Artillery, Pvt. Worthington was twice wounded but never seriously. He was paroled at Appomattox Courthouse with the cannoneers of the 1st Maryland who at the time had been fighting as infantry. Going to Baltimore he studied pharmacy and was engaged as an apothecary there. Later at Belvoir near Annapolis he was the cashier of the Annapolis Savings Institute. Besides being a member of the Society of the Army and Navy in the Confederacy in the State of Maryland, he was chosen Lieutenant Commander of the George H. Steuart Camp of Confederate Veterans when it was formed on January 22, 1895.

GEORGE LITTLETON GALE (1843/1862) - Watercolor photograph - Raised at Princess Anne, he was one of three brothers who joined the Confederacy. On July 16, 1861, he and his brother Frank became privates while his brother John, a physician, was commissioned a lieutenant in the Maryland Flying Artillery. They subsequently became the 1st Maryland Artillery and George was among the members who were sent to the Hampton Legion South Carolina Artillery, Company B, in the summer of 1862. He became company bugler and was wounded on the Old Battlefield at Manassas. As the enemy pressed forward in overwhelming numbers, the battery would limber its piece to the rear about 100 yards, halt and renew the fight. The was done several times until the enemy was driven back with heavy losses. The following day on August 29, 1862, he died as a result of his wounds.

WILLIAM HUNTER GRIFFIN (1836/1896) - Ambrotype - This businessman from Baltimore crossed the Potomac and assisted in organizing the Baltimore Light Artillery in August of 1861. They subsequently became known as the 2nd Maryland Artillery and he was elected 1st lieutenant. At Sharpsburg, when their commander J.B. Brockenborough was promoted to major for the gallantry of the 2nd Maryland, Griffin became commander. At Yellow Tavern his guns were so effective the enemy massed a heavy body of cavalry determined at any sacrifice to capture the guns that had been wreaking such dreadful havoc in their ranks. During this charge Griffin resorted to grape and canister. At every discharge whole companies melted away and the enemy fell back in confusion. As they advanced again the Confederate cavalry gave way for an instant which left the battery to the mercy of the enemy who dashed upon it. General J.E.B. Stuart had witnessed all the action and rallied his broken cavalry by seizing the colors of the 1st Virginia. While riding forward to save the brave Marylanders he was killed. The battery suffered severe losses in men, horses and two guns along with its commander. Griffin was imprisoned in the dungeons of Morris Island and Fort Pulaski until finally being released on June 16, 1865.

38 - Artillery

ELABORATELY CARVED PIPE made with a common pocket knife by Private J. Thomas Earnest bearing the coats of arms of Maryland and Virginia. Also depicted is a design with figures of a soldier holding a Confederate flag while beneath Justice draws aside a curtain to disclose a Star of Hope. The stem is inscribed "Made in Camp of Balto. Lt. Art. Feb. 1863, near New Market, Va." while on the bowl is carved "Presented to Lt. W.B. Bean by J.T. Earnest."

WILLIAM RITTER (1835/1928) - Carte de Viste - He was a native of Carroll County and was a mail agent in the first rural route delivery in the country prior to the war. Leaving home on October 12, 1861, he was one of the organizers of the 3rd Maryland Artillery, in which he became an orderly sergeant. They were organized at Richmond and trained at Camp Lee at the New Fairgrounds. On February 4, 1862, the company was ordered to Knoxville, Tennessee. On March 17, 1863, he was promoted to 2nd lieutenant and commanded the 2nd Battery. During the long siege of Vicksburg, Ritter became 1st lieutenant and received his second wound at Resaca, where his section lost half its men. He dressed his own wound and continued to command. Of the cannoneers who worked the guns, Ritter, along with another lieutenant and two sergeants, were the only ones to escape uninjured from this disastrous field. They overtook the reserve on foot and moved with the army to Mississippi. After Captain Rowan was killed at Columbus, Ritter became captain on May 10. In February of 1865 they were ordered to Mobile where he commanded Battery D. During the battle he and his men were surrounded and forced to surrender. They were later paroled at Meridian. In February of 1866 he returned to his native state after an absence of four years and four months. The next year he married the widow of his former commander. Moving to Reisterstown, he entered the business world. He held memberships in the Society of the Army and Navy of the Confederate States in the State of Maryland, of which he was vice president in 1898, the Franklin Buchanan Camp and the Isaac R. Trimble Camp of Confederate Veterans where in 1899 he served as adjutant.

HARRY HALE BROGDEN (1835/) - Carte de Viste - He left his home at Davidsonville and enlisted in Richmond on March 4, 1861, in the 2nd Company, Maryland Zouave Regiment. The formation of the regiment did not occur because of the capture of its proposed colonel, Richard Thomas Zarvona. Brogden became associated with the artillery in the Signal Corps and was appointed a sergeant on October 18, 1862, which was officially accepted on November 18. On April 15, 1863, a letter to the Federal Occupying troops stated that Harry Brogden, an officer of the Confederate Army and wearing the uniform of that Army, was with Captain W. Knows 13 miles from Annapolis. He was captured on the Chesapeake Bay on May 7 and tried as a spy and confined in prison. On May 28, 1864, he was exchanged and returned to the Signal Corps. On September 7, 1864, he was appointed adjutant of the 37th Virginia Cavalry but after a short period declined due to ill health. On January 23, 1865, he was detailed for special service in the Signal Corps and reported to the Secretary of State.

ALEXANDER HAMILTON BAYLY (/1929) - Carte de Viste - Leaving his ancestral home at Cambridge, he enlisted on April 26, 1861, in Peyton's Virginia Artillery for one year as a private. After being discharged in the summer of 1862 he re-enlisted in the Orange Light Artillery. On October 9 Bayly was detailed to the Danville, Virginia, Hospital. On July 6, 1863, he was appointed a hospital steward gaining the rank of sergeant and remained at Danville. He was paroled on May 1, 1865, at the hospital and after several months returned to his native town.

ROBERT H. GOLDSBOROUGH (/1865) - Carte de Viste - Born and raised in Queen Anne's County he was a 1st lieutenant in the Scott Rifles of the Maryland Militia prior to the war. Upon the advancement of the Southern Army into Maryland, Goldsborough became captain of Company C, Chambers Independent Maryland Artillery Battalion. They were organized at Frederick and eight days later were in action at Antietam. Chamber's Artillery Battalion was almost completely destroyed and the survivors were absorbed into other artillery units. Goldsborough became a private in Company B, 39th Virginia Cavalry on October 29, 1862, but was soon detailed as a courier for General Ewell. He was appointed 1st lieutenant on May 16, 1863, as an aide-de-camp on the staff of General J.E.B. Stuart. He was captured on June 9, 1863, at Beverly Ford and was confined first in Capitol Prison at Washington and then at Point Lookout. On August 5, 1883, General Stuart suggested Goldsborough be offered in exchange for an aid of General Buford. The exchange was granted but in the mean time Stuart was killed at Yellow Tavern. Goldsborough served as an aide-de-camp on the staff of General Curtis Lee and was mortally wounded at Saylor's Creek on June 6, 1865.

FREDERICK MORGAN COLSTON (1845/1922) - Carte de Viste - Born in Leesburg, he came to Baltimore and in 1853 graduated from Georgetown University. Passing an examination for appointment in artillery he became an officer on December 2, 1862. Serving in the ordnance department as a 2nd lieutenant he was with Richard Snowden Andrews through the early part of 1863. In March he joined Alexander's Battalion of Artillery. After Gettysburg he was sent to the Army of Tennessee for a short period and then returned to the Army of Northern Virginia. On September 10, 1864, he was advanced to the rank of captain. In October he was ordered to mount the heavy guns from Wood's, Semmes' and Brooke's Batteries. They arrived by rail and were mounted by night on the southeast side of the James River on Howlett's Bluff. On February 28, 1865, he was sent to Amelia Courthouse in charge of ordnance stores. His artillery always occupied the ground after

every fight and buried their own dead. Throughout the campaigns of Charlottesville, Gettysburg, East Tennessee, The Wilderness, Spottsylvania and Petersburg he never ran. In fact, throughout his service, he never ran until Saylor's Creek, three days before the surrender at Appomattox, when their train was captured and he barely escaped. He surrendered with the Army of Northern Virginia on April 9, 1865. After returning to his home, he was forced to take the oath of allegiance at Catonsville on June 12, 1865. The following year he formed a banking firm of which he became president. In 1867 he was captain of Company F, 5th Maryland Militia Regiment. Colston was a member of the Society of the Army and Navy of the Confederate States in the State of Maryland.

RICHARD S. CONTEE (1836/1908) - Carte de Viste - He was born and raised on the plantation "Pleasant Prospect" in Prince George's County. Travelling to Virginia, he enlisted as a volunteer aide on June 1, 1861, on Colonel Arnold Elzey's staff. He received a commission as a 1st lieutenant on September 11, 1861, as an aide-de-camp. Richard resigned on June 20, 1863. Meeting his wife who had run the blockade, they proceeded to Winchester to nurse his wounded brother, Charles Snowden. Knowing that the army was going into action, he remained only a week. Attaching himself to General Richard Ewell as an aide-de-camp, he was wounded in the arm at Gettysburg on July 3, 1863. In late 1864 he was raised to the rank of major by President Davis and received a staff appointment with General G.W. Smith. Returning to his home in the fall of 1865 he farmed until April 2, 1907, at which time he became a resident of the Maryland Line Confederate Soldiers Home.

THOMAS ALEXANDER SYMINGTON (1843/1900) - Tintype - He was the brother of Major W. Stuart Symington and a member of the Maryland Guard, Baltimore militia, in 1860. Leaving his home in Catonsville, he enlisted on May 24, 1861, in Richmond for the war as a private in Blunt's Light Virginia Artillery. In January of 1864 he was transferred to the 10th Virginia Cavalry and shortly thereafter to Darling's Headquarters where he became ordnance sergeant of the 38th Virginia Artillery Battalion. In May he served on the staff of General Darling and was officially made 1st lieutenant on October 8, 1864. By the end of the war he was aide-de-damp on the staff of General G. Pickett. Returning to Baltimore County he was a member of the Society of the Army and Navy of the Confederate States in the State of Maryland and the Franklin Buchanan United Confederate Veterans Camp.

JOHN D. KLINE (1837/) - Carte de Viste - Leaving his family home in Baltimore after hearing that the Southern Army had crossed into Maryland, he proceeded to Frederick where, on September 9, 1862, he joined Chambers Independent Artillery. This battalion was formed in Frederick by Marylanders and participated in the Antietam Campaign. They were so devastated by casualties that the men were then absorbed into other artillery units. Kline received a commission in the ordnance department and was assigned to the staff of E.F. Paxton. While advancing at Chancellorsville on May 3, 1863, he was captured and sent to Johnson's Island. Upon being exchanged, Captain Kline was sent to the Army of the Gulf where he became chief of ordnance with W.K. Patterson. He was captured again on June 28, 1864, at Courtland, Alabama, and sent to Louisville, Kentucky, where he was held until his release on June 14, 1865. He lived in Columbia, Tennessee, for several years before returning to Maryland.

AUBREY PEARRE (1838/1915) - Ambrotype - He and his brother, Oliver Hazzard Pearre, left their farm near Unionville and rode with Harry Gilmor's command. At Antietam, they were met by another brother, James Warfield Pearre, but persuaded him not to join. Before returning home, James volunteered as a hospital aide at the Dunkard Church. On Sepember 20, 1862, Aubrey and Oliver enlisted in Company D, 1st Maryland Cavalry. A month later they were transferred to the Army of the West. There they joined their first cousin, Lieutenant Charles Morgan Pearre, also from Unionville, and second cousin, Major Charles Baer Pearre from Comus. Oliver became a member of the Signal Corps, and Aubrey a 1st lieutenant and ordnance officer of General P.R. Cleburne. Aubrey surrendered at Greensboro on April 26, 1865. While returning to his wife and home, he took the amnesty oath at Harpers Ferry on July 1. He settled in Baltimore where he and Oliver formed the dry good business of Pearre Brothers.

42 - Artillery

LYWELLYN GRIFFITH HOXTON - Ambrotype - He was born and raised in Georgetown and was appointed to the Military Academy at West Point. Upon graduating with the class of 1861 he received a 2nd lieutenant's commission in the Federal Army on May 6. Not accepting it, he through in his lot with the cause of the south and was listed as dismissed on May 25. He became 1st lieutenant in Captain Tobin's company of Virginia Infantry on June 26, 1861. Hoxton was ordered to Memphis, Tennessee, and assigned to the artillery. By June 5, 1862, he was a captain serving in ordnance with the Army of Mississippi. As a member of the staff of General Hardee he was promoted to major in January of 1863 and served with the Army of Tennessee. He became chief of artillery and obtained the rank of lieutenant colonel. In March of 1865 he commanded batteries on the left wing in the Department of the Gulf, surrendering at Meridian, Mississippi. He was paroled on May 1, 1865. He went to Catonsville where he received an appointment as instructor of mathematics and English literature in the Maryland Military Institute.

JAMES BREATHED (1838/1870) - Paper Enlargement - Breathedsville was the place of his birth and he was educated at St. John's College and the University of Maryland Medical College before becoming an apprentice under Dr. James Macgill at Hagerstown. Breathed resettled in Missouri to practice his profession which he abandoned at the outbreak of the war. He returned to his father's home in Washington County to cast his fortune with those of his state. On his journey east his travelling compaion was J.E.B. Stuart. Departing for Virginia, he joined Company B, 1st Virginia Cavalry, as a private. Stuart recognized young Breathed from a few weeks previous and assigned him to detached service as a scout. On March 23, 1862, he was elected 1st lieutenant under Captain John Pelham, in a battery of horse artillery organized by General Stuart. On August 9, 1862, Dr. Breathed was promoted to captain and recruited well over 100 Marylanders into Stuart's Horse Artillery. This battery of horse artillery also would include 10 Maryland commissioned officers along with many enlisted men. Serving as a warrior and not a physician during the fighting he was wounded four times. After the war he quietly resumed his professional work and established Hancock as his home.

Chapter 5

CAVALRY

The first complete company of Maryland horsemen rode under Turner Ashby as Company G, 1st Virginia Cavalry, captained by Dr. Frank J. Mason. Out of the ranks of this company rose a number of fearless riders destined for cavalry commands. These were Lieutenants Thaddeus L. Thrasher, T. Jeff Smith, Richard Grubb, Rodney C. Howell, Charles Owen, S. Clapham Smith, and Blanchard Gowen Pilpott; Captains Benjamin Pilpott Crampton, and Thomas Benton Gatch; Major Warner G. Welsh; and Lieutenant Colonels Harry W. Gilmor, Elijah Viers White and T. Stragis Davis. General Ashby was killed on June 6, 1862, near Harrisonburg while leading Marylanders and Virginians.

Gus W. Dorsey drew Free Staters around him as he organized Company M, 1st Virginia Cavalry. Through their courageous riding they won the heart of General J.E.B. Stuart, and were placed on the right of the battalion and their company designation changed to K.

Eighteen young men who had served in Company K, 1st Virginia Cavalry, upon completing their 12-month enlistment, proceeded to Richmond and organized a complete Maryland regiment in May of 1862. As they were organizing, Ridgely Brown's first company was assigned to the 2nd Virginia Cavalry. On November 25, 1862, the 1st Maryland Battalion was officially organized in the Confederate service at Winchester with Company B under the command of Captain George W. Emack and Company C under Captain Robert Carter Smith, formerly of the 1st Maryland Infantry. Warner Griffith Welsh resigned his captain's commission of Company F, 12th Virginia Cavalry, and mustered in men from Frederick and Carroll counties as Company D. William Independence Rasin had formed a company known as Winder's Cavalry which became Company E. Three rich young Baltimoreans ran the blockade to Baltimore for all their arms and accoutrements except for the horses and formed Company F. In July, 1864, Company K, 1st Virginia Cavalry, was finally transferred to their brother Marylanders in the 1st Battalion, retaining their company designation.

Elijah Veirs White was authorized to raise a company in late 1861. The men were used as couriers until the first company was mustered in on March 19 of the following year. On June 20 they received news that Captain George W. Chiswell had organized a full company of men in Montgomery County and was prepared to join White's Cavalry. By October, Bradley T. Johnson mustered in the 35th Virginia Cavalry. At Frederick during the Antietam Campaign, White was ordered to take his men back to Virginia to protect the flank. He incurred the displeasure of General Stuart when he objected to being left out of this chance to help free his home state. He is quoted as saying "I am a Marylander by birth and have fought as hard as any man for the privilege of fighting upon the soil of my native state." He requested to see General Lee concerning this matter and Stuart, realizing that White was from Maryland, relented and allowed the 35th to remain with the main army. There were at least 272 Marylanders in the 35th Virginia Cavalry.

Harry W. Gilmor obtained permission from Turner Ashby to organize a Maryland company with the 7th Virginia Cavalry Regiment in early March of 1862. Instead of being affiliated with their state kinsmen of Company G, they were sent to the 12th Virginia Calvary as Company F on April 10, 1862. On May 7, 1863, Gilmor resigned his commission when authorized to organize a battalion. While recruiting, his mounted men were scouts for General's A.G. Jenkins and J.E.B. Stuart. Gilmor's battalion, when ordered to the Maryland Line, became known as the 2nd Maryland Cavalry, with Company A under Captain Nicholas Burke; Company B, Captain Eugene Diggs; Company C, Captain David M. Ross; Company D, Captain John Burke; Company E, Captain John E. Sudler, and Company F, Captain James L. Clarke. After their commander was captured at Moorefield his brother, Richard Tilghman Gilmor, commanded the 2nd Maryland Battalion from February 4 until they were disbanded on April 29.

44 - Cavalry

In late 1864 Harry Gilmor was placed in command of the 1st Maryland Cavalry and McNeill's Rangers in addition to his 2nd Maryland Cavalry. McNeill's Rangers contained at least 23 known Marylanders. After Gilmor was captured young Captain McNeill, who had replaced his deceased father, sent John Lynn to his home in Cumberland during the early part of February in 1865 on reconnaisance. Another Cumberland boy, Sergeant John B. Fay, was also dispatched to Cumberland and returned on February 19. On the information received, 65 rangers rode 75 miles and, in the early morning hours of February 21 in Cumberland, captured Major Generals Kelly and Crook. Even though Cumberland was occupied by 8,000 troops, they returned with the captured generals without the loss of a man. There were three troopers in this command with the last name Clary. One was Dr. Richard L. Clary, who was killed on June 12, 1861, the first fatality of the command. Lloyd L. and Thadeus W. Clary also rode in this unit.

Philip Henry Lee put together a cavalry troop in 1862 that furnished scouts, guides and couriers for the Maryland Line. William W. Dallam also organized a group of 62 mounted Marylanders that was later dissolved into other commands and he became a lieutenant in the Engineer Corps. A unit of mounted riflemen under William H. Jacobs was organized, but before their ranks could be completely filled, they were consolidated with the Bradford Rangers and later became Company I, 2nd Virginia Cavalry.

T. Sturgis Davis mustered in six companies of partisan rangers and became lieutenant colonel of Davis' Maryland Cavalry. The company commanders were Company A, Captain Thomas Benton Gatch; Company B, Captain Charles E. Bishop; Company C, Capain John G. Phillips; Company D, Captain George M.E. Shearer; Company E ,Captain William C. Nicholas, and Company F, Captain A.D. Irwin.

John Singleton Mosby's original 15-man unit included three Marylanders, Daniel L. Thomas Jr., Edward S. Hurst and Thomas Turner. These 15 men were the nucleus of Mosby's Partisan Rangers. There were at least 251 Marylanders contained in the ranks of the 43rd Virginia Cavalry.

GEORGE RIDGELY GAITHER JR. (/1899) - Ambrotype - He was born and educated in Baltimore but made his home in Ellicott City. He was captain of the Howard County Dragoons, Company B, a militia unit composed of 40 men. They were disbanded when the Federal Army took over the state. Twenty three men, mounted and equipped with their militia accoutrements, hastily gathered up the company's arms and made their way to Point of Rocks. At Leesburg they were joined by Montgomery countians. On May 14, 1861, Gaither was made captain of a cavalry unit performing picket duty at Edward's Ferry for some weeks before being mustered into the 1st Virginia Cavalry as Company M. At the Second Battle of Manassas Captain Gaither was captured. After three weeks he was paroled and returned to his command just prior to the Battle of Sharpsburg. After the Battle of Brandy Station he was advanced to the rank of lieutenant colonel. The Marylanders with Stuart's cavalry acted as guides during the summer of 1863 as they proceeded through Darnesville, Westminster, Hanover, and Carlisle on their way to Gettysburg. In December of 1863 he was obligated to resign his commission because of physical disabilities. Hospitalized at Staunton, Greenwood and Charlottesville until November of 1863, he was transferred to Richmond. The following month he had the opportunity to go to Europe for three months. Afterwards he travelled to Nassau and St. John's where he remained until the hostilities had ended. In August, 1865, he returned to Baltimore and entered into the cotton trade business until his retirement in 1879. In 1871 he began a long association with the 5th Maryland Militia. That year he was commissioned major; 1875 lieutenant colonel, and 1895 colonel of this veteran corps. In 1899 he was vice president of the Army and Navy Society and a manager of the Maryland Line Confederate Soldiers Home.

NATHAN CHEW HOBBS (1837/) - Ambrotype - Departing his Cooksville home, he enlisted for one year in Company M, 1st Virginia Cavalry, on May 14, 1861, at Leesburg. He was appointed sergeant prior to the company's designation being changed to Company K. Upon re-enlisting, he was elected 2nd lieutenant on May 14, 1862. While returning from the Gettysburg Campaign, he was wounded in the right thigh and captured at Hagerstown on July 12, 1863. He was confined at Fort McHenry until being exchanged on March 2, 1864. While in prison he was promoted to 1st lieutenant. Shortly after Company K was transferred by the War Department to the 1st Maryland Cavalry, he was wounded in the right forearm on September 19, 1864, and admitted to General Hospital No. 4 at Richmond. In an attempt to stay with his command, he reported at the end of the month to Wayside Hospital in Lynchburg and by October 21 was in Charlottesville General Hospital. After a 30-day furlough he returned to his regiment from Petersburg, Virginia. After surrendering at New Market, Virginia, he signed the amnesty oath at Winchester on April 19. Returning to his native Howard County, he was active in the Society of the Army and Navy of the Confederate States in the State of Maryland.

GEORGE MURRAY GILL JR. (1842 /1865) - Carte de Viste - He was a Baltimorean and was graduated from Princeton majoring in law. As a sergeant in Company E, Maryland Guard, 53rd State Militia he mustered in the spring of 1861 when Federal troops first entered the southern states. In the early part of the war he attached himself to the infantry but soon enlisted in Company K, 1st Virginia Cavalry. He was severely wounded in 1862 during a skirmish on the Little River Turnpike. After Gettysburg he was captured at Hagerstown and spent five months in captivity. After exchange he joined Mosby's Partisan Rangers, Company D, 43rd Virginia Cavalry. On March 30, 1865, Private Gill was wounded near Berryville. In attempting to return to Upperville he was compelled to stop at a house in the Blue Ridge from a loss of blood. John Gill, a cousin, joined George and, realizing the seriousness of his wound, started for a physician, riding all night and returning the next day, only to find George had died. The last words he uttered were, "I died at least in a good cause." He was buried in a little graveyard on the mountainside.

46 - Cavalry

THOMAS SHERWIN (1839/) - Carte de Viste - Enlisting at Martingburg on Spetember 10, 1862, he became a private in the 1st Virginia Cavalry, Company K. His original enlistment was for two years, but he served with the company throughout the war. In July of 1864 Company K was finally transferred to the 1st Maryland Cavalry. At Fisher's Hill on September 21, 1864, his horse was killed in the initial action. He was paroled at Staunton on May 13, 1865.

RIDGELY BROWN (1833/1864) - Paper Enlargement - This Montgomery Countian went to the aid of the Confederacy on June 1, 1861. After serving a year as a lieutenant in the 1st Virginia Cavalry, Company K, he was among the organizers of the 1st Maryland Cavalry. Until the regiment could be completely formed, this company, of which he was elected captain, was attached to the 2nd Virginia Cavalry and was designated Company B in early 1862. After the regiment was formed they became Company A and Brown subsequently won promotion to major. In April of 1863, at Greenland Gap in the long West Virginia Expedition, he was painfully wounded in the leg while leading a dismounted attack. Continuing on duty, he rose 168 miles before examining his wound. Promotion to lieutenant colonel also brought him command of the battalion. On June 1, 1864, at South Anna Bridge, while contesting the Federal advance on Richmond, the battalion was in contact with the enemy from daylight until 2 o'clock before the fighting subsided. During this engagement Brown was killed by a stray bullet, which struck him in the forehead, and he died without speaking a single word.

GUSTAVUS W. DORSEY (/1911) - Carte de Viste - He was reared on a farm near Brookville and was one of the eager young soldiers to go to Virginia in 1861. He enlisted with the Marylanders of the 1st Virginia Cavalry which became Company K. Shortly after joining the unit his qualifications secured him a promotion to orderly sergeant and a year later to 1st lieutenant. He was wounded in the desperate engagement at Fredericksburg in 1862 and again at Fisher's Hill during the Valley Campaign of 1864. This wound disabled him for six weeks. At Yellow Tavern when General Stuart was wounded Captain Dorsey immediately rushed to his assistance, taking the general from his horse and placing him against a tree. Stuart expressed his belief that his wound would be fatal and that he could be of no further use so he ordered Dorsey back to his command. Dorsey declined to do this until he saw him safely from the field and called upon some of his men to place Stuart upon a horse and lead him to a place of safety where an ambulance could then be secured. Shortly after Stuart's death, Company K was transferred to the 1st Maryland Cavalry. Dorsey was promoted to lieutenant colonel of the 1st Maryland Battalion after Colonel Brown fell on June 1, 1864, near South Anna. The regiment was prepared to go to the aid of the Army of the South after Appomattox, but on April 28 Dorsey received orders from General Munford to disband the regiment. He returned to his home in Montgomery County where he turned to farming.

Cavalry - 47

WARNER GRIFFITH WELSH (1834/1895) - Albumin Print - Welsh was born in Anne Arundel County and came to Frederick County in the early 1840s. He was a farmer near Libertytown. He was a member of the Liberty Riflemen who were formed in the fall of 1859 and became part of the 20th Regiment, Maryland Militia. He enlisted early in the rebellion in Company G, 7th Virginia Cavalry, composed of Marylanders. In March of 1862, he assisted in organizing a company and was elected first lieutenant in Company F, 12th Virginia Cavalry. That fall he resigned to organize his own company which would be in the 1st Maryland Cavalry as Company D composed of men from Frederick and Carroll counties. They enlisted on September 20, and among the ranks were two of his brothers, Luther Brooke Welsh, Jr., who rode as a private, and Milton Welsh, who was chosen a 2nd lieutenant. On May 20, 1863, he was labeled a bushwhacker when captured while checking enemy headquarters near Winchester and was sent to Fort McHenry. He was confined on May 22, and during the night of June 13 or the morning of the 14th he made his escape and returned to his unit. In the early fall of 1864, after Gilmor had been seriously wounded, General Lomax proposed to consolidate the two Maryland battalions and appointed Gilmor as colonel, Gustavus W. Dorsey lieutenant colonel and Welsh as major. Welsh and his two brothers, along with numerous others of the command, headed for General Johnston's Army in Salisbury, North Carolina, where he surrendered in early May. He returned to his home near Libertytown, which had now been renamed, "Capsylvia," in his honor.

HAMMOND DORSEY (1841/1898) - Albumin print - He was born on a farm near Ellicott City in Howard County and on May 14, 1861, enlisted in K Company, 1st Virginia Cavalry at Leesburg. He refused to re-enlist in the Virginia regiment, preferring to be in a Maryland cavalry unit. He was suffering from acute diarrhea because of his diet and on June 25, 1862, entered the General Hospital No. 21 in Richmond. In early 1863 he became a sergeant. During the Gettysburg Campaign, Company A was attached to General Ewell's Headquarters. During the withdrawal from Pennsylvania, Ewell's wagon train was attacked near Hagerstown by a strong Union cavalry command. Sixty-four men of A Company turned and counter-charged at full speed. Sergeant Dorsey was the first man of the company to reach the enemy's lines and five men fell from his saber before the company retired. Near Appomattox, Dorsey, having lost his horse, was on foot and was compelled to surrender on April 10, 1865. He returned to his home and was made to report to the provost marshal of the Middle District at Relay House on April 23 to take an amnesty oath. After returning to Howard County he was forced to report and take the oath again on May 25.

48 - Cavalry

EDWARD W. BEATTY (/1864) - Carte de Viste - Leaving the Rockville area, he travelled to Harpers Ferry where he enlisted as a private in Company D, 1st Maryland Infantry. Being advanced in years, he was constantly called upon for leadership, but steadfastly refused promotion, preferring instead to carry a musket. After his discharge, he became 2nd lieutenant of Company A, 1st Maryland Cavalry. Wounded in the shoulder at Greenland Gap, Beatty was captured at Brandy Station on October 16, 1863, and sent to Johnson's Island where he died on March 24, 1864.

ALLEN C. REDWOOD & SKETCH OF THE 1ST. MARYLAND CAVALRY (1844/1922) - Carte de Viste - He attended private school in Baltimore and the Polytechnic Institute, Brooklyn, from which he left at the outset of hostilities to enlist on July 24, 1862, at Urbanna, Virginia. He became a private in Company C of the 55th Virginia Infantry, serving as military secretary and courier on the staff of General L.L. Lomax. In January of 1864 he became a member of Company C, 1st Maryland Cavalry. During the war he was wounded three times and captured twice, finally being released on July 3, 1865. With the end of the war he went to Warren County, North Carolina, and then returned to Baltimore. He worked as a lithographer and became one of the state's most renowned oil and watercolor artists of the Confederacy. His name was on the rolls of the Society of the Army and Navy of the Confederate States in the State of Maryland but he resided in Port Conway, Virginia, in the early 1900s.

EDWARD HOWARD HALL (1844/1917) - Carte de Viste - He left his home in Harford County enlisting as a private in the 1st Maryland Cavalry, Company A, on July 15, 1862. At Pollard's Farm on May 21, 1864, he was taken prisoner in a flanking movement where the 1st Maryland lost between 50-60 men in the dreadful hand-to-hand combat before they were given the order to retreat. He was exchanged on February 18, 1865, and returned to his company. Again, he was captured at Hanover Courthouse on March 13 in an all-day skirmish and was incarcerated at Point Lookout until his release on April 20, 1865.

JAMES WILCOX JENKINS JR. (1844/) - Carte de Viste - The impetuous desires of youth caused him to leave his studies at Georgetown University and go to the aid of the Confederacy. He enlisted in Winder's Cavalry on October 13, 1863, in Richmond. He served as a private in Company E, 1st Maryland Cavalry, until being captured near Hagerstown on July 6, 1863, while guarding the wagon train retreating from Gettysburg. He was sent to Fort Delaware and later to Point Lookout. On February 18, 1865, he was exchanged and returned to the cavalry battalion that escaped Appomattox. He was paroled on April 13, 1865, at Lynchburg and on June 15 took the oath of parole in Baltimore while returning to his native home.

THOMAS P. WILLIAMS JR. (1842/1891) - Carte de Viste - He was a sailor from Caroline County who came to Baltimore. Travelling to Virginia he enlisted in the Maryland Guard of the 21st Virginia Infantry on May 1, 1861. After Company B's term of enlistment had expired, he re-enlisted on February 23 in the Marion Light Georgia Artillery. Under General Order No. 65, which enabled Marylanders to proceed to distinctive Maryland commands, he was among the few who were relieved by their commanders and transferred on March 24, 1864, to Company C, 1st Maryland Cavalry. He was captured on August 27 by the 1st New York Calvary at Moorefield where the two Maryland cavalry battalions were taken by surprise in camp. Williams was sent to Atheneum Prison at Wheeling and then to Camp Chase, Ohio. On March 18, 1865, he was transferred to Point Lookout and exchanged. Returning to the Maryland Line Cavalry, he was paroled two months later and signed the oath of allegience at Burkittsville on May 18 after returning to the state.

FRANK LOUIS HERING (1835/1909) - Carte de Viste - He was a miller from Carroll County and enlisted on July 1, 1864, in Frederick just prior to the Baltimore Raid, attaching himself to Lieutenant Colonel Harry Gilmor's Battalion. Being among the last Maryland volunteers, he summed up his feelings in a letter of July 4. "I came from Maryland building no castles in air consequently feeling perfectly satisfied. I do not regret the step I have taken. I expected to suffer many privations consequently and prepared for almost anything and if the Good Lord sees fit to spare my life so that I may see my friends again I hope I might find you all alive and well and when we can sit down and enjoy a good talk together. Tell father and Jenny and all the rest to keep in good spirits, that all that I can desire I ask is your earnest prayers and with the assurance of this and a grace of an all wise God I am sure I will get back again to enjoy the comforts of home." After the Baltimore-Washington Raid he mustered into Company D, 1st Maryland Cavalry. Private Hering received his parole on May 5, 1865, at Staunton after breaking through the Appomattox Line. He remained in the valley for nearly a year before returning to the Finksburg area.

SILK LAUREL WREATH presented by the Ladies of Leesburg to Colonel E.V. White.

ELIJAH VEIRS WHITE (1832/1907) - Tintype - He lived near Poolesville and was educated at Lima Seminary, New York, and Granville College, Ohio. White went to Kansas to participate in the 1855 insurrection returning to Montgomery County in 1857. White farmed and was a member in the Loudoun Cavalry during the John Brown incident. At the onset of hostilities, he joined Frank Mason's Company G, 7th Virginia Cavalry, consisting of Marylanders. In December of 1861 he organized and became commander of the 35th Virginia Cavalry, known as White's Rangers and later the "Comanches." Lige White, as he was familiarly known, gathered together a battalion of six companies composed of men from both sides of the Potomac and it became part of the Laurel Brigade. During the war he was wounded three times and was paroled on May 9, 1865, near Leesburg, Virginia, where he continued to reside. White was sheriff of Loudoun County in 1867 as well as a wheat shipper and opeator of a ferry between Maryland and Virginia. In 1892, he was elected president of the People's National Bank and served as commander of Clinton Hatcher Camp of United Confederate Veterans.

GEORGE T. ELLMORE (1843/) - Ambrotype - Leaving the Old Land of Sanctuary he and his brother John D. along with a number of other young lads from Montgomery County enlisted at the same time in Company A, 35th Virginia Cavalry on October 4, 1863. He was captured on April 12, 1864, at Aldie in Loudoun County. Sent to the Old Capitol Prison in Washington, from where his brother was recently exchanged, George ended up in the prison hospital on May 7 for eight days and again on June 13 for 29 days. George was transferred to Fort Warren and released on June 13, 1865 when he proceeded home to again meet his brother.

JOHN D. ELLMORE - Ambrotype - He enlisted for the war on October 4, 1863, in Loudoun County in Light's Border Rangers. The rangers became Company A of the 35th Virginia Cavalry. In the beginning, the unit had a terrible time getting troopers to serve as teamsters because everyone wanted to be a combatant. As the war dragged on, however, teamster volunteers became more numerous. In December of 1863 Ellmore served as a teamster. He was captured on June 9, 1863, during the Battle of Beverley Station. He received his parole at Winchester, and upon crossing into Maryland at Edward's Ferry on April 26, 1865, was forced to take the oath of allegiance.

52 - Cavalry

WALLACE SELLMAN (/1864) - Albumin print - Reared in the Old Medley's area of Montgomery County near Clarksburg, he and his brother, Alonzo, left their home and joined Company B, 35th Virginia Cavalry. Alonzo remained in the comanches and became a sergeant, while Wallace enlisted in Lee's Maryland Cavalry. They were to be a part of the Maryland Line but, when it was not formed, became scouts and guides. In the summer of 1864 as a courier under Captain Philip Henry Lee, he was taken ill with typhoid fever and died.

JOHN POOLE SELLMAN (1840/1908) - Carte de Viste - He was born at Comus in Montgomery County and ran away from the Brookville Academy. On September 1, 1863, he joined Company K, 1st Virginia Cavalry, and served there until February 10, 1862, when he transferred to Company A, 1st Maryland Cavalry. While on picket duty in Loudoun County, Virginia, on September 6, 1864, he was captured and taken to the dungeons of Old Capitol Prison. He was exchanged in February of 1865, and then rode with White's Comanches of the 35th Virginia Cavalry. Sellman was again captured and returned to Old Capitol Prison until the rebellion was over. Going to Loudoun County, he was married and soon returned to his home to raise stock. In 1888 he was elected county commissioner for two terms and in 1902 represented Montgomery County in the state legislature. Sellman was a member of Ridgely Brown Camp of Confederate Veterans.

HARRY W. GILMOR (1838/1883) - Albumin Print - He ventured to Wisconsin and Nebraska to try his hand at homesteading, but returned home in 1860. He was arrested for his secessionist activities and imprisoned in Fort McHenry for two weeks. He then left his home near Glen Ellen where he had been a corporal in the Baltimore County Horse Guards of the state militia. He crossed the Potomac on August 30, 1861, and enlisted as a private in Mason's Maryland command, Company G, 7th Virginia Cavalry. On March 26, 1862, became commander of a cavalry company of Marylanders he had organized, which was designated Company F, 12th Virginia Cavalry. By September of 1863, he organized a battalion of six companies which was mustered in as the 2nd Maryland Battalion, and served as partisan rangers. Gilmor's daring exploits rang through the army, and they were affectionately known as "the band." In July of 1864, he was put in command of the consolidated Maryland cavalries in the Maryland Line. During the war, he was wounded four times, captured four times and imprisoned twice, becoming Maryland's most renowned cavalry commander. Gilmor was released from Fort Warren on July 24, 1865. After spending several years in New Orleans and Europe, he returned to Baltimore and became police commissioner.

GEORGE WASHINGTON PURNALL (1841/1899) - Carte de Viste - Born at Snow Hill by the age of 12 he was an orphan. Graduating from the Snow Hill Academy and, after attending the University of Virginia, he entered Princeton University in 1859. With the outbreak of war he left college and returned to his home before making his way south. Worcester County Federal Enrollment Records show that his name was stricken and beside it was written "Gone South." In May of 1863 he helped organize Company B of Gilmor's Battalion and was chosen 2nd lieutenant. They became the 2nd Maryland Cavalry. While pursuing Hunter's troops, he was captured near Piedmont, Virginia, on June 5, 1864, and sent to Johnson's Island. In a letter to his family members of April 11, 1865, he stated that the events of the surrender were too sad to talk about. Released on June 15 when persons of his rank were enabled to obtain release by taking the oath of parole, he proceeded to Baltimore where, on August 12, he was caused to go before the provost marshal to again signify the oath of his allegiance. He studied law at Snow Hill and returned to the University of Virginia, passing the bar in 1868. As an attorney at Snow Hill he was also a member of the Society of the Army and Navy of the Confederate States in the State of Maryland.

54 - Cavalry

CHARLES R. FAVOUR (1844/) - Ambrotype - This young student left his Harford County home and enlisted for two years or the war in Company F, 12th Virginia Cavalry, on July 22, 1862, at Orange County Courthouse. On May 22, 1863, Favour signed a petition with the other members of Gilmor's old company, which was forwarded to the adjutant general, requesting that they be attached to the 2nd Maryland Cavalry. The company was ordered to Gilmor's Battalion but in August it was recalled to the 12th Virginia. This was in response to the protest of Colonel Harman who felt that, although they were Marylanders, they were critically needed in the Virginia Cavalry. Not until the spring of 1864 were they finally added to the 2nd Maryland Cavalry. After a short hospital stay at Staunton in 1864 Favour was captured during heavy fighting on May 3 when Gilmor's Battalion drove back the advance of 500 Federals and then wheeled and retreated under fire while giving the pickets of Davis' Maryland Battalion time to form. Favour was sent to Wheeling and then Camp Chase until exchanged on February 25, 1865. He returned to the remaining remnants of what was once a fine command which did not surrender with the main army. Favour was paroled on April 15, 1865. He travelled to Winchester and was required to take the oath on May 17 while stating that he was proceeding to Martinsburg. By June 3 he was back in Maryland and was again submitted to the oath at the provost marshal's office of the Middle District before making his home in Sykesville.

JOHN B. WILLIAMSON (/1895) - Carte de Viste - Leaving his Allegany County home, he went south and became a member of Jacob's Mounted Riflemen, a Maryland unit. After consolidation with the Radford Rangers they were pressed into service with the 30th Virginia Volunteers. Later he was among the members who became Company I, 2nd Virginia Cavalry. During his service he was wounded several times by sabre and ball until finally being discharged. He became a member of McNeill's Rangers which was made up of a number of Allegany countians. After the war he returned to his home and was a member of the James Breathed Camp No. 1046, United Confederate Veterans of Cumberland.

HENRY RIEMAN DUVAL - Oil Painting - Departing from his Baltimore home he went to Virginia and enlisted in the fall of 1862 in Barry's Maryland Volunteers. They were recruited at Camp Maryland and designated to become Company C when the 1st Maryland Infantry was reorganized. This failed to materialize and Barry's men were ordered to report to General Elzey who placed them in command of detectives on the Rappahannock. They transported prisoners and goods across the lines and worked in independent service until October 29 when they were ordered to report to Major Elias Griswold, the provost marshal of Richmond. Their headquarters was at Hedgesville. In the fall of 1864 they were assigned to duty at Andersonville Prison where Duval re-enlisted again as a private in McNeill's Rangers.

SPRIGG S. LYNN (1845/) - Carte de Viste - Departing from his Washington County home he became a member of Company A, 18th Virginia Cavalry, until discharged in March of 1863. He re-enlisted for three years or the duration in McNeill's Partisan Rangers on May 9 at Rockingham. During the Gettysburg Campaign the elegant dwelling of his father in Washington County was burned by Federal troops in response to the southern sympathy of the family. He was captured in Hardy County on January 14, 1864, and sent to Wheeling. From there he was imprisoned at Camp Chase and later moved to Fort Delaware, escaping on July 1, 1864. Returning to McNeill's Company, he rode with the rangers until paroled on April 15, 1865, at Richmond. After the war he made his home in Cumberland and was a member of the James Breathed United Confederate Veterans Camp No. 1046.

JOHN B. FAY (1843/1925) - Carte de Viste - Leaving his studies and his Cumberland home he enlisted for one year on May 4, 1861, at Winchester in Company F, 7th Virginia Cavalry. He was captured in Hampshire County on January 5, 1863, and sent to Camp Chase in Ohio. On March 28, after being exchanged, he served along side the many Marylanders in Stuart's Horse Artillery, Shank's Company. He re-enlisted on August 25, 1863, as a private in McNeill's Partisan Rangers at Augusta. Fay was paroled at New Creek, West Virginia, on May 5, 1865. He made his home at Dunn Loring in Fairfax County, Virginia.

56 - Cavalry

THADDEUS W. CLARY (1840/) - Carte de Viste - On June 12, 1861, when news reached Thaddeus that his brother, Dr. Richard C. Clary, had been killed at the age of 25 years, 11 months and 5 days, he immediately left his Frostburg home to take up the southern cross. He travelled to Bolivar where he enlisted in the first company he found, Company K, 13th Virginia Infantry. After his 12-month term expired he re-enlisted in June of 1862 in McNeill's Rangers, the same company in which his brother had served. On June 3, 1864, he was captured at Harrisonburg, Virginia, and was sent to Johnson's Island where he gave his rank as 1st lieutenant in Company G, Davis' Maryland Battalion. He took the oath of allegiance on June 14, 1865, and was released and returned to make his home in Cumberland.

JESSE W. BRANDENBURG (1840/) - Carte de Viste - Leaving Carroll County he travelled to Virginia and there was elected 1st lieutenant of Lee's Maryland Cavalry. They were organized in the late winter and early months of 1862. With the spring campaign and the wounding of George Hume Steuart Jr., the Maryland Line failed to come to fruition. Lee's Maryland Cavalry Company was used as scouts, guides and couriers for the Army of Northern Virginia. Late in the war he re-enlisted in the 2nd Maryland Cavalry, Company C, as a private. He was paroled on April 25, 1865, at Winchester.

ELIJAH W. BISHOP - Carte de Viste with the backmark of Henry Moltz, Baltimore - Leaving his home in Baltimore County he went to Virginia and enlisted in the Lee Rangers of the 27th Battalion, Virginia Mounted Rifles. They subsequently became Company I, 25th Virginia Cavalry. Corporal Bishop served as a trooper with the Army of Northern Virginia until being paroled on April 27, 1865, at Cumberland Gap, Kentucky.

THOMAS BENTON GATCH (1840/1933) - Carte de Viste - Born in Lauraville in Baltimore County he was a member of the Baltimore County Horse Guard Militia Cavalry prior to the War. After going to Romney he was one of the first recruits and on June 21, 1861, joined a new company of Freestaters who became Company G, 7th Virginia Cavalry. Colonel Delaney, commander of the 7th Virginia, was to present a pair of warm stockings to the best soldier of the regiment. This coveted prize was won by Orderly Sergeant Gatch. In 1863 he was severely wounded three times with minnie balls passing through his shoulder, thigh and foot. Upon recovering he recruited a company of Maryland men who were scheduled to become Company G, 2nd Maryland Cavalry. Instead, they became A Company of T. Sturgis Davis' Maryland Battalion. Gatch was captured while under the command of Lieutenant Colonel Harry Gilmor on September 24, 1864, at Harrisonburg as they charged the advancing Federal cavalry. He was sent to Baltimore, developed pneumonia and recuperated in the West Building Hospital. Upon recovery he was imprisoned on October 19 at Fort McHenry, later being transferred to Fort Delaware. He was released by a general order of June 9, 1865. Graduating from the Old Columbia College of Medicine in Washington, he became a dairy farmer and founder of the Bellview Dairy. In 1870 he represented Baltimore County in the Maryland House of Delegates and held a position in the clerk's office of Baltimore County at Towson in 1892. Gatch was a member of the Harry Gilmor United Confederate Veterans Camp No. 673 of Towson.

JAMES W. DAVIS (1837/) - Carte de Viste - Davis was raised in the Darnestown area and the Montgomery County Federal Enlistment Records show that he went south. He enlisted on April 27, 1861, in Company G, 7th Virginia Cavalry. Following his former mess mate E.V. White, he enlisted in the 35th Virginia Cavalry and became a sergeant in Company B. He was captured at Moorefield on September 11, 1863, and was sent to Fort McHenry. He escaped on November 16 and proceeded to the eastern shore and finally made his way back to southern lines. Davis did not return to his command but re-enlisted as a private in Davis' Maryland Cavalry. While  scouting in Maryland he was again captured on October 20, 1864, and again sent to Fort McHenry. He was then transferred to Point Lookout and scheduled to be exchanged on February 20, 1865. By order of General Wallace he was retained and not released from prison until May 9, 1865. Travelling to the eastern shore he made Cambridge his home.

58 - Cavalry

HAMILTON LEFEVRE (1840/) - Ambrotype - Born and raised in Harford County, in the August of 1862 he travelled by rail from Baltimore to Westminster. He then made his way on foot towards Frederick, purchased a horse and joined Company L, 1st Virginia Cavalry. On September 9 he enlisted for the war in Company C, 1st Maryland Cavalry. Lefevre was promoted to sergeant on August 12, 1863. He was captured on November 17, while on a two-week furlough. Being held as a spy, only the wearing of his Confederate belt-plate saved him from going before a firing squad. He spent six months in Camp Chase, and six months more in Fort Delaware where he contracted measles, typhoid fever and pneumonia. He refused a pardon from President Lincoln, which was brought by his father. Persuaded by his comrades that he could not last long, he took the oath of allegiance and was taken home. He settled in Baltimore where he was an accountant, and later entered the Maryland Line Confederate Soldiers Home on May 2, 1914.

JAMES DICKSON POLLOCK (1841/1915) - Ambrotype - He was born near Cumberland and enlisted on June 1, 1861, in Company F, 7th Virginia Cavalry, and became a 3rd corporal. He re-enlisted as a corporal for another 12 months in June of 1862. On April 24, 1863, he re-enlisted as a private for 24 months. At Gettysburg, he was wounded, captured on July 5, sent to Fort McHenry and then to Point Lookout, until his exchange on February 13, 1865. After the war, he farmed near Barton and was a member of the James Breathed Camp of United Confederate Veterans of Cumberland.

JAMES ATHEY (1843/) - Carte de Viste - On March 17, 1862, he left his home in Cumberland and joined Company D, 12th Virginia Cavalry. After the Battle of Chantilly in the autumn of 1862, Lee's Army advanced into Maryland, but Athey was destined not to see his cherished home state. On September 7 he was captured near Martinsburg and sent to Wheeling Military Prison. From there he was sent to Camp Chase to await exchange that fall. Returning to the 12th Virginia Cavalry he continued to ride with the troopers until he was paroled on April 19, 1865, at Harpers Ferry.

DAVID G. WHITE (1837/) - Carte de Viste - Receiving an appointment to the U.S. Military Academy he matriculated West Point on July 1, 1857. As a member of the second class, he was among the four Maryland cadets of the six at the academy to resign their commission. Receiving transportation to Annapolis, he wrote President Jefferson Davis that he had resigned on April 23, 1861, and wished to join the Confederacy. White returned to his home in Cecil County but stayed but a brief time, when on August 24 he was commissioned a 1st lieutenant on the staff of General W.J. Hardee. In the spring of 1862 he was adjutant of the 6th Battalion, Arkansas Cavalry. On August 1 he was promoted to captain and assistant adjutant general of staff. He was advanced to the rank of major on December 31 and was listed as chief of ordnance. On September 20, 1864, White reported to General Hood to command the 5th Georgia Cavalry with the rank of colonel. He continued with this regiment until February 11, 1865, when he was assigned to be acting assistant inspector general. Colonel White was paroled at Greensboro on May 1, and later made his home at Davidsonville. In 1871 he was elected 1st lieutenant of Company F, 5th Maryland Militia Regiment.

FRANCIS THOMAS GROVE (1845/) - Ambrotype - Born and raised in Sharpsburg, he enlisted at Harpers Ferry in Company B, 2nd Virginia Infantry for a 12-month term. After the expiration of his time he re-enlisted in Company F, 1st Virginia Cavalry for three years or the war. During Sheridan's Raid up the Shenandoah Valley, Grove was wounded in the right leg at Strasburg on September 22, 1864, and left on the field through the night. The next morning he was picked up by the enemy and sent to Baltimore and housed in the West Building Hospital. After 60 days he was exchanged. His wound healed enabling him to return to his unit. After the war he settled in Baltimore where he became a merchant and on August 4, 1910, a resident of the Maryland Line Confederate Soldiers Home at Pikesville.

MOSBY'S MARYLANDERS - This cabinet card, and the two which follow, were taken in 1866 during John S. Mosby's highly publicized visit to Baltimore. From the left are J. Monroe Heiskell, Henry Slater, Dan Murray Mason, Claiborne Robinson, Colonel Mosby, James C. Blanchard, Charles E. Grogan, D. Giraud Wright, J. Henry Smith, Joshua Riggs, Alexander G. Carey and Gresham Hough.

MOSBY'S BALTIMOREANS - Cabinet Card - From the left are John T. Dixon, J.R. Watson, Colonel Mosby, Daniel L. Thomas, James Jackson Mitchell, Daniel G. Carlisle, John W. Corbin and Richard McVeigh.

RICHARD NEWTON McVEIGH (1828/) seated on the right with John Singleton Mosby - Carte de Viste - McVeigh was born at Middleburgh, Virginia, but moved to Baltimore. When the war broke out he was in Alabama. Enlisting at Huntsville in Gaston's Company, he remained about a month before transferring to a Mississippi regiment. The regiment was transferred to Pensacola, Florida, where McVeigh was able to secure his release. Quickly proceeding to the Army of the Potomac he acted as a scout and guide for General Joseph E. Johnston at Manassas. McVeigh became a trooper in Company H, 4th Virginia Cavalry, and after his 12-month enlistment became a ranger in Mosby's 43rd Virginia Cavalry, Company B. While leaving Arundel's Farm his retreating column was cut off by the 8th Illinois Cavalry and he was severely wounded on April 10, 1865, a day after the war was officially over for the Army of Northern Virginia. Being captured he was sent to Fairfax where he took the amnesty oath and five days later was admitted to the 3rd Division U.S. General Hospital of Alexandria. While hospitalized a carbine ball was removed from his right breast. McVeigh returned to Baltimore becoming a salesman and entered the Maryland Line Confederate Soldiers Home on June 30, 1901. He was expelled by order of the board of directors but returned to the home on December 6, 1905, by order of the board.

RICHARD DAVIS MURPHY (1835/1902) - Carte de Viste - Reared at Martinsburg, West Virginia, Murphy graduated from Princeton with the class of 1858 and took up the study of engineering. He was employed at the Baltimore and Ohio Railroad Company shops at Mount Clare in Baltimore. When General B.F. Butler occupied Relay, just outside the city, he issued orders for Mr. Murphy's arrest for participating in the riots of April 19, 1861. Upon receiving news of his impending arrest, Murphy went to Harper's Ferry and joined an independent cavalry command, the Fort Lewis Volunteers. This service was not congenial to him so he resigned and followed Johnston's Army to Manassas where he enlisted on the day before the battle as a private for one year in the Company B, 1st Virginia Cavalry. He re-enlisted on February 11, 1862, and in July became 1st sergeant. At Gettysburg, he was severely wounded by fragments of a shell. He became adjutant in the fall of 1863 when John Singleton Mosby, then adjutant of the regiment, resigned to embark upon a career as a partisan. On June 20, 1864, he was officially appointed adjutant with the rank of 1st lieutenant. He held this position until the end of the war when he returned to Baltimore and was later connected with the City Water Department.

DANIEL GIRAUD WRIGHT (1840/1922) - Carte de Viste - He was born in Rio de Janeiro and reared in Baltimore. Wright enlisted at Suffolk on May 28, 1861, in Company D, Weston's Maryland Battalion. When the battalion was divided Company D was sent to the 21st Virginia Infantry as Company B. He soon received a transfer and became a private in Company H, 1st Maryland Infantry. After his 12-month service he re-enlisted in Lee's Maryland Cavalry. He served under Captain Philip Henry Lee as a scout and guide with the Army of Northern Virginia. Re-enlisting once again, Trooper Wright became a member of Company D, 43rd Virginia Cavalry. While riding with Mosby's Rangers he was captured on April 15, 1864, in Loudoun County, Virginia. Sent to the Old Capitol Prison and later to Fort Warren, Wright finally gained his release upon giving the oath of allegiance on June 21, 1865. Returning to Baltimore he became a criminal court judge and a member of the Murray Confederate Association and the John S. Mosby Confederate Veterans Camp, 821, of Baltimore.

DAVID STONE BRISCOE (1840/1914) - Carte de Viste - Leaving Leonardtown he enlisted as a private in the 1st Maryland Infantry, Company H, on June 18, 1861. A year later Briscoe mustered out with the rest of the 1st Maryland. He applied to the Naval Department and secured a position as an acting master not in line for promotion. With the atrition of southern naval vessels he was without a command by the end of 1863. He enlisted as a private in Mosby's Rangers in Company D, 43rd Virginia Cavalry. Briscoe was elected 2nd lieutenant to fill the vacancy of Lieutenant William Trundle, who was killed in an ambush near Bunker Hill on March 27, 1864. Paroled on April 22, 1865, at Winchester, he made Baltimore his post-war home and was a member of three United Confederate Veterans groups: the Franklin Buchanan Camp, the Murray Confederate Association and the John S. Mosby Camp.

WILLIAM E. COLSTON (1839/1864) - Painting - After leaving his home in Baltimore, Colston enlisted on June 1, 1861, in Weston's Maryland Battalion of Infantry at Richmond as a member of Company B, Maryland Guard. Weston's Battalion was divided and dispersed into various commands, Company B being sent to the 21st Virginia Infantry. Colston gained a transfer to the 1st Maryland Infantry, Company H. At the Battle of Cross Keys on June 8, 1862, he was severely wounded with a shot through the body. When he was able to ride but not fully recovered, he served as a volunteer aide to General Isaac R. Trimble. The general was wounded and had to be left at Gettysburg so Colston volunteered for Mosby's command. He became a member of Company A, 43rd Virginia Partisan Rangers. He was killed on January 10, 1864, in an attack on Cole's Federal Maryland Cavalry camped near Harpers Ferry. The Federals were surprised during the night and Colston fell in front of a tent with powder burns from the close carbine ball which killed him. His brother, Captain Frederick M. Colston, furnished a memorial room in his memory in the Maryland Line Confederate Soldiers Home in Pikesville.

HUGH T. WATERS (left) - Carte de Viste - His first term of service in the C.S.A. was with the Maryland Guerrilla Zouaves. They were assigned to Velligan's Louisiana Infantry as the 2nd Company C. After being discharged from infantry service, Waters was with the Alabama troops until his transfer to Mosby's Rangers. He was wounded while serving with A Company, 43rd Virginia Cavalry, on June 6, 1864, on the Aldie Turnpike near Mt. Zion. That summer, in a scouting expedition near Georgetown, Waters related to John Alexander, who was riding by his side, that he had a premonition he would be killed that night. Waters divided up his few assets and the spoils of many chases among his friends. Finally patting his horse Bess on the neck he said that he wanted her to be given to Mollie L. This last request aroused Alexander's interest. "To Mollie L.? he asked. Why, what's your reason for that? Well, I suppose I'll have to tell you, as it won't make much difference now. And his voice became a shade more doleful. Well, the truth is, I am in love with her - and - she's my sweetheart! The mischief you say! You are not engaged to her? Yes, I am, Johnnie, old fellow. You see I had to tell you, although I promised her not to. By George! I am engaged to her myself! I answered, an incipient feeling of rivalry imparting some warmth to my tones, perhaps, in spite of the solemn business we had in hand. Just at this interesting point our conversation was interrupted by a pistol shot. Both rangers were spared and in the darkness made their escapes separately. Alexander, going to the home of Mollie  L., was surprised to find Hugh Waters already there resting in their best arm chair, playing invalid over some bruises and scratches he had obtained that night." Waters made his home in Washington, D.C., and Alexander in Albemarle County, Virginia, but it is not known if either ended up with Molly.

EDWARD S. HURST (1838/) - Tintype - Hurst was born and raised at Gypsy Hill near New Windsor. Making his way to Virginia, he enlisted on April 9, 1861, for one year with the Loudoun Light Horse Cavalry. They rode under Turner Ashby before being mustered into the 1st Virginia Cavalry as Company H. At the end of his enlistment he assisted James Louis Clark in organizing a Maryland Cavalry Company. They were prevented from carrying their men into the field due to the lack of horses the government had promised. A number of men from Clark's Independent Cavalry accompanied their commander to Stuart's Horse Artillery. Three Marylanders, including Hurst, were among the first detail transferred to John Singleton Mosby. These original 15 men selected to report to Mosby became the corps of the Partisan Rangers. Although Hurst served as a private, he was the head of various detachments and during the course of action was wounded seven times, twice in the fight at Warrenton Junction on May 3, 1863. He was paroled at Winchester and settled in Fairfax County, Virginia.

64 - Cavalry

JAMES GERALD WILTSHIRE (1842-1922) - Carte de Viste - Leaving his father's farm at Funkstown, he enlisted as a private in the 2nd Virginia Infantry, Company G. On April 17, 1862, he re-enlisted for two years in the 12th Virginia Cavalry, Company B. He was captured on October 13, 1863, and imprisoned in Fort McHenry and Point Lookout. Wiltshire was exchanged and became a 2nd lieutenant in Company H of the 43rd Virginia Cavalry. He was with a group of Mosby's Marylanders in the latter part of September, 1864, when they went to Annapolis in an attempt to capture the governor. At Port Tobacco, they captured 17 soldiers and near Rockville, his commander, Lieutenant Walter Bowie, was killed. Wiltshire lost his horse within 15 yards of the enemy but managed to escape. This occurred on March 30, 1865, and was the last raid in the rear of Sheridan's Army. After being paroled, he came to Baltimore where he became a physician. Dr. Wiltshire held membership in three Confederate Veterans organizations: the Isaac R. Trimble Camp, the John S. Mosby Camp and the Society.

STACY B. BISPHAM (1847/) - Carte de Viste - Enlisting on November 21, 1863, in Company A, 43rd Virginia Cavalry, he later transferred first to Company B, then D, the latter containing the largest number of Marylanders. Bispham was captured at Upperville on April 29, 1864, and spent the duration of the war in Fort Warren. Making his home in Baltimore he went to New York City working for Russell & Erwin Manufacturing and upon retiring returned to Baltimore.

ROBERT BOWIE CHEW (1842/1919) - Carte de Viste - Reared in Calvert County, Chew enlisted at Frederick for three years on September 1, 1862, as a private in the Maryland Flying Artillery. Wounded in the right arm at Stevenson's Depot on June 15, 1863, he was sent to Chimborazo Hospital in Richmond. After leaving the 1st Maryland Artillery in April of 1864, he joined his cousins in Mosby's 43rd Virginia Cavalry, Company D. He was badly wounded on Christmas Eve while scouting with J. West Aldridge near Point of Rocks. Aldridge led Chew's horse 15 miles through the back country before dressing his wounds. Chew signed his parole as a sergeant in the 1st Maryland Artillery at Appomattox Courthouse with the Army of Northern Virginia. On April 22, his parole was violated when he was arrested and imprisoned in Washington by the Federal Government. After his release he made his residence in Anne Arundel County and then Baltimore, becoming a salesman. He was admitted to the Maryland Line Confederate Soldiers Home on July 20, 1901.

THOMAS BOOKER (left) and **CHARLES PAXSON** (1843/1864) right - Cabinet card with painted backdrop - Thomas Booker, of Washington County, enlisted on October 15, 1861, at Yorktown in Company K, 1st Virginia Artillery, which later became the 2nd company of the Richmond Howitzer's. Upon the expiration of his 12-month enlistment, Booker re-enlisted and on January 29, 1863, was detailed to the quartermaster department. On August 20, he returned to the Howitzer's but, soon being discharged, joined Company E, 43rd Virginia Cavalry. He became 4th sergeant with Mosby's Rangers and surrendered on April 22, 1865, at Winchester. Returning to Washington County, the displeasure of the federal authorities caused him to move to Richmond where he made his residence and in latter years became a resident of the Virginia Old Soldiers Home. Charles Paxson was born in Baltimore and went with his family to Washington County and then across the river into Virginia. He enlisted in Company A, 43rd Virginia Cavalry, and was one of the 106 rangers who, on the night of January 10, 1864, rode into the snow-covered camp of Cole's Maryland Cavalry on Loudoun Heights and attacked the sleeping Federals. The fight was fierce and the night so dark that the Rangers could not see to reload their revolvers. Paxson fell from his horse and called out, "You are not going to leave me here on the field." Captain William R. Smith was advancing to assist him when a shot from one of the tents put an end to his career. The Federals suffered six killed, while the Confederates left five dead in the camp and four mortally wounded who died soon afterwards. Of these nine, Paxson, William E. Colston and William H. Turner were Marylanders. When morning broke, an officer of Cole's Cavalry found Paxson upon the field, wounded in the face and neck near the jugular vein. Raising up the dying lad's head, the officer asked his name and heard the name Paxson. The officer immediately knew who he was for in 1862 his father had cared for five men of Cole's Cavalry who were wounded at the Crossroads near the Paxson farm. All that could be done for the lad was to ease his last moments. Thomas Booker was paroled at Winchester on April 22, 1865. Returning to Washington County, the displeasure of Federal authorities caused him to go to Richmond where he made his residence, and in later years resided at the Virginia Old Soldiers' Home.

Chapter 6

INFANTRY

After having gone south, Richard Zarvona Thomas returned to St. Mary's County and organized Zarvona's Maryland Zouaves. Thomas was commissioned colonel with Captains William C. Walters and Thomas Blackistone commanding the first and second companies, respectively. After participating in the capture of the ship St. Nicholas, Colonel Thomas was captured. The unit was broken up and the first company was absorbed as Company H of the 47th Virginia Infantry. The second company became guards at Castle Thunder Prison.

The Lanier Guards were organized and equipped in Baltimore by George Lanier of Lanier Brothers, wholesale and dry good merchants. The scheme adopted to get out of the city in a body was based on a funeral procession to Loudoun Park Cemetery. There the coffin containing their guns and accoutrements was unloaded. They became Company G of the 13th Virginia Infantry.

Major J. Alden Weston organized a battalion of Marylanders at Richmond. The secretary of war began utilizing these companies to fill existing regiments. Every man in Weston's Maryland Battalion signed a petition to Jefferson Davis requesting that the battalion not be separated, but to no avail. On June 21 the Weston Guards, under Captain Edward R. Dorsey, became Company C of the 1st Maryland Infantry. The Maryland Guards, under Captain J. Lyle Clarke, became Company B of the 21st Virginia. Captain Michael Stone Robertson's Southern Marylanders of Company C were not completely equipped or uniformed and were used as prison guards at Richmond until August 1 when they became Company I of the 1st Maryland Infantry. Captain William H. Murray's Company D, Maryland Guards, was also sent to the 1st Maryland Infantry as Company H on June 21.

The Harpers Ferry Companies of the 1st Maryland were organized on June 16, 1861 under Colonel Arnold Elzey, Lieutenant Colonel George H. Steuart Jr., and Major Bradley T. Johnson. Company A was commanded by William Worthington Goldsborough; Company B, Charles C. Edelin; Company D, James R. Herbert; Company E, Harry McCoy; Company F, J. Louis Smith, and Company G, Wilson Carey Nicholas.

The National Volunteers of the District of Columbia, after offering their services to the City of Baltimore following the Pratt Street massacre, crossed the river to Virginia and became Company E of the 1st Virginia Infantry. The National Rifles, known as the Beauregard Rifles, under Captain Francis B. Schaeffer, also from Washington, offered to guard the Maryland frontier and later became Company F, 1st Virginia Infantry.

An artillery unit under Captain John D. Myrick, known as the Baltimore Artillery, was assigned to the 9th Virginia Infantry and became Company B on June 5, 1861. After gaining his release from Fort McHenry, Ogle S. Tilghman went to Richmond and formed a company of mostly Talbot Countians which was then sent to Tennessee. At the same time Captain William J. Maddox recruited a company known as the Maryland American Rifles.

The majority of the men of Company B, 21st Virginia Infantry, mustered out after 12 months of enlistment to re-enlist as Company E of the 30th Virginia Sharpshooters, again under Clarke.

In the late fall of 1862, Edmund Barry, a Mexican War company commander, recruited a company at Camp Maryland for the 1st Maryland Regiment. Barry's Maryland Volunteers were commanded by General Elzey, who placed Barry in command of the detectives on the Rappahannock transporting goods across the line. They continued independent service under Major Elias Griswold, the provost marshal of Richmond, and by 1864 were taken by General John H. Winder to Andersonville Prison as guards.

Louis Keepers was elected commander of a company called the Maryland Guerrilla Zouaves, organized in Richmond. They later became the 2nd Company C of Belligan's Louisiana Infantry.

68 - Infantry

The Confederate government employees at Richmond organized into a local defense battalion, the 3rd Battalion, Virginia Infantry. On June 4, 1863, Captain Albert Ellery was chosen commander of Marylanders who formed the 2nd Company D, known as the Treasury Guards.

After their terms of enlistment, a number of veterans from the 1st Maryland Infantry went to Richmond and organized a regiment which became known as the 2nd Maryland Infantry. Company A was commanded by William H. Murray; Company B, J. Parran Crane; Company C, Ferdinand C. Duvall; Company D, Joseph L. McAleer; Company E, John W. Torsh; Company F, Andrew Jackson Gwynn; Company G, William Worthington Goldsborough, and Company H was under James Thomas Bussey. Company D contained a private named David Hammett, from St. Mary's County, whose twin brother, Daniel, was serving as a private in the 2nd Maryland Artillery. The 2nd Maryland Infantry served with the Army of Northern Virginia until Appomattox. On April 9, 1865, only 63 men remained to surrender.

J. LOUIS SMITH - Carte de Viste - Smith was a member of the Garrison Forest Ranger Militia. He left his Baltimore County home venturing to Harpers Ferry where he enlisted on May 22, 1861, in Thomas Holbrook's Company. Upon the consolidation of Price's and Holbrook's companies in the reorganization of June 16, he was chosen captain of Company F, 1st Maryland Infantry, on July 1. After his 12-month term of service he was mustered out and assisted in recruiting the 2nd Maryland Infantry. On October 13, 1862, Smith became provost marshal of Winchester. On January 8, 1863, he became captain in the assistant adjutant's department, dated from December 2, 1862, and was ordered to General Elzey. He was relieved on April 30, 1863, from the adjutant general's department and ordered to the Maryland Line Camp. On October 4, 1864, Smith reported to Richmond to the inspecting staff department from where he was later sent to the Signal Corps.

JOHN HENRY FOSTER (1838/1908) - Carte de Viste - He enlisted on June 18, 1861, in Weston's Maryland Battalion of Infantry. They were sent to the 21st Virginia Infantry as Company B. On May 24, 1862, with the expiration of his term of enlistment, he re-enlisted in the 2nd Company B of the 6th Virginia Infantry. On June 14, 1862, his abilities led him to the rank of orderly sergeant. In 1864 Foster was a member of the 43rd Virginia Cavalry, Company A, again as a private. He was wounded on March 23, 1865, in a skirmish near Middleburg. Foster received his parole with the majority of Mosby's Partisan Rangers at Winchester on April 26, 1865. He returned to his native Baltimore and became a resident of the Maryland Line Confederate Soldiers Home on April 24, 1905.

CHARLES ECCLESTON HAYWARD (1840/1898) - Carte de Viste - Departing from his Dorchester County home he enlisted on May 18, 1861, in the Maryland Guard of Weston's Maryland Battalion. They were sent to the 21st Virginia Infantry as Company B. On September 1 he was appointed a sergeant. The company was ordered to Corinth, Mississippi, where he was appointed a 2nd lieutenant by General Bragg on April 15, 1862. He re-enlisted in Company A, 1st Florida Infantry, and was elected a 1st lieutenant. On July 6, 1862, he requested a transfer under General Order No. 8 from the War Department. The Confederate Congress had passed the act authorizing the organization of the Maryland Line and that all natives or adopted citizens of Maryland, who were or should be in voluntary service, might, at their option, be re-enlisted into this unit. He stated in his resignation, "Now that our army has been successful in Virginia and there is every possibility that very soon entering Maryland, I wish to avail myself of the privilege granted under the Act of Congress to the citizens of the state of Maryland by being transferred to the Maryland Line under Brigadier General Steuart." General George Hume Steuart, Jr. however, was given command of a brigade in Ewell's Division and was seriously wounded at Cross Keys and the Maryland Line did not materialize at this time. Hayward then served in Holbrook's Independent Maryland Artillery with the Army of the West. After the seige of Vicksburg, he returned with a portion of the command who still desired service with the Marland Line. They proceeded to Camp Howard at Hanover Junction and found that General Elzey had been reassigned and they were subsequently absorbed into the 64th Virginia Infantry. After the hostilities he spent two years in the south before becoming a resident of Washington, D.C., until the latter part of his life when he returned to his native Cambridge.

70 - Infantry

GEORGE MALCOLM EMACK (1842/1886) - Carte de Viste - He was born on the family's estate of Locust Grove near Beltsville in Prince Georges County. Shortly after the start of the war he was arrested at the home of his father but escaped by fatally stabbing the Union officer in whose custody he was being held. This incident persuaded him to join the southern cause and he was appointed from Maryland as a 2nd lieutenant of infantry on October 18, 1861. His brother, James W. Emack, was commissioned a lieutenant in the 7th North Carolina Infantry. Upon the formation of the 1st Maryland Cavalry, George assisted in raising a company and was elected commander of Company B on November 12, 1862. In the spring of 1864 he was wounded in the thumb and forefinger. On July 29 of that year he had his bay horse killed out from under him while receiving a wound in the right forearm. On August 14, 1864, he was admitted to Charlottesville General Hospital and was later transferred to Richmond. During the course of the fighting he was wounded a total of 10 times. He was again admitted to Charlottesville General Hospital on March 1, 1865, with diptheria. Eight days later he was in Stuart Hospital in Richmond and returned to duty on April 2. After the war he returned briefly to Prince Georges County, then went to New Orleans for six years before finally moving to Versailles, Kentucky.

EUGENE DIGGS - Ambrotype - After graduating with the class of 1857 from Georgetown University, he left his Port Tobacco home and proceeded to Richmond and enlisted on June 15, 1861, in a company composed of Marylanders. On July 19 he was elected 3rd lieutenant. The company was unable to join the 1st Maryland Regiment due to their inability to secure uniforms and equipment. After Manassas, they were detailed to guard prisoners in Richmond and were finally ordered to join the 1st Maryland at Fairfax Station as Company I. On May 17, 1862, Lieutenant Diggs was court martialed for allowing a prisoner to escape while officer of the guard. After his term of enlistment expired, he raised Company B, 2nd Maryland Cavalry, in May of 1863 for Gilmor's Battalion. In October of 1863, while scouting through the Blue Ridge Mountains, he was captured while staying in a home and sent to Fort McHenry, then to Fort Delaware and later to Point Lookout. Diggs was finally transferred to Hilton's Head, South Carolina, on August 20, 1864, and placed under the fire of Confederate guns with 600 other Confederate officers. Held at Fort Pulaski he was later returned to Fort Delaware where he was paroled on June 1, 1865, along with the release of officers of that rank. Four days later he was back in Maryland and was made to take the amnesty oath.

WILLIAM HENRY RYAN (1846/) - He was a coach maker in Baltimore before proceeding south and mustering into Company A, 1st Maryland Infantry, as a private for one year. After being discharged, he re-enlisted in Company C, 2nd Maryland Cavalry. On May 12, 1864, he was captured near Hawkinstown in the Shenandoah Valley. The "Band" was chased about two miles by the enemy who were strung out, but the 2nd Maryland had retreated in order without breaking a single section. They were ordered by fours, to right about, wield and charge. In this countercharge Ryan was captured by members of the 1st New York Cavalry. He was sent to Athineum Prison at Wheeling and then to Camp Chase, Ohio. He was transferred to City Point and exchanged on February 25, 1865. He surrendered at Accotink, Virginia, on April 1, 1865, and took the oath of allegiance before being sent to Washington.

JAMES WILLIAM LYON - Carte de Viste - From Baltimore County, he enlisted as a private on June 18, 1861, in Company H, 1st Maryland Infantry. He was appointed sergeant, and soon thereafter called to the staff of General Isaac R. Trimble. He was commissioned major on February 13, 1862, to rank from January 26. On March 23, 1863, he was assigned to Hoke's Brigade. Throughout the war he served as commissionary of supply. He was paroled on April 24, 1865, in North Carolina.

RICHARD CURZON HOFFMAN (1839/1926) - Carte de Viste - As a stockbroker in his native Baltimore he was active in the pre-war militia as a 1st lieutenant in Company F, Maryland Guard. After resisting the northern invasion in defense of Baltimore, Hoffman, along with many of his company, crossed into Virginia where he was elected 1st lieutenant of Company B, 21st Virginia Infantry. On April 4, 1862, he became its captain until the unit was mustered out. Hoffman then commanded another unit of Freestaters who became Company E, 30th Virginia Sharpshooters. He led this Maryland unit from the battle of Kernstown to Cold Harbor. Being unfit for field duty because of illness, he resigned his commission on February 10, 1865. He returned to his native city after the war and became president of the Reed Island Iron Company, Seaboard Air Lines Company and the Baltimore Steampackers Company and also served on the boards of directors for five other companies. He was one of the founders of Franklin Buchanan United Confederate Veterans Camp in 1896 and held membership in the Isaac R. Trimble Camp.

72 - Infantry

WILLIAM NORRIS (1820/1896) - Tintype - Norris left the family estate of Brookland, near Reisterstown, to go to Yale where he graduated in the class of 1840. As a successful businessman and lawyer, he became judge advocate to the United States Pacific Squadron. In May of 1861 he moved south with his wife and five children to cast his lot with the Confederate cause. Serving as a volunteer civilian aide on the staff of General J.B. Magruder, he soon received a commission of captain and signal officer in the Army of the Peninsula. The Confederate Congress authorized the establishment of a Signal Corps in the spring of 1862 with Norris as commander. With a modest expansion of the corps on October 8 he was promoted to major. In late 1863 Norris also organized and became head of the Secret Service Bureau. Exiles from Maryland were well known to him and became his mainstay not only for the Secret Service Bureau but also the Signal Corps. With the evacuation of Richmond in March of 1865, Colonel Norris was travelling southwest with the presidential party when he became commissioner of exchange. On April 26 he signed the oath of allegiance but was later arrested and held until June 30 when he was finally able to return to his Brookland estate. He was a member of the Society of the Army and Navy of the Confederate States in the State of Maryland.

ELIAS GRISWOLD (1819/   ) - Carte de Viste - Born in Ohio he had resided in Georgia and Florida before coming to Dorchester County where he practiced law. Leaving his home in Cambridge he ran the blockade and was commissioned a captain in the Quartermaster Department on November 15, 1861, at Richmond and was then sent to Tuscaloosa, Alabama. On April 17, 1862, he was promoted to a major and returned to Richmond where Griswold became provost marshal of the city. He surrounded himself with native Marylanders while working in that capacity. On February 29, 1864, as assistant adjutant general, he was sent to Camp Sumter near Andersonville on special duty in charge of prisoners. He was transferred on November 1, 1864, to General Hardee's command at Columbia and later in Greensboro. By March 25, 1865, he was back in Richmond serving under General Ruggles. With the evacuation of the capital he left and proceeded to Salisbury, North Carolina, where he was paroled on May 3, 1865. Afterward he returned to his home on the Eastern Shore.

HENRY KYD DOUGLAS & SPURS (1840/1902) - Tintype - He was born on Ferry Hill Place overlooking the Potomac in Washington County. In 1859, after graduating from Franklin and Marshall College near his home, he came upon an overloaded two-horse wagon and was told by the driver, an "Isaac Smith," that the wagon contained miner's tools. Douglas got his father's carriage horses and

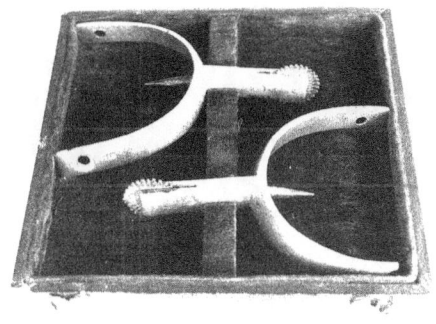

assisted them in reaching the Kennedy Farm. It was not long afterward that Douglas learned Smith was actually John Brown and the boxes contained pikes for the insurrection. In April of 1861 he enlisted in the 2nd Virginia Infantry, Company B. A year later he was promoted to lieutenant and ordered to report for special duty at the headquarters of General T.J. Jackson. Stonewall soon realized his abilities and appointed Douglas assistant inspector general becoming the youngest member of his staff. After Jackson was killed Douglas served on the staffs of Generals E. Johnson, J.B. Gordon, J.A. Early, J.H. Pegram and J.A. Walker. As a major, Douglas led the 13th and 49th Virginia Regiments, was wounded six times and was captured at Gettysburg. Exchanged on March 18, 1864, he assumed command of the Light Brigade as a colonel. He was soon recommended to become a brigadier general but the request was not forwarded before the surrender at Appomattox. At Shepherdstown, a lady suggested he have a picture taken with her. He carried his uniform coat over his arm to Darnell and had this picture taken. Douglas was arrested on May 5, 1865, for donning his Confederate uniform for the photograph and was sentenced to two months imprisonment at Fort Delaware. Afterward, he opened a law office in Hagerstown, became a judge and was raised to the rank of major general in the Maryland National Guard. Also pictured are his spurs.

CHARLES MARSHALL (1830/1902) - Frontace in <u>An Aide-De-Camp to Lee</u> - He graduated from the University of Virginia in 1849 and until 1852 was a professor of mathematics at the University of Indiana. Coming to Baltimore and passing the bar, he practiced law until April of 1861 when he went to Richmond and offered his services in the fight for southern independence. He was commissioned a 1st lieutenant and by April 21, 1862, was a major in the cavalry service. Marshall was appointed aide-de-camp on May 10 on the staff of Major General Robert E. Lee. By March of 1864 Marshall had received his second star as a lieutenant colonel. He continued to serve Lee by writing many of his documents in the capacity of adjutant general. At Appomattox he was the only staff member to accompany the general when he met with Grant. In an ambulance near Lee's tent the following day, Marshall wrote the general order of Lee's farewell address. Only one line was changed by Lee before it was read. Marshall took the oath of allegiance at Alexandria on May 21, 1865, and returned to Baltimore where he was soon allowed to continue his law practice. He was a member of the Franklin Buchanan United Confederate Veterans Camp No. 747, the Isaac R. Trimble Camp No. 1025 and the Society of the Army and Navy of the Confederate States in the State of Maryland.

THOMAS WILLIAM HALL (1833/1901) - Paper Enlargement - He was editor of the South Newspaper in Baltimore. He was arrested on September 12, 1861, at his home and was sent as a political offender to Fort McHenry. The following day he was transferred to Fortress Monroe and later to Fort Lafayette and Fort Warren. Hall was unconditionally released in November of 1862 after which he ran the interior blockade. He was commissioned a captain on the staff of General John Gregg with whom he was a fellow prisoner at Fort Warren. After Chickamauga, Gregg was transferred from the Army of the West to Hood's Brigade. Hall was later reassigned in the Army of Northern Virginia where he continued the duties of assistant adjutant general. Late in 1864 Hall was promoted to major a week before the lines were broken at Petersburg. Afterward he was assigned to special duty under the direction of the secretary of war. By a direct order from President Davis, he was enroute to Louisiana when he learned of Lee's surrender. He reported to President Davis at Washington, Georgia, where he was paroled. Hall resided in Marengo County, Alabama, until the ironclad oath system in Maryland was removed in 1867. He returned to Baltimore to practice law and later served as city solicitor. He was a member of the Isaac R. Trimble and Franklin Buchanan Camps of the United Confederate Veterans.

CLEMENT SULIVANE (1838/1920) - Tintype - He was born in Mississippi and, as an infant, came to Cambridge. He received degrees from Princeton and the University of Virginia. In 1857 he began to read law in Cambridge and was admitted to the bar in 1860. At the beginning of hostilities he went to Pensacola and, on April 19, 1861, enlisted in Company A, 10th Mississippi Infantry. Learning that a Maryland regiment was being formed, he proceeded to Virginia, but finding the 1st Maryland filled, fell in with Company B, 21st Virginia Infantry. In November he was commissioned a 1st lieutenant and aide-de-camp on the staff of General E. Van Doren. As assistant adjutant general on the staff of G.W.C. Lee he was promoted to captain. In early 1865 he commanded Curtis Lee's Brigade and was captured at Sayler's Creek on April 6. Returning to Cambridge he practiced his profession and later was elected to the state senate.

HENRY E. SHEPHERD (1842/) - Frontace from Narratives of Prison Life - He was born in Cumberland County, North Carolina, and enlisted on May 1, 1861, in Company D, 43rd North Carolina Infantry. He was promoted to 2nd lieutenant on April 2, 1862, and one month later became 1st lieutenant. He was wounded in the right knee at Culp's Hill at Gettysburg, and captured on July 5, 1863, during the retreat on South Mountain. After spending one month in a hospital in Frederick, he was moved to West Hospital Prison in Baltimore. On September 29, he was transferred to Johnson's Island. Shepherd was exchanged on March 14, 1865, and after the war settled in Baltimore.

FREDERICK GUSTAVUS SKINNER (1814/1894) - Carte de Viste - He was born in Annapolis and educated in France as a result of his father's friendship with Lafayette. He spent the early part of his manhood in Baltimore and, going to the cause of the South, he enlisted in the 1st Virginia Infantry and was elected major in May, 1861. By November 18 he was promoted to lieutenant colonel. Skinner carried a large, heavy saber similar to the one used by Von Borke of J.E.B. Stuart's staff. At Second Manassas, while leading a charge on a gun battery, he cut through the collar bone of a gunner, almost severing his head. Another artilleryman seized the bridle of Skinner's horse and fired a pistol into his face. The colonel turned to one side but was wounded in the area of his ear. His sabre passed under the shoulder and through the heart of the man who immediately fell to the ground. Skinner was then shot through the right side and his left arm was shattered between the elbow and wrist. On partial duty, he was promoted to colonel effective July 3, 1863, and he was officially retired to the Invalid Corps on February 6, 1865. After the war he proceeded to Rappahannock County, Virginia, and later to Charlottesville and did not return to Baltimore until his burial.

WELLS J. HAWKS (/1873) - Albumin Print - Although he was born in Massachusetts, he moved to Ruxton in Baltimore County before going to Charles Town, West Virginia. He was twice elected to the General Assembly and chosen Mayor of Charles Town and was active in politics prior to the war. Although he was beyond the stage of military service, he was one of the first to answer the call. He proceeded to Harpers Ferry and was commissioned in the Commissary Department and attached to the 2nd Virginia Infantry. From the position of regimental commissary he gradually rose to become a major and chief commissary of General Stonewall Jackson. After the war he returned to Charles Town where he was in the carriage and lumber business but frequently visited his son, A.W. Hawks, in Ruxton.

EDWARD MURRAY (1819/1874) - Carte de Viste - He was born in Howard County and secured an appointment to West Point, graduating from the U.S. Military Academy, class of 1841. Receiving a commission as 2nd lieutenant, he served with the 2nd U.S. Infantry. In 1847 he advanced to 1st lieutenant and in 1853 made captain of the same regiment. Resigning in 1855, he returned to Central Maryland to farm. In the summer of 1861 Murray travelled to Fauquier County, Virginia, and raised Company C, 49th Virginia Infantry, becoming its commander. On July 19 he was elected lieutenant colonel and led the regiment for 2 years and 4 months. Because of failing health he was reassigned as an assistant adjutant general by Robert E. Lee on November 4, 1864. His health continued to decline and he was finally released from duty. After the war he returned to his native state and resided at West River.

76 - Infantry

JAMES HENLEY SMITH (1843/1907) - Ambrotype - This student left his Centerville home in Queen Anne's County and proceeded to the defense of the south. In the spring of 1863 he enlisted in D.M. Snovell's Local Defense Company, composed of Marylanders, and formed an additional company for the Maryland Line. The Maryland Line was not organized under General George H. Steuart, Jr., at that time so they continued service in the Richmond area. After his 12-month enrollment expired he enlisted in Company D, 43rd Virginia Cavalry. He rode with Mosby's Rangers until the war was over and he was paroled on April 22, 1865, at Winchester. On May 31 he was in Baltimore where he was required to take the amnesty oath. He returned to Richmond, reported to the provost marshal's office on June 12 and did not return to the eastern shore of Maryland until the following year and later made the District of Columbia his home.

HENRY G. ROBERTSON OF JONATHAN (/1865) - Carte de Viste - Leaving his Port Tobacco home he enlisted in the Maryland American Rifles at Richmond. The U.S. Enrollment Records of Charles County for 1862/1864 show that he could not be drafted because he had gone south. He enlisted at Richmond on August 27, 1862, for three years or the war, as a private in Company B, 2nd Maryland Infantry. Wounded in the trenches at Petersburg by a ball that passed through his left lung, he was captured on April 3, 1865, while in the Fair Ground Post Hospital. Henry died on April 22 and was buried in the cemetery attached to the hospital.

THOMAS A. PRICE (1836/) - Carte de Viste - Leaving his Baltimore home, he departed for the South and became a volunteer aide with the rank of a 2nd lieutenant, appointed from Maryland. On May 16, 1861, he was with Company A, 6th North Carolina Infantry. By October he was promoted to 1st lieutenant, and continued with the company in the Army of the Potomac. By July 31, 1863, he had contracted a fever and had been placed in General Hospital No. 4 in Richmond. He was captured on November 7, 1863, at Rappahannock Station and sent to Old Capitol Prison, and then to Johnson's Island. He was released on June 27, 1865, and returned to his home in Baltimore, and later moved to Salisbury, North Carolina.

JAMES INNIS RANDOLPH - Carte de Viste - Leaving his home in Charles County, he went to Richmond and received a commission as a 2nd Lieutenant in the Engineer Corps. General Richard Ewell requested him for his staff on June 24, 1862 when he consented to serve as an engineering officer. After Spotsylvania and Ewell's declining health, Randolph followed the general to Richmond and served in the capital city's defenses. After the war he returned to Charles County and is best remembered for penning the poem "I'm A Good Old Rebel".

DENNIS H. POOLE - Carte de Viste - Departing from Frederick County, he ran the blockade and joined the Sothern army as a volunteer aid - de - camp. Receiving a commission as a 2nd. lieutenant he was assistant adjutant general on the staff of General W.J. Hardee.

GEORGE SMITH NORRIS (1841 /1912) - Carte de Viste - In the spring of 1862 he, his brother Alexander, and a friend, left there farm in Harford County and went south. In Southern Maryland while crossing the Potomac in a row boat, they were pursued by a Federal gunboat. When they neared the Virginia shore they jumped out of the boat and waded ashore and hid. Going to Richmond, George enlisted on August 4 in the 1st Maryland Cavalry as a private. He was detailed to the Signal Corps. By July 1, 1864, he was 1st sergeant. He was paroled at New Market on April 20, 1865 and made his home in Bel Air.

78 - Infantry

THEODORE O. CHESTNEY - Carte de Viste - From Georgetown, he was appointed a 2nd lieutenant on May 20, 1861, from the District of Columbia. He became an assistant adjutant general on the staff of General Arnold Elzey. In December, he was appointed captain, this time being recorded from Maryland. On January 8, 1863, he was appointed major, and was again listed as being from Maryland. The last two years of the war he was in the Department of Richmond in the Assistant Adjutant and Inspector General Headquarters Department.

RICHARD I. MANNING - Carte de Viste - He enlisted as a private in Company C, Hampton Legion. On October 24, 1861, he was transferred to the staff of General Samuel Jones as an aide. On January 11, 1864, he was announced as a captain and aid-de-camp to General J.E. Johnston. An appointment of April 13, 1864, shows Manning with the rank of 1st lieutenant with General Johnston in the Department of Tennessee. He was paroled at Greensboro as a major on April 26, 1865. He was a member of the Society of the Army and Navy of the Confederate States in the State of Maryland, even though he resided in Stansburg, South Carolina.

WARFIELD P. SEMMES - Carte de Viste - A resident of Georgetown, he enlisted in Balfour's Company of Mounted Riflemen. In the fall of 1862, he received permission to form an artillery company. With Semmes as captain, the company was assigned on January 7, 1863, to the 5th Regiment, Virginia State Line. Because it was a skeleton regiment it was soon disbanded. He then commanded Thomas E. Jackson's Company of Horse Artillery through the summer of 1863. After transfer to the Engineer Corps, he was a captain in the 2nd Regiment.

RICHARD LAMAR SPRIGG (1842/1918) - Carte de Viste - Living in Cumberland, he was educated at York, Pennsylvania, but left school at the age of 18 to join the Confederate Army. He enlisted on April 18, 1861, at Charles Town in Company G, 2nd Virginia Infantry. After his 12-month enlistment expired, Sprigg joined the Nitre and Mining Bureau, and was commissioned 1st lieutenant on August 26, 1862. In February of 1864, he was promoted to captain. He married during the war, and afterwards they lived in Baton Rouge, Louisiana, but finally settled in Cincinatti, Ohio. He worked in the linen thread industry, representing the Smith & Dove Manufacturing Company.

SAMUEL D. BUCK - Portrait used as a frontace in With the Old Confeds - After hearing of the fight between North troops and the citizens of Baltimore, he enlisted in the Warren Rifles, and was appointed 4th sergeant. After 12 months of service, he was advanced to 2nd sergeant of Company H, 13th Virginia Infantry. At Sharpsburg, he was promoted to 1st lieutenant, and on March 28, 1864, became captain. At the Battle of the Wilderness on May 6, he was wounded. With Company H almost nonexistent after this fight, Buck transferred to cavalry service. He surrendered in Page County, and opened a store in Middletown before permanently settling in Baltimore. He was a member of the Society of the Army and Navy of the Confederate States in the State of Maryland.

JAMES R. HERBERT (1833/1884) - Painting - He was born in Woodstock and at the age of 13 left school and went to sea. He became a businessman in Baltimore in 1854 and was 2nd lieutenant in Company A, Independent Grays. Departing for Harpers Ferry, Herbert was elected captain of Company D, 1st Maryland Infantry. After the expiration of their term, he was elected major of the 2nd Maryland Infantry. On March 17, 1863, he was appointed lieutenant colonel to rank from January 6. On July 2, at Culp's Hill, he was wounded by three balls in the leg, arm and abdomen. Herbert was in Litterman Hospital and then on Johnson's Island. Exchanged on October 12, 1864, he returned to his unit. After the war he was one of the Southerners to re-establish the militia in 1867 and became colonel of the 5th Maryland regiment.

WILLIAM WORTHINGTON GOLDSBOROUGH (1831/1901) - Carte de Viste - He was born at Graceham, Frederick County, and educated at Hanover, Pennsylvania. During the Mexican War he ran away from home to enlist but his father found him in Baltimore and took him home. He learned the trade of a printer and worked in Pittsburgh before coming to Baltimore about 1850. In 1857 he joined Woodburn's Company of the Baltimore City Guards. Sent to Harpers Ferry to subdue the John Brown raiders, he was among the first militia men to enter the engine house with the marines. In May of 1861 he enlisted in the 1st Maryland Infantry with the Frederick Volunteers and soon was elected captain of Company A. At Front Royal his men captured his brother, Charles, who was a member of the Federal 1st Maryland Infantry. At 2nd Manassas he was wounded while commanding the 48th Virginia Regiment. After his recovery he organized a company at Richmond in December of 1862. They were sent to the 2nd Maryland and became Company G. Soon thereafter he received the star of a major for his collar. While commanding the left wing of the regiment on Culp's Hill at Gettysburg, he was hit by a minnie ball that passed through his left lung and out his back. Being left upon the field, he was captured and later was among the 600 Confederate officers placed within range of the Confederate batteries at Charleston, South Carolina. He remained a prisoner until the war was over. He established the Winchester Virginia Times newspaper, then travelled to Philadelphia to start the Philadelphia Record in 1870. Following his death bed request, his body was sent to Baltimore where it was interred in the Confederate plot in Loudoun Park Cemetery with full military honors from the Society of the Army and Navy of the Confederate States in the State of Maryland, of which he was a member.

JAMES PARRAN CRANE (1838/1916) - Tintype - After returning from the University of Virginia, this St. Mary's County native exhibited previous military training when he took command of the Factory Riflemen, a militia unit, in February of 1860. Just prior to the war, he replaced Simeon B. Gibbons as head of the military department of Charlotte Hall Military Academy, founded in 1774 as Charlotte Hall Academy. Going south in the summer of 1862, Crane formed one of the first companies that mustered into the 2nd Maryland Infantry while his brother, William S., entered into cavalry service. James' company, along with that of William H. Murray, both enlisted on the same date and a dispute erupted over which would be the senior company. After three different decisions in favor of Murray, Crane's unit became Company B. No regimental officers remained after the 2nd Maryland had charged up the rough slopes of Culp's Hill at Gettysburg. As a senior line officer, Crane commanded the battalion. At the Battle of Weldon Railroad he received a severe concussion. On September 27, 1864, he was appointed major. By October 24 he was in General Hospital No. 4 at Richmond suffering from his old wounds. He was furloughed on November 14 with partial paralysis in the left arm and leg from injuries to his spinal column caused by a blow from a musket. On December 24 he was detailed to General Ewell as an inspector near Petersburg. Major Crane was paroled on May 1, 1865, at Salisbury, North Carolina. He returned to southern Maryland and became a member of the Bradley T. Johnson United Confederate Veterans Camp No. 1110 of Leonardstown.

WILLIAM HENRY MURRAY (1839/1863) - Engraving - He was born and educated in Anne Arundel County at the settlement of West River before moving to Baltimore in 1855. He was elected commander of the Maryland Guard City Militia. After participating in the April militia buildup in Baltimore he went to Virginia where he organized many of his former men into one of Weston's Maryland Battalion. On May 21, 1861, his Company D was sent to the 1st Maryland Infantry where they became Company H. After the termination of their one-year enlistment, he proceeded to Richmond and formed the first company of the 2nd Maryland Infantry. While commanding the right side of the regiment on July 3, 1863, in the advance on Culp's Hill at Gettysburg, he was instantly killed. The ground all around him was torn up by bullets as his body was partially covered with dirt from the volleys fired at them.

CLAPHAM MURRAY (1838/1925) - Carte de Viste - Born and educated at West River in Anne Arundel County, he came to Baltimore on January 1, 1855. He was a member of his brother William's company of Maryland Guard in the militia. After resisting the Federal invasion of the state, he departed and on June 1, 1861, enlisted as a private in the 1st Maryland Infantry, Company H, and was soon appointed sergeant. After the regiment was mustered out, he assisted his brother William in organizing Company A, 2nd Maryland Infantry, and was elected 1st lieutenant. At Gettysburg, Murray assumed command of the company after his brother, Capt. William Henry Murray, was killed. On August 5, 1864, Clapham was captured while commanding Company A on the Petersburg-Weldon Railroad. He was confined in Fort Delaware until the conclusion of the war. In 1867 he was elected captain of Company D, 5th Regiment, Maryland National Guard. Upon the formation of the United Confederate Veterans Organization, he was elected vice president of the Murrary Confederate Association in 1871. During that same year he was elected tax collector of Baltimore.

WILLIAM DORSEY SKINNER (1849/1909) - Ambrotype - He was born and raised in Calvert County and enlisted for three years or the war on September 19, 1862, in Company C, 2nd Maryland Infantry. At Gettysburg, Private Skinner suffered a contusion of the thigh and was captured. He was admitted to the West Buildings of the General Hospital in Baltimore on July 28. He was taken to Point Lookout on August 21. After eight months imprisonment he felt that he would not be exchanged and was bearly able to continue to exist so he sought his own release. On April 6, 1864, he was paroled under an oath of allegiance that he would become a peaceful citizen, not take up arms against the United States nor support the Confederacy.

JAMES THOMAS BUSSEY (1838/) - Carte de Viste - He was born in Cecil County and moved to Baltimore where, during the civilian buildup, he served in the Winan's Guards to resist the passage of Northern troops. He travelled to Point of Rocks, and enlisted in Company C, 1st Maryland Infantry. He served as a private for 12 months, then re-enlisted on September 11, 1862, in the 2nd Maryland Infantry, being chosen 2nd lieutenant of Company D. On January 27, 1864, Bussey was elected captain of Company H. He was wounded in the left hip at Weldon Railroad on August 19, 1864, and sent to General Hospitals No. 4 and No. 9. He was captured during the fall of Richmond, and sent to Libby Prison. He was paroled on April 19, 1865, and started home to Baltimore in June.

JAMES McKINNEY WHITE (1842/1924) - Carte de Viste - He was born and raised in Cambridge and enlisted for one year on July 27, 1861, in Company H, 1st Maryland Infantry. While posted in a woods at Cross Keys, White helped drive back the enemy three times until he was severely wounded in the head. This caused him many months of pain and deprived him of nearly two years of active service. After finally recovering, he re-enlisted on April 20, 1864, in Company A, 2nd Maryland Infantry, as a private. He was wounded again at Cold Harbor where the bayonet was the weapon of the day. He was captured on April 2, 1865, after the fall of Petersburg. White was held as a prisoner of war until June 12 when he returned to his home and by August was residing in Baltimore. He represented Maryland in the Baltimore and Ohio Railroad Company and, as a brigadier general, served on the staff of Governor Jackson in the Maryland Militia.

CHARLES M. TRAIL - Carte de Viste - Crossing the Potomac in defense of a great cause, Trail enlisted for three years or the war on September 6, 1862, at Richmond in Company A, 2nd Maryland Infantry. He served with the company as a private until Gettysburg, where he was wounded on July 3, 1863. He was with the troops during the evacuation but was forced to remain in Seminary Hospital at Hagerstown where he was captured. By August he was sent to the General Hospital at Chester, Pennsylvania, before being exchanged. He convalesced in the Episcopal Hospital at Williamsburg, Virginia, until the spring of 1864 when he was transferred to the General Hospital. By fall he was fit for active duty with his company but on October 26 was detailed as a courier in the quartermaster and commissary departments. After the bitter end had come he took the amnesty oath in Richmond on May 12, 1865. He returned to Baltimore after several years and was a member of the Murray Confederate Association.

WILLIAM P. ZOLLINGER (1839/1889) - Carte de Viste - A resident of Baltimore, he enlisted on June 18, 1861, in Company H, 1st Maryland Infantry, and was chosen 1st lieutenant. After they disbanded, he assisted in organizing Company A, 2nd Maryland Infantry, and Zollinger again had the rank of lieutenant. His brother Jacob E. Zollinger, died from wounds received at Gettysburg while serving under William. In February of 1864, Zollinger and William Smith ran the blockade, and secured $25,000 from the patriots of Baltimore. Separating on their return, Smith was captured carrying the money. Zollinger was wounded at Weldon Railroad, and again at Pebble's Farm. He was captured on April 2, 1865, and sent to Johnson's Island, being released on June 21. In 1867 he was captain of Company H, 5th Maryland Militia Regiment, and colonel the following year.

JAMES WINDER LAIRD (1838/1864) - Carte de Viste - Born and raised near Cambridge he enlisted on July 27, 1861, as a private in Company H, 1st Maryland Infantry. He was mustered out with his company and re-enlisted in the newly formed 2nd Maryland Infantry. He was soon appointed adjutant of the regiment. On August 18, 1864, Laird was shot through the head and instantly killed in the desperate two-day fighting during the Battle of Weldon Railroad. James F. Pearson, Summerville P. Gill, Ridgely Howard and Spencer M. Grayson would not leave their comrade's body to be insulted by the foe. They placed his body on their muskets and hurried off to the Davis House by the railroad where each took a blanket from his scanty stores, wrapped them around Laird, dug his grave and buried him.

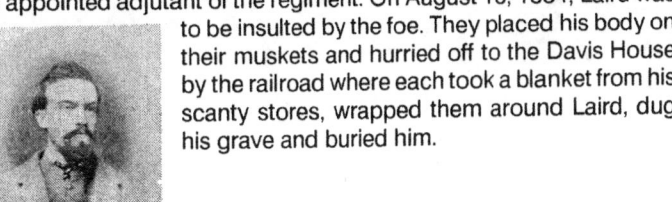

Chapter 7

NAVY

During the War Between the States Maryland's sons played a prominent role in the Confederate navy. There were three admirals from Maryland who served during the war, one Federal and two in southern service. These two Free Staters were the only admirals in the Confederate Navy. Franklin Buchanan entered the navy as a midshipman on January 28, 1815. He was the first superintendent of the Naval Academy. In the Southern navy he commanded the ironclad Virginia and was wounded in the first day's action. On August 19, 1862, he became a flag officer. Raphael Semmes entered the navy as a midshipman on April 1, 1826, and served during the Mexican War. He entered the Confederate navy as a commander and outfitted the first Southern warship, the Sumter. Fourteen months later he was captain of the raider Alabama. On February 10, 1865, he became a rear admiral.

The Confederate Navy was top heavy with Marylanders. Besides the two admirals, Maryland furnished one commodore, seven captains, four commanders, seven lieutenants commanding and 15 lieutenants. There were 163 recorded Marylanders who would serve as officers in the relatively small Southern Provincial Navy. The majority of career men resigned from the old navy, but their resignations were not accepted. Instead, their names were stricken from the roll and marked as

CAPTAIN JAMES IREDALL WADDELL (1824/1886) - He was born at Pittsboro, North Carolina, and was appointed to Annapolis on September 10, 1841. After graduating, he was assigned to duty on the U.S. ship, Pennsylvania. A few months later at Portsmouth, Virginia, he was shot in the hip during a duel with another midshipman and the injury caused him to limp the rest of his life. In 1858 he was promoted to lieutenant and made an assistant professor of navigation at the Naval Academy. In 1859 he was ordered to the East India Squadron and, after learning that the war had begun in 1861, mailed his resignation from St. Helena. Returning to Annapolis, he married his betrothed, Miss Inglehart, the daughter of James Inglehart, whose family was very strongly inclined to the South. The marriage took place in December of 1861 and he was listed on the Naval Registrar as being dismissed from service on January 19, 1862. After remaining in Annapolis for a short time, he rode the blockade to Richmond in February of 1862 and enlisted in the Confederate Army, receiving a commission of 1st lieutenant dated March 27, 1862. Waddell was sent to New Orleans for a short period and then returned to Virginia to Drewry's Bluff as an ordnance officer. He was ordered to Charleston Harbor for a short while and then to Europe for foreign service, arriving in England in May of 1863. The Confederate Naval Department purchased a British

merchant steamer and in October of 1864, rendezvousing off Liverpool, she was commissioned the C.S.S. Shenandoah and was commanded by Waddell. This was the last of the Confederate cruisers and, with the exception of the Alabama, inflicted the largest amount of injury upon the U.S. commerce vessels during the war. The Shenandoah wiped out most of the New Bedford whaling fleet off Alaska, taking many prizes and more than 1,000 prisoners. At one time, her decks and cabins were so crowded that she was forced to place her captives in whaling boats and tow them through the Arctic Sea. From prizes taken on June 23, 1865, Waddell read accounts in the newspapers of the April proceedings between Grant and Lee relating to the surrender. The paper also informed him that the seat of the Confederate government had been moved from Richmond to Danville and President Davis had issued the proclamation giving assurance of the continuation of the struggle by the South. With this knowledge he had no right to suppose that the war had ended and so he continued his operations until August 2. On November 6, 1865, he and his crew surrendered to the English government. Not until 1875 did Waddell leave England and return to this country. After re-establishing his home in Annapolis, the white-haired, limping sailor was once more called to the service of his nation. The governor of Maryland appointed him in the 1880s to take charge of the war that the state was waging against the Chesapeake Bay oyster pirates. After several days, Waddell's small force had completely wiped out the pirates. Upon his death in Annapolis, the legislature recessed its session for the day of his funeral.

being dismissed. Heroic deeds by Maryland's sea-going sons were recorded from the onset of hostilities beginning with the capture of the St. Nicholas by Richard Thomas' Zarvona Maryland Zouaves on June 28, 1861. The last deed of heroism occurred on August 2, 1865, when Captain James I. Waddell of the C.S.S. Shenandoah learned that President Davis had surrendered and the Confederacy was no more. The Shenandoah's guns were at once dismounted, portholes closed, funnels whitewashed and the ship transformed into an ordinary merchant vessel. After holding a conference with his officers, they all decided to go to England. They carried on hostilities for six months after the end of the war and finally surrendered to the English government on November 6, 1865, when the Confederate flag was hauled down and saluted for the last time. The Shenandoah and her captain became the subject of a violent discussion within North America with many wanting to try him as a traitor and impress the damages upon Her Majesty's British government. This, of course, caused a furor in the English Parliament. The American Congress and the whaling industry demanded Waddell's neck. Finally, in 1871 a treaty was signed between the United States and England which resulted in the claim of $15,000,000 being paid by Great Britain, an award for damages done by the Confederate cruiser.

The commissioned and warrant officers employed by the Naval Department were nominated as "in line" for promotion or "not in line" for promotion. There were very few advancements in rank because of the few ships which regulated the number of officers required. In April of 1862, the Confederate Congress passed an act authorizing the president to nominate officers to be promoted on account of gallantry. There were 209 promotions for distinguished valor and only two from the navy were twice advanced. In the army distinction was received by George W. Booth on September 25, 1863; Samuel D. Buck on May 20, 1863, and Gustav W. Dorsey on February 17, 1865. Naval

LIEUTENANT COMMANDING JOHN W. BENNETT (1822/1903) - After his preliminary education at the academy in Easton, located in Talbot County where he was born, he entered Delaware College. He was appointed a midshipman in the Navy in 1840. After seeing five years of sea service, Bennett went to the Naval Academy at Annapolis and graduated in 1846 with the first class. He served on various sloops during the war with Mexico. He also served in the West Indies Squadron, and sailed to Japan with Commodore Perry, holding the position of navigating officer. At the beginning of the movement for secession in South Carolina, Lieutenant Bennett was on duty at the observatory in Washington. After waiting several days, he resigned from his department and proceeded with his family to his home in Talbot County. After waiting a month, he was informed his name had been stricken from the Navy rolls and he immediately hastened to Richmond where he was appointed a lieutenant in the Confederate Navy. At Manassas he worked on the entrenchment of guns and commanded two of the eight batteries at headquarters. In the fall of 1861 he was assigned to the steamer Nashville. After returning from a European tour of service, he became an executive officer on the gunboat Gaines as a lieutenant commanding. The crew fought until, in a sinking condition, the Gaines was run aground and the crew was able to escape to Mobile in six boats. Bennett was then in charge of the Naval battery called Buchanan at Choctaw Point near Mobile until taking command of the new Nashville. He remained in defense of Mobile until the evacuation to Demopolis, Alabama. After being paroled on May 9, 1865, he returned by way of New Orleans and Norfolk to his old home. Bennett later moved to Sykesville and resided in the former home of his father-in-law Commodore Charles Lowndes.

COMMANDANT WILLIAM HARWAR PARKER (1827/) - Son of Commander Foxhall Parker Sr. he entered the navy in 1841 and graduated from the Naval Academy at the head of his class. He became an assistant professor of mathematics at the academy. Resigning his commission at Annapolis, he joined the Confederacy while his brother, Foxhall Jr., remained in the Union Army. William was commissioned a lieutenant and took part in the battles in the North Carolina Sounds. He commanded the gunboat Beauford and was executive officer of the ironclad Palmetto States. In March of 1863 he was selected as commandant of the newly formed Confederate States Naval Academy. The steamship Patrick Henry of the James River Squadron was chosen as the schoolship. On April 2, 1865, the midshipmen evacuated Richmond and Parker disbanded the corps of cadet midshipmen on May 2 at Abbeville, South Carolina. After the war he commanded the vessels of the Pacific Mail Steamship Company, subsequently became president of the Maryland Agricultural College and, in 1887, was U.S. Consulate at Bahia.

PAST MIDSHIPMAN DANIEL MAURY LEE (/1916) - Lee was born in Virginia and was a cadet at the Virginia Military Institute when the war broke out and he entered the naval service. He was sent to Norfolk as an acting midshipman and was aboard the Confederate relief ship, U.S. States. He saw action on the C.S.S. Jamestown in the engagement at Hampton Roads and off Drewry's Bluff in 1862. Transferred to the ram Chicora, he participated in three engagements in 1863. After advancement to midshipman, he was ordered aboard the C.S.S. Patrick Henry. He served with the James River Squadron and was then ordered to the Charleston Naval Station where he was on board the steamer, Juno. After promotion to past midshipman, Lee participated in the two attacks on Port Fisher, North Carolina. His last sea duty was aboard the C.S.S. Chicamauga. After the war he came to Baltimore where he was active in the Socity of the Army and Navy of the Confederate States in the State of Maryland and the James R. Herbert United Confederate Veterans Camp No. 657. In the early 1890s he moved to Stafford County, Virginia, where he farmed.

LIEUTENANT COMMANDING WILLIAM FITZHUGH CARTER - Carter enlisted on April 19, 1861, as a captain in the 4th Battalion, Virginia Volunteers, but the battalion failed to organize. He received a naval commission as a lieutenant not in line for promotion. He was an acting master on the James River during the summer of 1862. Later he became superintendent of transportation on the James. On April 27, 1863, he was detached from the steamer Torpedo and sent to Charleston. In 1864 Lieutenant Carter was ordered to Europe under James D. Bullard for the construction and equipment of Confederate vessels. In January of 1865 he left London in command of the C.S.S. Louisa Ann Fanny. He returned to his native home and worked in the Baltimore City Hall while holding memberships in the Society and the Buchanan and Trimble Camps.

88 - Navy

MASTER RICHARD FLEMING FOLEY - He was recorded in the Federal enrollment records of Annapolis as "gone south." On March 15, 1861, Foley was serving on the staff of W.H.C. Whitney as an engineer with the rank of captain. Upon receiving a naval commission as master he was ordered to the ironclad Richmond. On May 1, 1863, he was aboard the blockade runner Robert E. Lee. Later, he saw service on the gunboat Caswell and the floating battery Artic. After the war, Foley was a member of the Society of the Army and Navy of the Confederate States in the State of Maryland and was listed with the rank of captain.

MASTER THOMAS EDWARD HAMBLETON (1828/1906) - A native Baltimorean, he departed for Richmond in 1862 with his wife and two sons. As a firm member of the Importing and Exporting Company of the Confederate capital city, he made two successful trips across the Potomac under the authority of the Secretary of War. On February 24, 1863, he enlisted at Camp Lee as a private in Winder's Cavalry. Four days later he was discharged by special instruction from the adjutant general with John A. Slingluff taking his place among the Marylanders. Hambleton was ordered by the Confederacy to proceed to Europe with cotton and to return with supplies for the government. He purchased and was acting commander of the blockade runner Virginia Dare. These blockade-running services were not performed for his personal gain but were carried out for the patriotic service of providing military materials. Hambleton's swift steamer ran in and out of various blockaded harbors. After leaving Bermuda the Virginia Dare attempted to run into Wilmington but was discovered. Seeing that escape was impossible, the captain beached her on January 7, 1864. At midnight, on Waccamow beach, 15 miles north of the Georgetown entrance, she was torched while the officers, crew and passengers made their escape. As a lieutenant, Hambleton was on the English built Coquette, a 3-masted, propeller driven sloop, taking 1,200 bales of cotton per voyage to Bermuda, Havana and Nassau. After the war he returned to Baltimore and founded a banking house. On May 2, 1905, he became a member of the Isaac R. Trimble United Confederate Veterans Camp.

ASSISTANT SURGEON JOHN THOMPSON O. MASON (1817/1891) - After becoming licensed as a medical practitioner he joined the Navy during the Mexican War as an assistant surgeon. With the onset of hostilities he resigned and offered his services to the Confederacy on June 10, 1861, and received an appointment as assistant surgeon. He was aboard the Patrick Henry under Franklin Buchanan at the Battle of Hampton Roads during the famous duel between the Monitor and the Merrimac. After hospital duty on shore he was reassigned in June of 1863 as medical officer aboard the ram Baltic in the Mobile Naval Squadron. His next tour of duty was on the C.S.S. Huntsville. Dr. Mason was not paroled but took the amnesty oath at Macon on September 8, 1864, and applied for a pardon that he might return to Maryland. In the latter aprt of his life he was a member of the Franklin Buchanan Camp of United Confederate Veterans.

QUARTERMASTER ADOLPHUS F. MARMILSTEIN (1837/1922) - Born in Baltimore he moved to Savannah, Georgia, at the age of nine. He enlisted early in the Republican Blues of Savannah, but in the summer of 1861 transferred to naval service. He became a master's mate and was ordered to Europe as a member of the crew of the Alabama. At 2 o'clock on August 24, 1862, while Captain Semmes read the formal commission of the cruiser, Marmilstein hoisted the Confederate ensign to the peak as a cannon fired. His service aboard this swift raider was that of quartermaster. After the Alabama was sunk off the French coast near Cherbourg Harbor, he ran the blockade and was captured off Wilmington, North Carolina. As a prisoner of war he was sent to New York and was housed in the Ludlow Street jail. Upon being released he returned to Liverpool, England, reported to Confederate authorities, and assisted in rigging vessels of war. At the collapse of the Confederacy he was in Europe performing shore duty while awaiting a ship. Returning to Savannah he became a master pilot, bringing in and taking out large vessels between the different outlets.

PAST MIDSHIPMAN JOHN THOMSON MASON (/1891) - He was born in Michigan of Maryland parentage and received his education at the Episcopal High School of Fairfax. He enlisted during May of 1861 in the 17th Virginia Infantry as a private and served for seven months. Upon the organization of the navy, Mason's qualifications led him to receive an appointment as a midshipman in December of 1861. He was ordered aboard the gunboat Hampton. After a few months he became executive officer until the summer of 1863 when he was ordered aboard a steamer that ran the blockade from Charleston to England. Mason then served on the Calhoun. In October of 1864 he was assigned to the Shenandoah as a past midshipman until November 6, 1865, when the flag was hauled down in Liverpool for the last time. He migrated to the Argentine Republic where he farmed for two years. After the return of constitutional rights to southerners, he returned to Baltimore and after further schooling was admitted to the bar to practice law. He was one of the founders of the Franklin Buchanan United Confederate Veterans Camp in 1896 and was also active in the Isaac Ridgeway Trimble Camp and the Society of the Army and Navy of the Confederate States in the State of Maryland.

MASTER MATE CHARLES HUNTER WHO, ALONG WITH HIS FATHER AND THREE BROTHERS, SERVED IN THE C.S.N. Thomas T. Hunter Sr. was born in Virginia and appointed to the navy from the District of Columbia in 1828. He resigned and the records show him as dismissed on April 23, 1861. He was appointed a commander when he joined the Southern Navy and commanded the C.S.S. Curlew, the gunboat Gaines and the C.S.S. Chicora. Sons Thomas T. Hunter Jr., William Hunter, Ferdinand S. Hunter and Charles Hunter were all appointed from Maryland and sometime during the war all served aboard one of their father's ships. Thomas Jr. was appointed as a ship's clerk and became an acting master's mate. He was captured on October 7, 1864, aboard the cruiser Florida at Bahia, Brazil, and sent north to prison. William, the youngest brother, was a midshipman and served in the Richmond Naval Station and the Mobile Squadron. On June 27, 1863, he was sent to the hospital ship Gaines and died on February 4 from typhoid fever. Ferdinand S. held the rank of past midshipman when captured on April 6, 1865, at Harper's Farm during the battle of Sailer's Creek and was sent to prison in Sandusky, Ohio. Charles was appointed acting master's mate and served on the C.S.S. Chicora. Upon the evacuation of Charleston, Charles, along with his father and Ferdinand, were ordered to the Richmond Naval Station. With the retreat from Richmond all three were in the Naval Brigade and captured at Harper's Farm. Charles and his father were sent to Fort Warren and held in lease mate No. 5, which his diary reveals contained 40 prisoners of whom 14 were Marylanders. He was released on June 13, 1865, and requested to stay with his father until men of that rank were released. Refused of his request, Charles returned to the old family homestead in Beltsville.

MIDSHIPMAN WILLIAM DICKINSON HOUGH (1834/1907) - He was a Baltimore native and one of four brothers to serve in the C.S.A. Enlisting for 12-months on June 18, 1861, at Fairfax in the Maryland Guard Company of Weston's Maryland Battalion he transferred with them when they became Company F, 1st Maryland Infantry. On October 8 he was elected 1st lieutenant. He resigned on June 12, 1862, because of ill health. Toward the end of the summer he secured a commission from the Naval Department and was appointed a midshipman. As a captain's clerk he served aboard the C.S.S. Florida. On October 7, 1864, he was captured at Bahia, Brazil, and was sent to Point Lookout. From there he was transferred to Washington and then to Fort Warren. On February 1, 1865, he was released by taking the pledge of honor to leave the United States within 10 days and to commit no further hostile acts. After the war he returned to Baltimore.

MIDSHIPMAN JAMES MORRIS MORGAN (1845/1928) - He was born in New Orleans, Louisiana, and then made his home in Mongtomery County. There were 13 midshipmen at the Naval Academy in 1861 who were either born in, appointed from or resided in the state of Maryland. He was one of seven whose principles were so deeply entrenched in the constitution under the Southern interpretation that they departed Annapolis to join the Confederacy. He became a steward to George Nicholas Hollins and in the early spring of 1862 Morgan accompanied him to Mississippi. The flagship McRae was his station until the fall of New Orleans when he proceeded to Norfolk. From there he was ordered to the naval batteries at Drewry's Bluff. He was present with his brother, a captain of a Louisiana regiment, at the Battle of Seven Pines and went through the Seven Days Battle around Richmond with the infantry. Assigned to Charleston Harbor, Morgan was appointed an aide to Commodore Maury and ran the blockade to England. He was advanced to a midshipman on the ironscrew steamer which was fitted up as a cruiser and christened, The Georgia, from April of 1863 through May of the following year. He returned aboard the Lillian which ran the blockade to Wilmington and he was then stationed at the naval batteries defending the James. When the beseiged city was abandoned he escorted Mrs. Davis to Abbeville, South Carolina, where he was directed by the president to report to Augusta. However, he was forced to surrender at Washington, Georgia. In 1870 he went to Egypt as a captain of artillery in the service of the Khedieve. Ten years later he was in Mexico where he was a railroad engineer before returning to assist in the erection of the Statue of Liberty. He received an appointment in 1885 as Consulant General to Australia and was in Melbourne for three years before returning to Cedarcroft plantation in Montgomery County.

MASTER'S MATE JAMES SAMUEL STERETT (1837/) - Leaving his home in Baltimore he proceeded to Richmond where he became a member of the Weston Guard on May 17, 1861, and was appointed 4th sergeant. The Weston Guard would become A Company of J. Alden Weston's Maryland Battalion but, when the company was shifted to the 1st Maryland Infantry, Sterett did not accompany them. He was the son of Captain Isaac Sterett of the Old Navy who, upon coming into the Confederacy, was joined by his son and both secured positions in the Confederate Navy, James as an active master's mate. James S. was arrested in Maryland in 1862 and was tried before a military tribunal. He was found guilty of treason and was sent to Fort McHenry and later to Fort Warren. J.W. Black & Company of Boston took this carte de viste in 1864 while he was a prisoner.

promotion was given to four native sons: Franklin Buchanan on August 19, 1862; Joseph Nicholas Barney on April 25, 1863; Raphael Semmes was advanced to captain on August 19, 1862, and to rear admiral on February 8, 1865, and John Taylor Wood was promoted to commander on August 23, 1863, and to captain on February 8, 1865. Charles Henry McBlair and Henry Ashton Ramsay held naval and army commissions. Commander McBlair was also an army colonel at Fernandina, and Chief Engineer Ramsay was appointed commanding lieutenant colonel of the defenses of Charlotte.

There were many instances of courageous deeds by Marylanders which are little known. Captain Beverley Kennon, during the Battle of Mobile Bay, commanded the little wooden side-wheeler Governor Moore. He was pursued by the Varuna and soon the Governor Moore began to sink. When Captain Kennon saw that his vessel was doomed he rushed forward determined to get a parting shot from his bow gun. Reaching the forecastle, he found that the entire gun crew had been killed or wounded, the carriage had been blown off the piece, and the rear transom resting against the heel of the foremast. Finding it impossible to depress the gun enough in its crippled condition, and not having the men or time to remount the piece properly, Kennon pointed the gun through his own deck, which was six feet inside the knighthead. He loaded the cannon and fired it through the heel of the bowsprit. The shot passed through his own deck and went crashing into the enemy's side a little below the water line. A second shot was fired in like manner while the smoke was too thick to allow Captain Kennon to see the other ship. When the air had cleared the Varuna was only 10 feet away and was slowly sinking by the stern. This was one of the few instances in which vessels engaged in battle together were both sunk and it was incredible that a captain would fire though the deck of his own ship to sink an enemy vessel.

There were 10 members of the Forrest family of Maryland who followed the Southern flag in the navy and 4 fought under the Stars and Stripes in the Federal army. The family had contributed many prominent sailors during the nation's past struggles, and the War between the State proved no exception. Captain French Forrest was chief of the Bureau of Ordnance and Detail; Dulany A. Forrest was a lieutenant; Douglas F. Forrest was a paymaster and acting masters mate; and W.S. Forrest served in the Southern navy. Lieutenant Moreau Forrest, acting Third Assistant Engineer Thomas Forrest and Masters Mate Henry Forrest all remained in the Union navy.

The amount of destruction to Union vessels by just three Maryland sailors was awesome. Raphael Semmes, commanding the C.S.S. Sumter, captured 18 ships, burned 8 and one was recaptured. While commanding the C.S.S. Alabama he burned 53 ships, scuttled 3 and ransomed 10. John Taylor Wood, of the C.S.S. Tallahassee, captured over 40, burned 16, scuttled 10 and ransomed 5 ships. James Iredell Waddell, of the C.S.S. Shenandoah, destroyed 34 ships and ransomed 4. These three Marylanders led both navies in the destruction of sea-going vessels. This destruction of shipping was to be felt for decades after the war ended.

CHIEF ENGINEER HENRY ASHTON RAMSAY (1835/1916) - Although he was born in Prince George's County he was raised in Washington and on May 24, 1853, joined the navy. He served for two years as an engineer aboard the Merrimac. When the Federals evacuated sailors loyal to the South he bored a number of holes in her bottom. As a consequence, when she was burned she sank so her machinery and parts were below the water line and were untouched by the flames. After resigning, Ramsay was commissioned in the Confederate Navy on June 10, 1861. Knowing every timber of the Merrimac, he was assigned as an assistant engineer and reconditioned her machinery as she was transformed into an ironclad. After participating in the engagements at Hampton Roads on the C.S.S. Virginia Ramsay was elevated to the rank of chief engineer. He was assigned to the Charleston Naval Station and was then sent to command the Naval Post at Charlotte, North Carolina. While guarding the city against ground raids by the enemy he received the army appointments of major and then lieutenant colonel. He was paroled at Charlotte on April 28, 1865. Ramsay made Baltimore his post-war home and worked as a consulting engineer. He was a member of the Confederate Veterans Camp that bore the grand old hero's name of Franklin Buchanan, No. 747, and the Society of the Army and Navy of the Confederate States in the State of Maryland.

Chapter 8

MARINES

The Confederate Corps of Marines was established on March 16, 1861, by act of the Congress of the Confederate States, then seated at Montgomery, Alabama. Although recruitment began immediately, Lloyd James Beall was not appointed commanding officer, with the rank of colonel, until May 21, 1861. The recruiting officers operated in the coastal towns of New Orleans, Mobile and Pensacola, as well as Richmond.

None of the officers of the companies organized by the individual states, prior to transfer to the provisional government, were above the rank of captain. As the corps expanded, the top positions were either allocated to Marylanders or Virginians. Commandant Beall, Major Algernon S. Taylor and Major Richard T. Allison were all Free Staters. The Cotton States had no marine officer above the rank of a company commander.

COMMANDANT LLOYD JAMES BEALL (1808/1887) - Beall was born in Rhode Island while his Georgetown family was away from their home. In 1826 he was appointed from Maryland to West Point and was graduated in 1830. He was commissioned a lieutenant in the 1st Infantry in the same regiment where he and Jefferson Davis both held 2nd lieutenant's commissions. Transferring to the 2nd Dragoons in 1836, Beall was soon promoted to captain. In 1840-1842 he attended the French Army Cavalry School at Saumur. He advanced to major and paymaster in 1844 and at the outbreak of the war was in St. Louis where he resigned effective April 22, 1861. Going to Charleston and then to Montgomery, on May 21 he was appointed colonel and commandant of the Marine Corps. On May 25, 1862, General J.E. Johnston wrote in a recommendation that Colonel Beall was imminently qualified for the grade of brigadier general. The small Marine Corps was never enlarged and Beall continued in the capacity of commandant until the end of the war. Settling in Richmond, he received a pardon on November 30, 1866, through contacts at his former residence in Georgetown and by recommendation of U.S. Grant and other influential people of the area.

The Corps' battalions followed the U.A. Marine principles rather than being developed into regiments of sea-going infantry. They were deployed as ships' detachments, or at scattered naval stations and harbors for defense. They were also used as mobile striking forces and for special assignments. James Thurston served as an instructor of artillery for the Baltimore Secessionists in the Charleston Harbor batteries before serving with the naval forces under Captain Isaac S. Sterett. He was discharged in order to receive a commission in the Marine Corps.

The Washington Volunteers, Company E of the 1st Virginia Infantry, were re-organized and sent to the 7th Virginia Infantry as Company H. Since most were Marylanders, they were not subject to the conscription act when their 12-month enlistment expired and so were discharged to seek other commands. From these ranks, five members entered the Marine Corps. William F. Phillips Jr. was a lawyer who became a quartermaster clerk to Major I.S. Taylor. Howard Benedict became a quartermaster sergeant while Redmond J. Darden and brothers Daniel and Joseph Parsons were privates in the Marine guard assigned to the C.S.S. Virginia.

On the high seas Marine detachments for naval vessels were considered a necessary part of the ship's complement. One or more musicians per detachment, be they fifer, drummer or bugler, wore a distinctive tunic so the officer could readily locate them to transmit his orders. The major role of marines in naval combat was to either act as boarding parties or to repel boarders by providing small arms musketry. Most of the time the Marines were used as a ship's police to maintain order. Joshua Charlesworth was a Baltimorean and a product of the pre-war U.S.M.C. While serving at sea in 1858 he got into a scuffle with another Marine and stabbed his antagonist. A court martial followed and Charlesworth was found guilty. However, dur to the other Marine only being slightly injured, he was only fined and demoted. Charlesworth enlisted in the C.S.M.C. as a sergeant and was sent to sea.

First Lieutenant Robert Young Fendall was captured at the surrender of Fort Gaines on August 8, 1864. He was imprisoned at New Orleans but escaped on October 13 along with Captain Julius E. Meiere, another Marylander, and two other Marine officers. He returned to duty on November 10 at Mobile.

CAPTAIN JULIUS ERNEST MEIERE (1833/1905) - New Haven, Connecticut, was the place of his birth and on April 16, 1855, he received an appointment as a 2nd lieutenant in the Marine Corps. After two years of sea duty in the Gulf of Mexico, and serving as acting council of Vera Cruz in June of 1860, he was ordered to the Marine Barracks in Washington. In January of the following year he was promoted to 1st lieutenant and on April 3 married Nannie Buchanan, daughter of Captain Franklin Buchanan. On April 20, while aboard the U.S.S. Anacostia at Washington he resigned his commission. Travelling to Montgomery, Alabama, he received the same rank in the C.S.M.C. on April 8. He was sent to Pensacola and then Savannah before being transferred to Richmond in the spring of 1862. Lieutenant Meiere was serving aboard the C.S.S. Virginia when she was abandoned and destroyed on May 11, 1862. After recruiting service in Richmond he was ordered to Mobile to command the Marine Station. While there he trained and organized marines for sea duty in the Marine Squadron. On August 8, 1864, he was captured during the surrender of Fort Gaines, Alabama. He escaped from imprisonment in New Orleans on October 13 and returned to duty. In February of 1865 he was ordered from Drewry's Bluff to Mobile, Alabama, where he surrendered on May 4 and took the oath of allegiance at Key West, Florida, on May 20. He returned to "The Rest," his father-in-law's home in Talbot County. He was graduated from the Medical College of the University of New York in 1869. After moving to Colorado in 1873 he applied for an appointment as an Army contract surgeon on March 28, 1874.

Daniel Lloyd Jr., of the 1st Maryland Light Artillery, was a nephew of Franklin Buchanan. Buchanan wrote the Secretary of the Navy recommending Lloyd for a commission in August of 1863. Toward the end of the war, General Order No. 38 was issued, which stated that any citizen of Maryland prior to the war could transfer to the Maryland Line. Many Marylanders accepted the benefit of this order and transferred from the Marine Corps. Consequently, under Special Order No. 84 in 1864, the following Free Staters transferred to the Line: Sergeant Gustavus Wagner, aboard the C.S.S. Charleston; Corporal William G. Huddleston, from the Richmond Naval Station; Private James Noal, of the C.S.S. Charleston; Private Stephen H. Ford, of the C.S.S. Indian Chief; Private Francis T. McHon, Private John Hafry, Private Robert Wright, all of the C.S.S. Palmetto State; Private J.B. Cooper, Private Thomas Nickoles, Private J.H. McCahan, and Private W.H. Harris, all of the C.S.S. Albemarle.

Upon the evacuation of Commandant Beall's headquarters in Richmond a number of books and papers of the Corps were ordered burned. Most of the records which have survived were the quartermaster's and commissary department's for the Corps under the direction and supervision of Major Algernon S. Taylor of Carroll County who was in the Maryland Line Confederate Soldiers Home. Also, the records of the paymaster department under Major Richard T. Allison remain intact. Allison carried these with him when he departed Richmond on April 2, 1865. He travelled first to

MAJOR RICHARD TAYLOR ALLISON (1823/1909) - Although born near Louisville, Kentucky, he moved to Maryland in 1845 where he passed the bar and started a practice of law. On October 30, 1849, he was appointed paymaster in the navy by his uncle, President Zachary Taylor. He accompanied Commodore Perry's expedition to Japan which was followed by duty with the China Squadron. Returning to this country in 1856, he was assigned as an inspector of provisions at the Washington Naval Yard. On April 20, 1861, he tendered his resignation but remained on duty until May 1 at the request of Secretary of the Navy Giddeon Wells. As he left for Richmond he telegraphed President Davis in Montgomery and was summoned there to receive a similar appointment in the C.S.M.C. on May 10, 1861. Advanced to the rank of major, the majority of Allison's service was spent in Richmond at the headquarters of the Marine Corps. He left the capital in April of 1865 and made his way to North Carolina where he surrendered with a part of Johnston's command. He was paroled at Greensboro on April 28. Returning to Baltimore, served many years as clerk of the Superior Court of the City of Baltimore. He made his home was near Phoenix in Baltimore County.

Danville, Virginia, and then on to Charlotte, North Carolina, in an attempt to rendezvous with the president and cabinet.

Many of Maryland's sons were never to see their native state again. Marine Corporal William Briggs died at Camp Beall at Drewry's Bluff on June 22, 1862. His brother, Private Daniel Briggs of Holbrook's Independent Artillery, was killed at Vicksburg. Both brothers, like so many Maryland casualties, lay far away in lonely, unmarked graves.

Chapter 9

PHYSICIANS

Of the 219 medical doctors from Maryland who served in the Confederacy, 12 served in the militia prior to the 1860s and one, Dr. Charles Macgill, was a militia major general. In the call to arms after the insurrection in Baltimore, general practitioners were asked to become a part of the volunteers. Thirty six doctors answered the call to compose the Baltimore Civilian Militia Surgical Staff. Of these, Edward Warren, Allen P. Smith, Alexander Clendenin, Richard Emory, William B. Everett, Arthur L. Foreman, Robert J. Freeman, Charles E.V. Nickerson, Samuel A. Raborg and Ignatius Davis Thompson ran the blockade and joined the Southern army. They administered to many of the volunteer militia who became Confederate soldiers. Eight career army physicians and eight naval doctors resigned their commissions to join the Confederate medical corps. There were five other physicians from this state who had seen previous military service and re-entered the military, this time against their former government. In proportion to volunteers, Maryland would contribute more medical men to the Confederacy than any other southern aligned state. This was because the aristocracy was southern in feeling and because of the three large medical schools located within the state: the University of Maryland Medical College and the Washington Medical College, both in Baltimore, and the Georgetown University Medical College. Of the 219 physicians, a number came out of predominantly Union areas: Allegany County gave 3 doctors to the cause, Washington 8, and Frederick an unbelievable 18. For some, the decision came easy but for others it was wrestled with for many sleepless nights. Dr. Memary Bonner, after receiving information concerning the death of two brothers killed in the southern army, withdrew from the faculty of the University of Maryland Medical College to render his services. In the army, 67 would gain the rank of surgeon and, of the 18 naval physicians, two would achieve the rank of surgeon. Charles Bell Gibson was surgeon general of Virginia, Cary Breckinridge surgeon general of Florida, Edward Warren surgeon general of North Carolina and Lucius Bellinger Northrop was a brigadier general and commissary general of South Carolina. In the nation's first dental corps, seven Marylanders would serve, two of which were M.D.'s. For a more indepth biography on these doctors, see Medical Doctors of Maryland in the C.S.A.

MEDICAL DIRECTOR THOMAS H. WILLIAMS (1829/) - He was born in Dorchester County and attended school at Washington Academy at Princess Anne and the University of Maryland Medical College, graduating with the class of 1848. On March 2, 1849, he was commissioned an assistant surgeon in the army and by 1857 Surgeon Williams was medical director of the army in Utah. He resigned effective June 1, 1861. Without selfish ambitions, he proceeded south and on June 26 was appointed a surgeon and ordered to report to General Beauregard at Manassas as his medical director. As the first medical director of the Confederate Army of the Potomac he was busy establishing the Field Medical Corps. Upon the reorganization of the army he continued as medical director of the Army of Northern Virginia. On June 6, 1862, Surgeon Williams became inspector of the general hospitals at Petersburg, Danville, Farmville, Lynchburg and Charlottesville. He established many of the large hospitals in Virginia except for those in Richmond and Petersburg. By December 15 he was assigned to temporary duty as medical director of General G.W. Smith's command. On January 14, 1863, he was ordered to the surgeon general's office in Richmond where he was placed in charge of the Medical Purveyors Department. He was paroled on May 9, 1865, at Augusta, Georgia. Returning to the Eastern Shore, he practiced in Cambridge and in 1898 Dr. Williams became a state member of the United Charities Hospital.

SURGEON ALEXANDER T. BELL (1826/1913) - Dr. Bell was appointed an assistant surgeon on July 19, 1861, and assigned to the 9th Virginia Infantry. In January of 1863 he was reassigned to the 3rd Virginia Cavalry at its organization but soon gained a transfer to General J.E.B. Stuart's Horse Artillery. Dr. Bell was thrilled to become part of a unit which was under the command of Dr. James Breathed. After being elevated to the rank of surgeon early in 1865, Dr. Bell became a member of the Exemption Board at Portsmouth. He was then assigned to the Prison Hospital at Libby in Richmond. When the city was evacuated he remained to attend the ailing Federals. After being paroled at the hospital on April 19 he was retained to continue his duties. He later established a medical practice in Baltimore where he held memberships in the Franklin Buchanan United Veterans Camp No. 747 and the Isaac R. Trimble Camp No. 1025. Dr. Bell was also active in the Society of the Army and Navy of the Confederate States in the State of Maryland and, on October 5, 1910, entered the Maryland Line Confederate Soldiers Home in Pikesville.

SURGEON WILLIAM PROBY YOUNG JR. - Practicing at Middletown in Frederick County he departed for the South and, in July of 1861, entered the 116th Virginia Militia. After his 12-month enlistment as a private expired, he appeared before the Army Medical Examining Board and was successful in receiving his commission. Assistant Surgeon Young was assigned to the 4th Georgia Infantry on July 15, 1862. During the Antietam Campaign that fall, he was wounded in his native county where, just a year and one half before, he had been treating patients. He returned across the Potomac with his regiment and continued to serve in the Army of Northern Virginia. On June 9, 1863, he was promoted to surgeon and was later transferred to hospital service. After the war he established his practice in Washington, D.C. As a member of a Confederate Veterans Association, Dr. Young was chosen as a pallbearer for the funeral of Major General Joseph E. Johnston which was held on March 24, 1891, at St. John's Church in Washington with the interment in Greenmount Cemetery in Baltimore.

SURGEON-IN-CHIEF JOHN RANDOLPH PAGE (1830/1901) - He was born in Gloucester County, Virginia, and received his medical degree from the University of Virginia in 1850. He then attended medical and surgical clinics in Paris and London for two years. He returned to the county of his birth and practiced until 1856. Dr. Page then moved to Carroll County, Maryland, and became a member of the Maryland Medical and Chirurgical faculty. When the hostile army held Maryland in subjection, he moved to the seat of war and became an assistant surgeon in the 10th Virginia Infantry on July 19, 1861. He was elevated to surgeon on February 5, 1862, and ordered to Yorktown where he organized and was in charge of the New General Hospital. By April Surgeon Page was assigned to the Reserve Artillery Corps of General Pendleton's command. He remained with Pendleton as head surgeon of the medical staff until August 17 when he was granted a leave of absence for 30 days for the benefit of his health. By mid winter he was surgeon-in-chief of Burkeville Infirmary. On April 24, 1863, he received orders to become medical director at Knoxville in the Department of East Tennessee, but this order was revoked on May 6. Sent to General Hospital No. 2 at Lynchburg he signed on as surgeon-in-charge on June 15. Within the next year he became surgeon-in-chief and on March 26, 1865, Dr. Page was called to report to Richmond but the war ended before he could arrive. His practice was established in the fallen capital where he was a member of the Richmond Academy of Medicine. Moving to Louisiana State Seminary at Lexington, he taught there until 1869 when he accepted a teaching position at the Washington Medical University in Baltimore. He was a member of the Association of the Maryland Line.

The Confederate clothing regulations specified that the medical corps were to wear gray frock coats with black collars and cuffs, dark blue trousers, green sash, and a hat emblem bearing the letters "MS". In reality, many wore undress sack coats devoid of color facings. Colonel George Peters, Ambulance Corps commander in the Army of Northern Virginia, had his men wear a red medical insignia on their hats. The 1st Maryland Infantry's hospital, under Surgeons Edwin Samuel Gallaird and Richard Potts Johnson, with Assistant Surgeons Styles Kennedy and Thomas Sargent Latimer, had their own flag. It consisted of white bunting (now faded yellow) with a long fly. In the center, placed horizontally, was a red and blue design in the shape of a hour glass.

SURGEON CHARLES MACGILL (1806/1881) - Macgill was educated at Baltimore College, class of 1823, and the Medical University, class of 1828. He entered the office of Dr. Charles G. Worthington to read medicine. In 1829 he started his doctoring in Hagerstown and became one of Washington County's most prominent physicians and politicians. He was a candidate for the presidential elector on the Van Doren ticket and in 1836 was one of the "Glorious Nineteen" electors of the state senate who brought about the constitutional reform. He was also active in the state militia rising from the rank of a 2nd lieutenant to colonel of the 24th Regiment and, on July 30, 1857, became major general of Western Maryland. Dr. Macgill raised the ire of the government early because he was a leading spirit among Southern sympathizers. He openly assisted his son-in-law, Robert Swan, a veteran of the Mexican War, to leave Hagerstown and join the C.S.A. Dr. Macgill was arrested and imprisoned in Fort McHenry, Fort Hamilton and Fort Lafayette as a political prisoner. In November of 1862 he was unconditionally released and returned to his home to resume his profession. When Lee's Army crossed the state in the summer of 1863 Dr. Macgill and his son, Dr. Charles G.W. Macgill, established a hospital at his residence in Hagerstown for broken down Confederate soldiers. When the army returned from Gettysburg on July 7 his hospital was used to treat the wounded Southerners. With the evacuation of Hagerstown five days later he cast his fortunes with the Confederacy, leaving his family in Maryland. He received an expression of gratitude from President Jefferson Davis. As a surgeon he worked in Lynchburg Hospital until he was captured and imprisoned on April 15, 1865. He was paroled three days later and went to Richmond where he remained to practice.

100 - Physicians

There were at least two father-and-son teams who were both physicians that would go into the medical corps of the C.S.A.: Daniel Smith Green, who was a surgeon in the navy, and his son William, a surgeon of artillery in the Second Corps; Charles Macgill and his son Charles G.W. Macgill. On June 15, 1863, when Southern forces entered Hagerstown, the Macgills established a hospital at their home for broken down Confederate soldiers. With the return of the army on July 7 from Gettysburg their hospital was used for wounded Southerners. With the evacuation of Hagerstown five days later, they both cast their fortunes with the Army of Northern Virginia.

ASSISTANT SURGEON JOHN FORNEY ZACHARIAS - He was born and raised in Frederick, the son of Dr. Daniel Zacharias, and received his educational discipline at the Frederick Academy and the Jefferson Medical College, class of 1860. Young Doctor Zacharias worked in the office with his father until the sentiments of the revolution led him into the Confederacy. On January 5, 1863, the resources of his training were utilized as he became an acting assistant surgeon at Danville General Hospital No. 2. By that summer he was an assistant surgeon. He was captured on May 13, 1864, and exchanged at Rough and Ready on September 28. Dr. Zacharias was assigned to General Hospital No. 1 in Danville until that fall when he was reassigned to the Army of Tennessee where he served at Shipp Hospital. He returned to Frederick immediately after the war and reported to the provost marshal. After finding out he would not be allowed to practice again in his native state, he crossed the Potomac to Leesburg and five years later settled in Cumberland. He was a member of Isaac R. Trimble United Confederate Veterans Camp of Baltimore even though he lived in the western portion of the state. In 1903 he was elected commander of all the United Confederate Veterans Camps within the state.

Surgeons kit with brass inlay engraved "DR. J. F. Zacharias" of walnut with a green velvet lining. Top tray contains three amputation knives, forceps, elevator, aneurism hook, tenotome; the bottom has lifting metacarpal saw, tourniquet, Key's saw and in the small compartment with an ivory knob is a small curved needle with a wire and cloth sutures, all instruments are marked "Gemrig Phila. Pa."

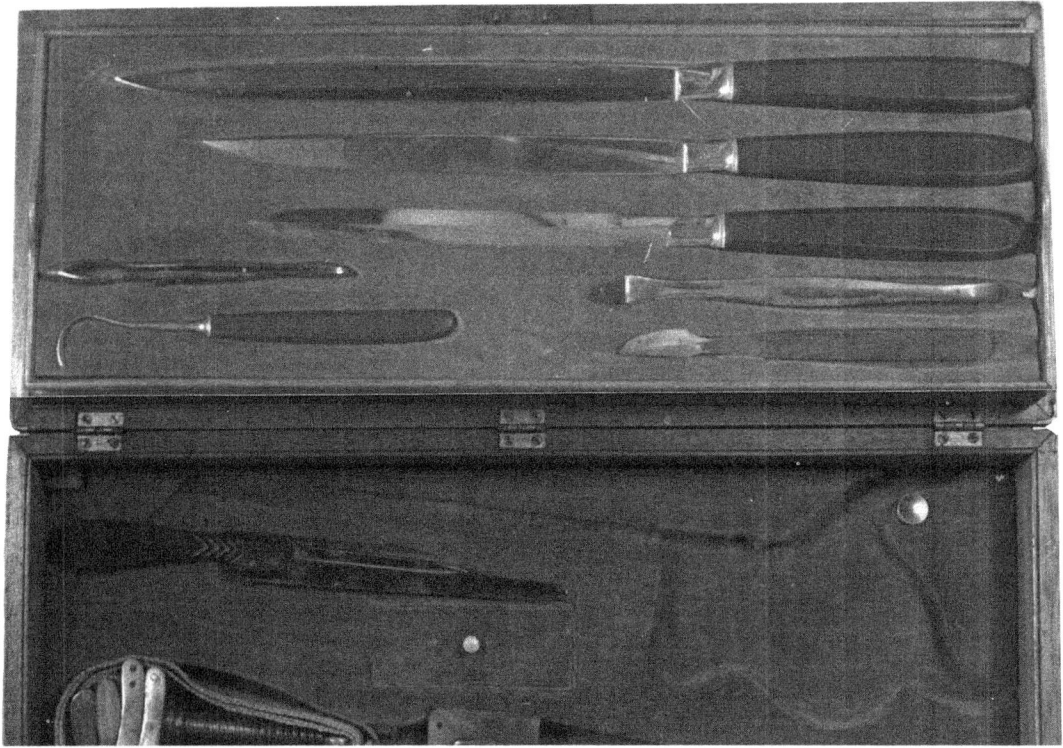

The great majority of these physicians entered the Confederate forces as privates in the enlisted ranks. Two of the four licensed doctors in the 1st Maryland Artillery were killed while fighting as cannoneers. Fifteen Maryland doctors continued to wear everything from the butternut of an enlisted man to the wreath of a brigadier general but did not perform medical duties. Seven medical practitioners from Weston's Maryland Infantry Battalion came out of the enlisted ranks, went before the Medical Board, and received their commissions. Doctors were conspicuous as line and staff officers in ordnance, engineer, signal and the quartermaster corps. One of these gallant heroes who gave up his medical valise for a sabre was Lieutenant Colonel James Breathed, who recruited over 100 Marylanders into Stuart's Horse Artillery. While his battery was being overrun Breathed is remembered for single handedly hitching the horses, jumping on the back of one and bringing them off of the field during which several of the horses were killed and dragged in their harness. His daring also included rallying some men and charging the enemy when the battery was in trouble, returning with blood on his sabre from the point to the hilt. The majority of these doctors entered the medical corps because of the dire need of skilled individuals to treat the wounded. Two Marylanders would write the only official medical texts published in the Confederacy. Julian J. Chisolm wrote <u>A Manual of Military Surgery</u> and Edward Warren wrote <u>An Epitome of Practical Surgery for Field and Hospital</u>.

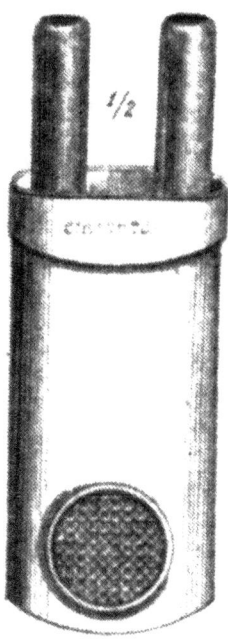

Metal chloroform inhaler invented by Surgeon Julian J. Chisolm during the war.

As medical officers', many practiced as contract physicians employed by the Confederacy before receiving commissions while eight contract doctors never did enter the corps.

This branch of service had the least number of casualties. Only 11 practitioners did not survive the war. There were 80 known former Confederate soldiers who, after the war, pursued the medical curriculum and became licensed practitioners within the state.

Chapter 10

CLERGY

There were 24 ordained, licensed clergymen of Maryland denominations who relinquished their pulpits to go into the service of the Confederate army. Most enlisted in the rank and file, serving as regular armed soldiers. Soon, many were stimulated by the deep sense of full-time Christian needs of their brothers around them.

Rev. James B. Avirett served churches in Allegany County and across the Potomac in northern Virginia. On June 17, 1861, he was appointed chaplain of Turner Ashby's 7th Virginia Cavalry. Many times he assisted Surgeon Arthur P. Burns with the wounded. Avirett carried a flask of whiskey in his ambulance which Harry Gilmor stole one cold winter's night because "he didn't believe in chaplains drinking." Many volunteered as chaplains, then sought regular commission appointments. As commssioned chaplains some still participated in combat. Rev. John Thomas Maxwell, of the 35th Virginia Cavalry, and Stephen J. Cameron, of the 1st Maryland Infantry, were each referred to as fighting chaplains. Rev. Maxwell carried a revolver and saber and was always at the front of Company B, not letting his sacred responsibilities as chaplain interfere with his patriotic duties as a soldier. Rev. Cameron, at Bailey's Cross Roads, "took a gun and fired once and was assured he had killed his man through or around a haystack, and, not doubting it, was filled with mixed feelings of triumph and remorse. It was not the last of his uncanonical acts." Others felt that spiritual leaders should not be engaged in the taking of lives. Rev. Randolph H. McKim was a private and then a staff officer before becoming an unarmed chaplain. He wrote that it took a good deal more nerve to go through a fight as a noncombatant than as a soldier. His choice was not easy when he resigned his

CHAPLAIN RANDOLPH HARRISON McKIM (1842/1904) - At the age of 18 this Baltimorean was a student at the University of Virginia and was a member of the Southern Guard, one of the two militia companies at the university. They were sent to Harpers Ferry for several weeks, after which he travelled to Baltimore to promise his parents he would finish the session at the university; however, on July 11, 1861, he joined Company H, 1st Maryland Infantry, as a private. This photo was taken after the Battle of Cross Keys he had been promoted to 1st lieutenant as an aide-de-camp on the staff of General George H. Steuart Jr. At Gettysburg he was struck by four different bullets but was not seriously hurt. In the autumn of 1863 McKim tendered his resignation in order to become a minister of the gospel. His resignation was accepted on September 1, 1863, and he began his studies at the Theological Seminary at Staunton. For the previous five years he had been working toward the Christian calling as a clergyman. On February 10, 1864, he was ordained and licensed in the Protestant Episcopal Church. Returning to the army, he received an appointment as chaplain of Chew's Artillery and subsequently was transferred to the 2nd Regiment, Virginia Cavalry. Paroled at Staunton, he returned to his native state where he continued to be a shepherd of his Lord's flock. He was a member of the Society of the Army and Navy of the Confederate States in the State of Maryland.

commission to prepare for ordination. He left the army with a heavy heart and was thankful that the people around him knew that this step was dictated by a higher sense of duty, but it was still a painful effort.

John M. Burke was messmate of McKim's during the first winter as enlisted men in the 1st Maryland Infantry. After Burke was discharged from his 12-month enlistment, he desired to finish his theological training which he had started prior to the war. He entered the Episcopal Seminary at Staunton and turned out in defense of the town as a volunteer during the Battle of River Bridge in June of 1864. He was serving with a musket in his hand when he raised his head above the breastworks and was instantly killed. Rev. Dalney Carr Harrison was first a chaplain and then resigned to become a company commander, only to lose his life at Fort Donelson. Rev. Charles Frederick Linthicum was killed by a sharpshooter on June 3, 1864. He mentions throughout his diary that the ministry was his special calling, and even though he accepted the staff appointment, he intended to return to the pulpit when the strife ended.

CHAPLAIN CHARLES FREDERICK LINTHICUM (1838/1864) - He was born and raised in the Urbana district of Frederick County. His early education was in the public schools of the state in which he later taught. In March of 1860 he was ordained as a minister in the Methodist Episcopal Church. He was sent by the Baltimore Conference to Loudoun County. He enlisted on May 8, 1861, in Company A, 8th Virginia Infantry. At the Battle of First Manassas, which was the first time the regiment was engaged, they were about to make a charge upon the enemy from the Henry House when a young soldier stepped forward from the ranks and asked permission of his officer to pray with his company. The wish was granted. In pathetic words he asked of Him who directs the destiny of armies to bless their cause and bring victory to their arms. After the battle he was detailed by Colonel Hunton, commander of the Bloody 8th, as chaplain of the regiment and soon after he received his commission signed by the War Department. Linthicum became known as "The Fighting Chaplain" for wherever and whenever fighting was going on he was found with his knapsack and musket in the front lines. Due to casualties suffered at the Battle of Gaines Mills, Colonel Hunton, after becoming commander of the brigade, detailed Captain Linthicum to temporarily act as adjutant general. So efficient and invaluable were his services that he was asked by General Pickett to accept the position of adjutant general. A new chaplain by the name of Reverend Ware was appointed and Linthicum accepted his new position. At Gettysburg, he had two horses shot from under him and he received a slight wound in the forehead from a spent minnie ball. Captain Linthicum was president of the Brigade Christian Association and raised considerable sums of money from his friends in Maryland for the relief of widows and orphans of his fallen comrades. His father became a political prisoner and was placed in the Old Capitol Prison while his younger brother, John Warren Linthicum, left Maryland to join Mosby's Rangers. At Second Cold Harbor, while bearing a message from General Hunton, he was crossing some fallen timber when he became the victim of a sharpshooter's ball.

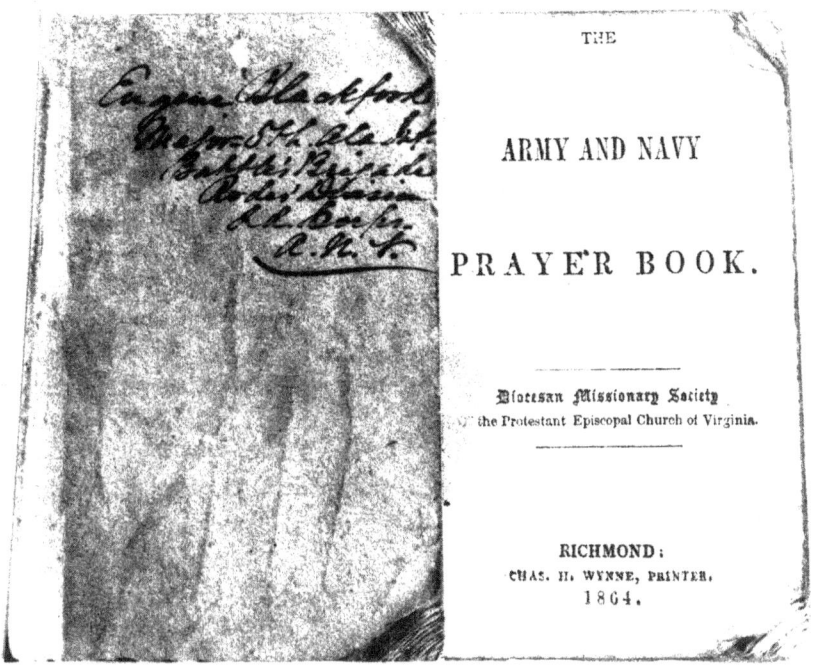

EPISCOPAL ARMY AND NAVY PRAYER BOOK of Eugene Blackford (1839/) with his name and rank self-inscribed on the front. He enlisted on May 15, 1861, in K Company, 15th Alabama Infantry. The prayer book was printed by Charles H. Wynne of Richmond in 1864 and was given to C.S.A. fighting men by the Diocesan Missionary Society.

At Camp Howard, the first winter camp for the 1st Maryland Infantry, a windowless church was built of pine logs chinked with mud, with a large fireplace on each side. The roof was made of hospital tent flies which admitted light but turned the rain. At the upper end was a platform to serve as a chancel, a reading desk and the pulpit, which consisted of a large round pine post capped with a board to hold a Bible. Behind this stood a large cross of evergreen that was kept fresh and bright. Over the front door was a gallery where the choir sat. On the outside above the door was a large wooden cross. The long building was capable of seating 500 and was not only used as a place of worship but also functioned as a library. It housed a glee club as well as the choir. Edward R. Rich recorded, "a goodly number were brought to the knowledge of Christ and confessed him before their fellow man in confirmation, took up the cross as the badge and ensign of their life-long battle with sin."

Army regulations called for chaplains to be clothed in cadet gray, but they wore almost any style or type of coat. They were permitted the use of one of the following badges: the letter C with a half wreath of olive leaves, a Latin or maltese cross, which later became the symbol used on Confederate graves. The Rev. Thomas Norton Conrad, chaplain of the 3rd Virginia Cavalry, was a secret agent for J.E.B. Stuart. "My wardrobe consisted of three suits - one a chaplain suit, a straight-breasted coat of black cloth; one a scouting suit, a drab-colored English felt jacket and black velvet pants; and a captain's suit of gray with yellow trimmings. The first mentioned I wore on my trips to Washingon posing as a Federal chaplain, the second was my scouting suit within our lines, and the third was used on dress parade occasions." Rev. Conrad was one of those chaplains who closed his prayer book, seized his saber and lead his men into a fight with as much enthusiasm as he led them in church services. Chaplain Conrad wrote "I met another Yankee plunderer on the highway. His horse was strung with chickens, hams, ducks and turkeys from its head to its tail. I shot him, took his feet out of the stirrups, and dropped him on the road. Led his horse far into the thicket and secured him until I could return and get him after dark." After the

106 - Clergy

CHAPLAIN WILLIAM F. GARDNER was in seminary training in preparation for ordination before leaving his Howard County home. He served as an enlisted man in Company H, 17th Virginia Infantry. After his 12-month term of enlistment Pvt. Gardner completed the Episcopal curriculum and, becoming licensed, was commissioned a chaplain assigned to Pickett's Division.

war this chaplain scout was an exiled fugitive who travelled to the depths of the Blue Ridge Mountains for sanctuary. Living among the hill people of Virginia's Fauquier and Frederick Counties, Conrad continued to wear his uniform, pistols and saber while eluding Federal troops. On October 4, 1866, he came out of seclusion, unbuckled his weapons, removed his uniform and left unmolested and unparoled.

Naval regulations for chaplains called for a black, single-breasted tailcoat with no cap device, shoulder boards, cuff, sleeve or collar decorations.

Dabney Ball was born in 1820 and, at the age of 15, converted to Christ and from that time until his death in 1878 followed the Christian faith. In 1843 he was admitted to the Baltimore Conference of the Episcopal Methodist Church. He served in the circuits of Wardensville, Virginia; Wrightsville, Pennsylvania; the Maryland charges of Westminster, Libertytown, Hagerstown, and Baltimore; Washington, D.C., and again in Baltimore before going south and being commissioned a chaplain in 1862. He was known by his men as the foraging pastor. He baptized in rivers, streams and even from a rusty tin cup. Chaplain Ball was chosen by J.E.B. Stuart for a position on his staff where he remained until the close of the war. He returned to Baltimore in the fall of 1866.

William Dame, of the Richmond Howitzers, went to a wounded Federal officer at Spotsylvania who begged of him, "Can you pray sir? Can you pray?" Dame bent over the poor fellow, who was from Maine, opened his blouse and saw that a large cannister shot had passed through his chest. Kneeling down beside him Dame took the enemy officer's hand and said, "You haven't much time left for prayer; but if you will say after me these simple words with heart as well as lips all will be well for you; God have mercy on me a sinner, for Jesus Christ's sake." The officer uttered the words over and over again with the death rattle in his throat.

Naval Paymaster Douglas French Forrest returned to the Monumental City in December of 1865 and began to practice law. Like many former veterans he was awarded a bachelor of divinity degree in 1873 in the Episcopal Church. He was a devout Christian during his early life. A former principal of a boys school in Baltimore wrote of an encounter he had with some of the lads who were determined to prevent him from saying his prayers. They attacked him while Forrest was on his knees but he maintained a stout defense and afterwards continued to pray unmolested. During his

CANNONEER WILLIAM MEADE DAME (1844/1923) - Charcoal paper enlargement used in his book <u>From the Rapidan to Richmond</u> - He was attending the Danville Military Academy when the war began. At the age of 17 he enlisted as a private early in 1862 in the Richmond Howitzers. He served in the 1st Company and was at his gun in every action except once, when he had typhoid fever. He was the number four man who pulled the lanyard of the number four brass Napolean. Dame was hit by several fragments but was never hurt seriously enough to leave his gun. After Appomattox he entered the Virginia Theological Seminary along with 25 other students, all of whom had been Confederate soldiers. After graduating, Dame served nine years in several parishes in Virginia. Moving to Baltimore, he served as rector of the Episcopal Memorial Church for over 50 years. He was also the chaplain of the 5th Regiment, Maryland National Guard, for over 30 years. Rev. Dame was active in the Franklin Buchanan Camp of the United Confederate Veterans. He officiated at the funerals of many brother Confederate soldiers over the years.

BIBLE OF WARNER GRIFFITH WELSH, one of three brothers in Company D, 1st Maryland Cavalry, which he commanded. He was a member of St. Peter's Roman Catholic Church of Libertytown which was founded by General James McSherry Coale, who was commander of the 9th Brigade, Maryland Militia, who remained loyal to the Union.

naval service, when Forrest was ordered to the C.S.S. Rappahanock for 16 months, he voluntarily served as chaplain. His naval wartime diary reflects his Christian beliefs.

In the last volume of Confederate Military History is found "The Morale of the Confederate Army" which records "It is believed that fully one-third of all the Southern soldiers in the field were praying men and members of some branch of the Christian church." Many found Christ from the revivals in camp. The best evidence of their Christian faith can be found in the lives of those who were fortunate to come home and tell their stories.

COLOR SERGEANT HORACE EDWIN HAYDEN SR. (1837/1917) - His preliminary education was at St. Timothy's Hall at Catonsville, his place of birth, before entering Kenyon College in Ohio. He left college to teach, and when the war broke out, enlisted on May 14, 1861, at Leesburg in the Howard County Dragoons. During the Battle of Manassas he carried the colors of Company K, 1st Virginia Cavalry. In March of 1862 he re-enlisted in the 1st Virginia Cavalry. This unit was later transferred and became Company K, 1st Maryland Cavalry. In the meantime, however, he had been detailed to Charlottesville Hospital where he became a wardmaster. On April 6, 1863, he received the rank of hospital steward and acting chaplain of Jefferson General Hospital, Division No. 2. On December 31, 1864, he was discharged in order to complete his theological studies. He entered the Theological Seminary of Virginia at Staunton, but the war ended before his ordination. As an Episcopal priest he served in West Virginia, Maryland and Pennsylvania. He was a member of the Franklin Buchanan Camp of the United Confederate Veterans and the Society of the Army and Navy of the Confederate States of Maryland.

Chapter 11

FLAGS

One of the first secession banners in the state was probably flown in Baltimore. On December 18, 1860, a militia unit called the Southern Volunteers, first raised South Carolina's palmetto flag to the breeze at the Liberty Engine House, and continued to parade under it. On February 6, 1861, the day after the organization of the Confederacy at Montgomery, Alabama, a palmetto flag was hoisted near St. Anne's Church. It was pulled down by an angry Unionist who was injured in the ensuing scuffle. In the spring of 1861, after the invasion of Northern forces, Southern and Maryland flags replaced the stars and stripes around the state. On April 23 at a large public meeting in Leonardtown, the highlight of the day was when the Raley Rifles of St. Mary's County were presented a handsome flag designed in the style of the Confederate flag by the ladies of the village. The Centerville Times in Queen Anne's County printed the following editorial. "There are 17 militia companies parading under the Confederate banner being avowedly for the state and local defense against Northern agression. In June (1861) a unit known as the Maryland Zouaves were organized. They numbered nearly 90 members and their uniforms consisted of navy blue flannel shirts trimmed in black, red flanneled zouave trousers, black leggings and dark blue fatigue caps trimmed in red. Their arms, Hall's breech loading carbines with bayonet attachment, were furnished by the U.S. government. This fine organization will carry no other banner than the stars and stripes. Have we not patriotic ladies enough to see that they shall soon have a standard to carry which shall once more gladden our eye?"

By the end of May, as the noose began to tighten from the Federal occupation of the state, military items were being confiscated from Southern sympathizers. In Manchester, news had leaked out about the Southern sympathizers' beautiful flag. Union troops arrived at the home of Adam Shower Jr. just behind the news that they were coming. Dr. Charles Geiger placed the Confederate banner under his vest greeting the troops on the porch and then leaving. When the troops searched the home they found a folded flag in the attic. Thinking it was the Confederate banner, the officer pierced it with his sword and was met with reprisal for destroying patriotic property. When the flag was opened it was found to be the flag of the Manchester Men under Adam Shower Sr. who had lead them to the Battle of Bladensburg during the War of 1812.

The first Maryland Confederates to form under the southern banner were the 500 men recruited in Baltimore for South Carolina service known as the Baltimore Secessionists. They were sent to Charleston and comprised three units, one being Rhett's heavy artillery. The wife of General R.S. Ripley presented a silk flag made by the ladies of Charleston to Rhett's Heavy Artillery. It was used at the surrender of Fort Sumter and they then marched under this flag to Fort Moultrie and then Fort Sumter where it was used daily on parade. When Charleston was evacuated in 1865 it was hidden since only battle flags were allowed in field service. After the surrender of Johnson's Army the men were told that rats had destroyed it. In late 1892, it was in the hands of a relic seller and was purchased for $100 by two former officers of the 1st Regiment Artillery. This recovered sacred emblem was formally presented to the Charleston city council.

Charles H. Claiborne had enlisted in Baltimore in the early spring of 1861 by enrollment officers from the Gamecock State. He was assigned to G Company, 1st South Carolina Infantry, as a private and rose to the rank of 2nd lieutenant. On June 20, 1863, mortars from Cummings Point firing on Fort Sumter cut the flag staff. Before the flag touched the ground it was seized by Lt. Claiborne who rushed with it through the smoke and bursting shells to the parapet. He ascended the parapet and reattached the broken staff. This prompted the Federals to begin a rapid fire on this tower. When the flag had been lashed to the staff, the enemy saluted with cheers and a wave of their hats. A number of engravings of the heroic act of Lieutenant Claiborne have survived.

A large portion of the Frederick volunteers, accompanying their commander Bradley T. Johnson, left Frederick on May 8, 1861, and travelled to Point of Rocks where they formally enlisted in the C.S.A. Carried with them was a silk banner made by the ladies of Frederick which had been presented to this company while they were resisting the northern invasion in Baltimore in April of 1861. It was proudly displayed as they crossed the Potomac to Harpers Ferry where they became Company A of the 1st Maryland Infantry. On the obverse was the 1854 Maryland state seal topped by gold letters on a red scrolled ribbon reading "Maryland expects every man to do his duty." It was used as the 1st Maryland Infantry regimental colors until the battle of Manassas. As the regiment

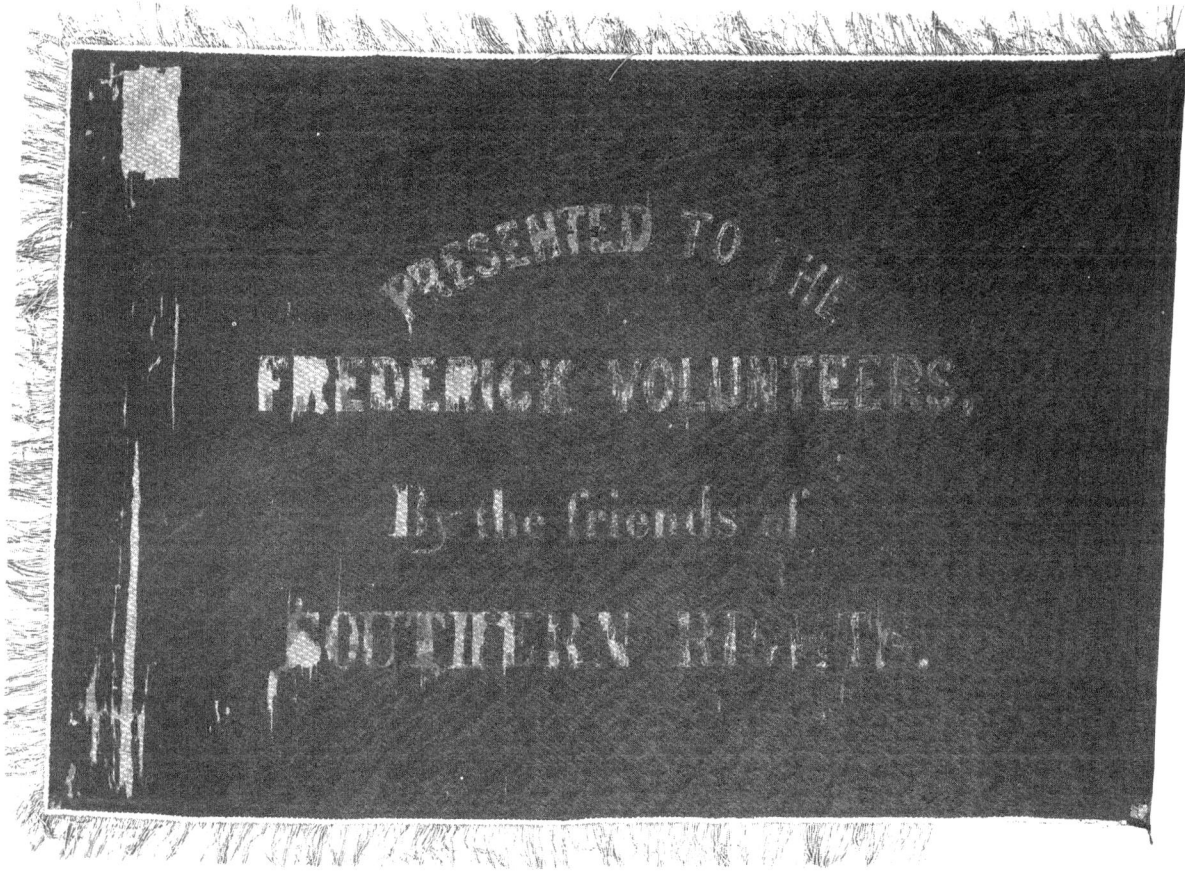

FIRST BANNER OF THE 1ST MARYLAND INFANTRY. This Frederick volunteers militia flag was carried by Company A. It is silk 56" on the fly and 35" on the staff. The edge has gold fringes that are 2-1/2". The design on the obverse is the Maryland state seal design with gold letters on a red scroll "Maryland expects every man to do his duty." The reverse, in dark blue paint, has gold letters "PRESENTED TO THE FREDERICK VOLUNTEERS by the friends of SOUTHERN RIGHTS." The means of attachment is missing. It was presented by General Johnson to the Maryland Line Confederate Soldiers Home and later to the state by the governor's after the home was closed.

marched into battle on July 21, 1861, Captain Charles Snowden presented them with a large standard which had been brought through the lines by Miss Hattie Cary. The silk flag bears on the obverse, "Presented by the ladies of Baltimore to the 1st Regiment Maryland Line." On the reverse is painted the state seal. Colonel William H. Steuart attached this new standard to the staff of the Frederick volunteers. The regiment went into the fight at Manassas with two flags on the same staff. On August 17, 1862, when the battalion was mustered out Mrs. Bradley T. Johnson was given the sacred banner. "... unanimously agree and resolve to present to you, as one true and trustworthy to receive it. Our Flag, which has been gallantly and victoriously born over many a bloody and hand

1ST MARYLAND INFANTRY REGIMENTAL COLORS. This flag was received upon the battlefield of Manassas. It is silk, 33" on the fly 26" on the staff, edged with 2-1/2" of white fringe. The obverse "PRESENTED BY THE LADIES OF BALTIMORE TO THE 1ST REGIMENT MARYLAND LINE," was painted in gold letters. The design on the reverse is the state seal using 14 colors of paint. The method of attachment is two pair of narrow red cords that are sewn to the top and bottom along the leading edge. To commemorate the regiment's defeat of the Pennsylvania Bucktails sharpshooters at Harrisonburg on June 6, 1862, the 1st Maryland was ordered by General R. Ewell to attach to the flag staff a bucktail taken from the Federal flag. Also attached to the staff are a pair of red, white, and blue tassels on blue and white cords. By a vote of the regiment when they disbanded, this standard was presented to Mrs. Jane Claudia Johnson and was laid on her bier in 1899 for the mass and burial in Louden Park Cemetery. It was in the relic room of the Maryland Line Confederate Soldiers Home until given to the state in 1907.

fought field, and under whose sacred folds Maryland's sons have fought and bled in a holy cause. Our attachment for our Flag is undying, and now that circumstances have rendered it necessary that our organization should no longer exist, we place in your hands as a testimonial of our regard and esteem, our little Flag, which is dear to us all."

At Fairfax Courthouse in August of 1861, Company H of the 1st Maryland Regiment was presented a variation of the first national flag by the ladies of Baltimore. In the canton on the reverse side was painted in gold letters, "My Maryland," surrounded by 15 stars.

COMPANY H, 1ST MARYLAND INFANTRY FLAG. It was presented by Miss Rider from the Ladies of Baltimore at Fairfax Courthouse on June 20, 1861. It is silk, 70" on the fly, 53" on the staff, edged with 1-1/2" of metallic silk fringe. The three horizontal red, white and red bars in the field are 17-3/4". The dark blue 35-1/2" square canton is painted "My Maryland," in gold letters and encircled with 15 gold five-pointed stars, each being 4" in diameter. This motif is painted on the reverse side of the flag and reads through the silk in reverse on the obverse side. The method of attachment is a 2" wide red silk heading that serves as a sleeve for the staff. The flag was given to the state by Mrs. George Thomas, wife of the company's first lieutenant.

According to the Richmond newspaper, in May of 1861 Captain Edward R. Dorsey's Company A of Weston's Maryland Battalion was presented a first national stars and bars flag in Richmond. It is not known what became of the flag of Weston's battalion because the companies were absorbed into other commands.

There are, however, four surviving banners associated with Captain J. Lyle Clarke's Maryland Guard. They were organized in J. Alden Weston's Maryland Battalion as Company B. On June 8, 1861, in the square at Richmond, a cotton state seal flag was presented by Mrs. Augustus McLaughlin, who had brought it from Maryland concealed on her person. The large buff-white field has the 1854 seal version set within a yellow circle with "Maryland" over the eagle. On June 21, 1864, the Maryland Guard were sent to the 21st Virginia Infantry where they became Company B. After they were discharged on May 24, 1862, the flag was conveyed to the newly formed 2nd Maryland Infantry. In October of 1862, it was used on the bier for the funeral of General Charles S. Winder who was killed at Cedar Mountain. At Hanover, Virginia, when the winter camp of 1864 was broken up it was given to Mrs. William T. Thelin, and after the war to Bradley T. Johnson.

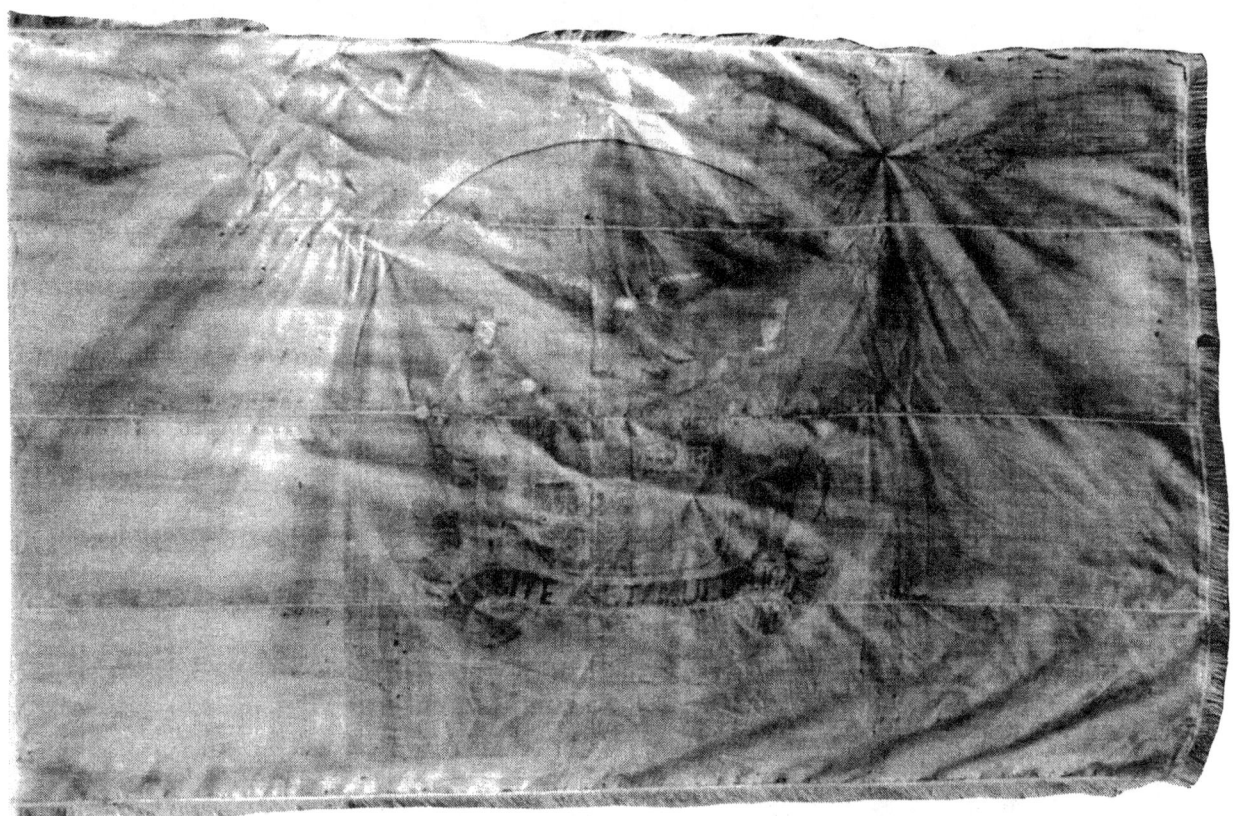

COMPANY B, 21ST VIRGINIA INFANTRY STATE COLORS. This flag was presented by the women of Baltimore. It is cotton bunting 116" on the fly, 70-1/2" on the staff and edged on three sides with gold 2-1/4" knotted silk fringe. The field is white buff made of four horizontal panels, one is 18" and the other three are 17-1/2". The 1854 version of the state seal is set within a yellow 53" circle painted in 11 colors under "MARYLAND" in large black letters which today are barely visible. The method of attachment is missing. The flag was loaned by Bradley T. Johnson to the Confederate Memorial Literary Society and is now in the Richmond Confederate Museum.

A silk first national was also carried by the Maryland Guard. The dark blue canton has 11 solid white stars and one that is outlined in white. The outlined star represented Maryland's southern sentiment and her commitment to fight so that the people of the state might have the opportunity to choose for themselves. Many believed the choice would be for seccession and joining the Confederacy.

COMPANY B, 21ST VIRGINIA INFANTRY 1ST NATIONAL FLAG. It is silk, 72" on the fly, 57" on the staff and edged with 3/4" red fringe with a white cord border. The red, white and red horizontal bars in the field are each 19" in width. The dark blue 38" square canton had 11 solid white five-pointed stars that are 6-1/2" in diameter and one white outlined star set in a 30" circle. The method of attachment is missing. This flag was given to the state by the daughter of the commander Miss Mary Lyle Clarke.

There is another large stars and bars camp flag of the Maryland Guard in the Maryland state collection. It was made by sewing together pieces of bunting.

CAMP FLAG OF COMPANY B, 21ST VIRGINIA INFANTRY. This stars and bars flag of the Maryland Guard is 105" on the fly and 58" on the staff. It is made of bunting with a dark blue canton containing 11 cotton five-pointed stars. The horizontal field bars are composed of 12 pieces of bunting. The header is of white canvas which is 2" in width making a sleeve. It was donated to the state by Mary Lyle Clark.

The fourth standard associated with the Maryland Guard was also a stars and bars flag. On May 24, 1862, the 12-month enlistment of the Maryland Guard expired and a large number had re-enlisted in the 30th Virginia Sharpshooters as Company E, under newly elected Captain Richard Curzon Hoffman. Their former commander J. Lyle Clarke had been promoted to major, and placed in command of the six companies of sharpshooters.

GARRISON FLAG OF COMPANY E, 30TH VIRGINIA SHARPSHOOTERS. It was presented to the state on November 12, 1907, by Miss Mary Lyle Clark of Baltimore, the daughter of J. Lyle Clark. The measurements are 142" on the fly and 77-1/2" on the staff. This bunting 1st National flag is believed to have been used by the Maryland Guard who re-enlisted in the 30th Virginia Sharpshooters as Company E and was commanded by Major J. Lyle Clark.

The first clash of arms at Manassas had determined that the stars and bars, or national flag of the Confederacy, resembled the Stars and Stripes too closely, especially in the heat and confusion of the battlefield. Responding to this problem, General P.G.T. Beauregard petitioned the congressional flag committee to remedy this problem. Beauregard, along with Generals Joseph E. Johnston and G.W. Smith, worked to design a distinctive field or battle flag. In September of 1861 this distinctive flag, designed by William Porcher Miles, was adopted. It consisted of a red square, bordered in white and traversed by a dark blue St. Andrews cross, also edged in white. Funds provided by the army quartermaster officials were used to purchase all available silk enrichment material, which varied from pink to crimson. Groups of Richmond ladies contracted to sew the new silk banners which were distributed to the Army of the Potomac in November of 1861.

The Cary sisters of Baltimore, Hattie and Jennie, along with their brother William Miles Cary, had incurred the displeasure of the military government garrisoned at Baltimore and were ordered to leave the city or be transferred to a northern bastille. The two sisters ran the blockade carrying drugs for hospitals and uniforms for friends, and resided with their cousin Constance Cary in Richmond. Their brother joined the 1st Maryland Cavalry troopers until receiving a commission in the quartermaster department. In the doorway of Captain Sterett's tent at Manassas in September of 1861, Free Staters in the Confederacy for the first time heard the refrain of "My Maryland," the stirring song by James Ryder Randall which would soon echo in every camp of the Confederacy. Constance wrote "In the autumn when my cousins had gone to Albemarle to visit relatives, we three had the honor of being asked by the committee of congress to make the first battle flags of the Confederacy after the design finally decided on by them. It was generally stated by historians that these flags were constructed from our own dresses, but it is certain we possess no wearing apparel in that flamboyant hue of poppy red and vivid dark blue required. We had a great search for material. I had to consider myself with a very poor quality of red silk for the field of mine, necessitating an interlining, which I regretted. I have alway been sorry we did not keep the model sketches with directions, assigned to us by the committee which decided the manner, and delivered by Major A. D. Banks. Our work, a gold fringe sewn around each flag, we were at liberty to present them as headquarter banners to our favored generals. Miss Hattie Cary, having first choice, sent hers to General Joseph E. Johnston, Miss Jennie Cary's went to General Beauregard and mine to General Earl Van Dorn."

ONE OF THE FIRST THREE BATTLE FLAGS OF THE CONFEDERACY. This banner was made by Jennie Cary and was presented to General P.G.T. Beauregard. This silk, 12-star flag was in New Orleans when the city fell and was smuggled to Havana. It was in the custody of a Washington Artillery member from the Crescent City and was donated to the Confederate Memorial Hall. It was used to drape the caskets of General Beauregard and President Davis during their funerals.

The first three battle flags of the Confederacy were made by Marylanders. The two Cary sisters were visiting their cousin Constance, who was a native and resident of Cumberland until the death of her father. After his death his wife and three children were taken by her mother to Alexandria.

Jennie Cary's flag to General Beauregard was used after the war to drape the coffins of Beauregard and Jefferson Davis at the time of their deaths. Constance's flag sent to VanDorn was used at his headquarters throughout the Virginia campaign and the Trans-Mississippi campaign. It was torn with bullets and stained with smoke from many battlefields. It was finally put back into her hands through the general's instructions by his nephew Clement Sulivane. Her name had been embroidered upon the flag in small gold letters.

The lack of uniformity of uniforms, large clouds of dust and white smoke from the black powder made the red and white St. Andrews cross that ran from corner to corner undistinguishable in battle. Even after the Army of Northern Virginia was issued these battle flags, the old 1st National emblems were used and not readily discarded. The Army of the Mississippi and the Army of Tennessee had even a wider diversity with Hardee, Polk and Van Dorn patterns. Military leaders tried to limit the number of flags per regiment, but nearly each company had at least one pennant that they wanted to carry into battle.

There are four standards which have survived that belonged to the 2nd Maryland Infantry. Two are silk, and of the 1st National pattern with a configuration in the dark blue canton of 10 five-pointed white stars in a circle with a center single star.

MARYLAND VOLUNTEER BATTALION FLAG. This silk flag was carried by the Marland Volunteer Battalion which officially became the 2nd Maryland Infantry. It is 72" on the fly and 49" on the staff. The dark blue canton is 32-1/2" square with 10 stars 2-1/2" in diameter and a center 6" star. The three horizontal bars are pink, white and pink. The white heading is 1-1/2" with five whipped eyelets. It was donated by the board of governors of the Maryland Line to the state.

118 - Flags

COMPANY A, 2ND MARYLAND INFANTRY FLAG. This silk flag was presented by the ladies of Baltimore. It is 48" on the fly and 30" on the staff with a metallic fringe. The dark blue field canton is 19-1/2" by 20" with 10 white stars 2-3/8" around a central star. The field is composed of pink, white and pink bars. The attachment is four pairs of silk ties. The top pair is red, the second pair blue, the third pair white and the bottom pair red along the leading edge.

2ND MARYLAND INFANTRY STARS AND BARS. It is another variation of the 1st National Confederate flag. It is made of silk with 15 gold painted 5-pointed stars in the blue canton. The bars are red, white and red with a metallic fringe on the upper and lower edges. The attachments are three pairs of evenly dispersed long silk ties, two pairs are blue and the lower pair is red.

The smallest is 48" on the fly, 30" on the staff and edged on three sides with 2" silver fringe. This flag was presented to Company A by the ladies of Baltimore. At Harrisonburg, the Confederate 1st Maryland defeated the Pennsylvania Bucktails. As they passed, General Ewell noticed that many of the men were wearing captured bucktails on their caps. Bradley T. Johnson called out to William H. Ryan, a tall, long-legged boy, to tie his trophy to the colors. The flag was brought home by Alexander Murray and given by Clapham Murray to the Richmond Confederate Museum. The larger one is 72" on the fly, 49" on the staff with a dark blue square canton and a large center star that is more than twice as large as the surrounding stars.

The silk regimental colors contained the 1854 state seal encircled in a ribbon device, flanked by the 1st National flag on each side. The signet is painted in 14 different colors on a dark blue field. The reverse side has a circle of 13 gold stars. At Camp St. Mary's at Hanover Junction the regimental colors were given to Mrs. William T. Thelin when the new St. Andrews battle flag was substituted for the state flag. The old 1st Maryland state flag was replaced for the state flag and the old 1st Maryland banner, because it was not thought advisable to carry the former colors to the front for fear of damage to what had become a sacred emblem. With tender reverence, these two state banners were packed in an old army chest. During the last year of the war it was requested that they be used on the bier of General John H. Winder, while his body lay in state in Columbia. A few days after the burial, Sherman's troops advanced and the pennants were hastily sewn up and pinned under the skirt of Mrs. William T. Thelin and worn to Charlotte.

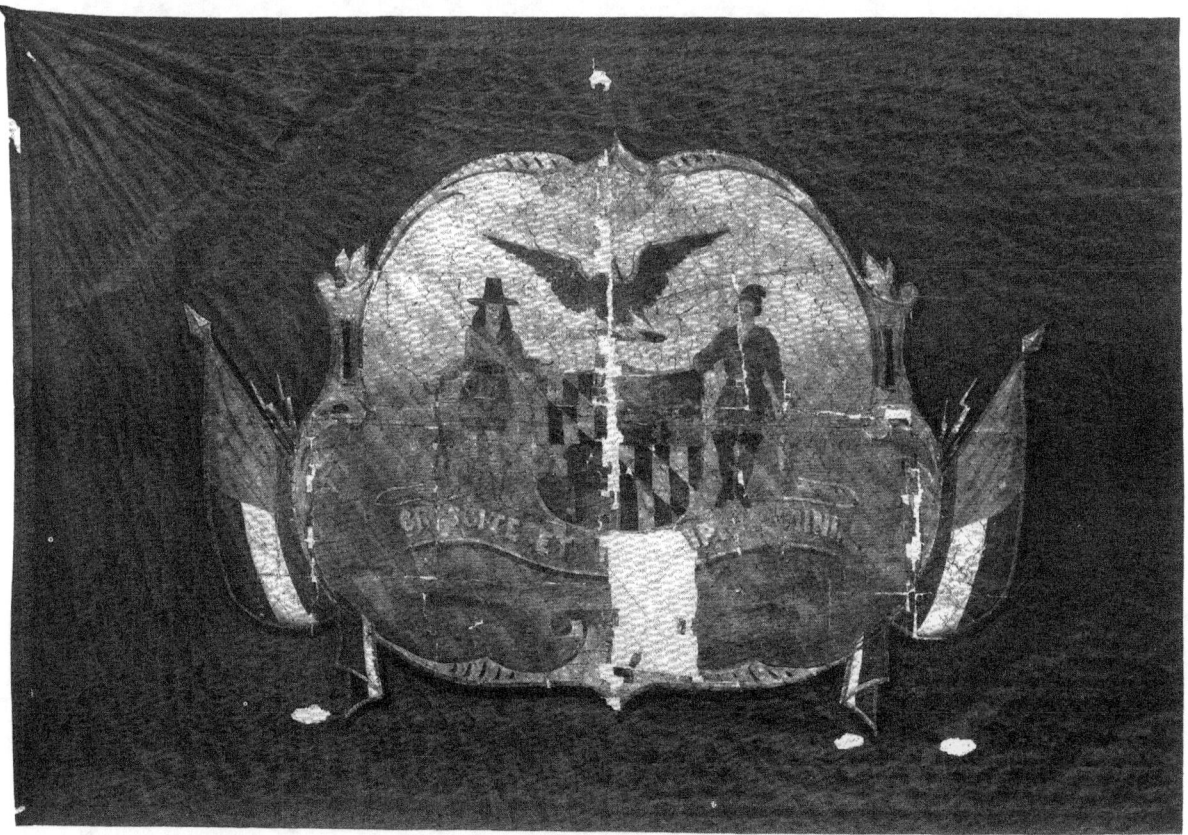

2ND MARYLAND INFANTRY REGIMENTAL STATE COLORS. It is silk, 60" on the fly, 40" on the staff, the dark blue field on the obverse is painted with the 1854 version of the state seal enclosed in a ribbon device flanked by 1st National Confederate flags. It is ornate in 14 colors of paint. The reverse contains 13 gold five-pointed 4-1/2" stars set in a 33" diameter circle. The stars were painted white then gilded in gold. The method of attachment is missing. This flag was given to the state by the wife of William T. Thelin.

The regiment's quartermaster department issued battle flag was made at the Richmond Clothing Depot. It is inscribed "1 MD B" for the 1st Maryland Battalion as they were referred to for quite some time before official designation as the 2nd Maryland Infantry. Battle honors of "Winchester No 2" and "Gettysburg" are also painted. This flag was issued in the summer of 1863 and carried until April 2, 1865. On this date at Hatcher's Run the enemy had broken through Lee's thin line and captured Fort Davis. The 2nd Maryland Infantry, only 200 strong, charged and recaptured the fort only to be overwhelmed in a few minutes by the mass of Federal troops. When all was lost, the battle flag was furled and hidden under a log. When the fighting was over it was discovered by the 123rd Ohio Infantry. There are two stars missing that appeared to have been removed as war trophies and taken home as souveniers.

2ND MARYLAND INFANTRY BATTLE FLAG. This flag is of the quartermaster issue pattern that was a complete division issue after Gettysburg. According to the diary of the Thomas Brothers of Mattapany on September 3, 1863, they received this banner which was already inscribed. The bunting red field is 48" on the fly, 46" on the staff, and is edged on the sides with a white 2" wide border. The dark blue bunting St. Andrews cross is 5-1/4" in width and edged in 3/4" white cotton. The 13 white cotton five-pointed stars are 3-1/2" in diameter. Over the center star is "1" and under the star "MD.B." painted in yellow. Also on the obverse in the field appears "Winchester No 2" and "Gettysburg" painted in black. The method of attachment at two large eyelets at each end and three small eyelets equally spaced in the 2" wide canvas heading. It was found under a log at Fort Davis on April 2, 1865, and was returned to the state in 1909 by Lieutenant Colonel Kellogy of the 123rd Ohio.

The regimental flag of the 1st Maryland Cavalry is a silk 1st National design. The configuration displays the state designation. In the dark blue square canton, there are 13 gold stars. They encircle the state seal painted in 12 colors in the center on both sides. It is edged on three sides with 2-1/2" of heavy white fringe.

1ST MARYLAND CAVALRY REGIMENTAL FLAG. It is silk, 66" on the fly, 48" on the staff, edged on three sides with 2-1/2" white fringe. The field has three 16" horizontal bars of red, white, and red. The canton is 32-1/2" square, dark blue with 13 gold five-pointed 3-1/2" stars painted in a 22-1/2" circle. The state seal in 12 colors is painted in the center on both sides. The method for attachment is missing. This banner was in the Maryland Line Confederate Soldiers Home and donated to the state by its Board of Governors.

In the fall of 1862, William I. Rasin recruited a cavalry company at Camp Lee. They were known as Winder's Cavalry and were presented a silk flag by the ladies of Kent County. On January 20, 1863, they were ordered to the 1st Maryland where they became E Company. This flag is a smaller version of the regimental banner, and was much more easily handled on a mount. Although it is similar to the regimental flag, the canton is rectangular with the state signet and no stars. It has a 2-1/4" wide white heading that serves as a sleeve for the staff.

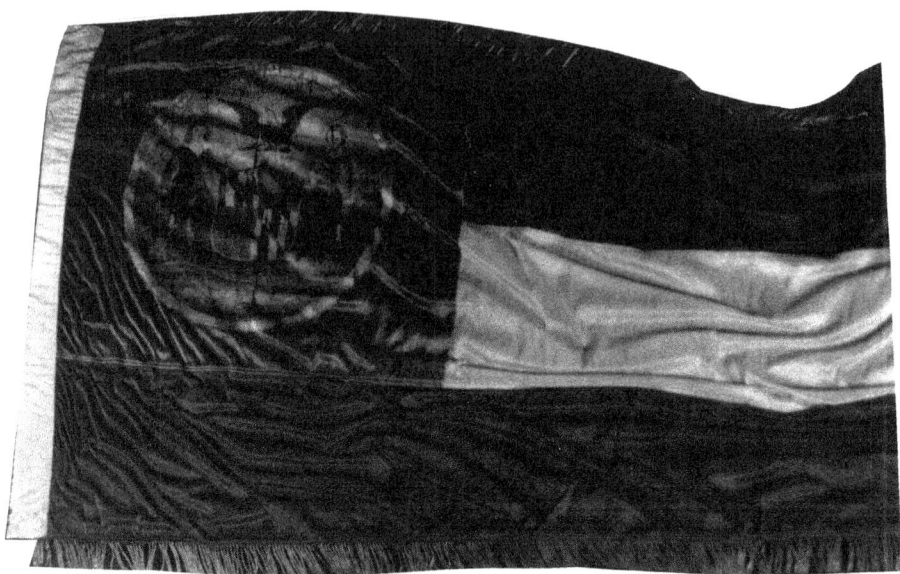

COMPANY E, 1ST MARYLAND CAVALRY BANNER. This flag is silk, 47" on the fly, 25" on the staff, edged on three sides with 1-5/8" gold fringe. The field has two red 8-1/2" horizontal bars and an 8" white bar in the center. The dark blue canton is 19" on the fly and 17" on the staff. The 1854 rendition of the state seal is done in 12 colors upon a 13-3/4" disk. The method of attachment is a 2-1/2" white header that serves at a sleeve for the staff. It was given by Mrs. Mary Garnett Rasin to the Richmond Confederate Museum in December of 1933.

The guideon of the 1st Maryland Cavalry is a small 1st National type. The horizontal bars in the field are made of a loose textured wool bunting. The dark blue canton is a woolen cloth with nap, a type of flannel. The 13 white 3-1/2" stars are cotton and form a circle, again displaying that the land of sanctuary was considered by these troopers as part of the Confederacy.

GUIDON OF THE 1ST MARYLAND CAVALRY. It is a 1st National style flag. The field is made of bunting with a top red horizontal bar of 8-1/2". A center white bar 8-1/2" and a lower red 9" bar. The dark blue flannel canton is 16-3/4" on the fly, 16-1/2" on the staff. There are 13 white cotton 3-1.2" five-pointed stars set in a 13-1/4" diameter. The stars are sewn on the obverse only. The method of attachment is missing. This banner was placed on loan by Bradley T. Johnson to the Confederate Literary Society and is now in the Confederate Museum.

The 1st and 2nd Maryland Cavalry were issued bunting quartermaster department battle flags. These St. Andrews, late war pieces are identical except for a small variance in size. The 2nd Maryland dark blue cross is 1/2" wider and the red field is also 2-1/4" longer on the fly. The panels of each vary in size but they are both 48-1/2" on the staff. The battle flag of Colonel Brown's troopers is penned in ink on the obverse white heading 8" from the bottom "1st Md. Cav."

1ST MARYLAND CAVALRY BATTLE FLAG. It has a red field of bunting 48-1/4" on the fly, 48-1/2" on the staff, and is edged with a 2-1/2" white border on three sides. The dark blue bunting cross is 4-1/2" in width and it is edged in 5/8" wide white cotton. The 13 white cotton five-pointed stars are 4-1/2" in diameter and sewn on. The method of attachment is three whipped eyelets piercing the 2" wide white canvas heading. On the lower edge towards the middle is penned in black ink "1st Md Cav".

The battle flag of Gilmor's Band is also designated on the obverse heading 4" from the bottom "2nd Md. Cav." in black ink that appears to have been done by a different hand. They had at least two other standards of which one was captured in the disaster at Moorefield at the break of day on August 7, 1864. Although color bearer John S. Phipps was not captured, he could not retrieve the flag in the surprise raid on the camp. Lieutenant Colonel Gilmor wrote that after the loss of the battle flag the ladies of the Moorefield area made them another. On August 27, 1864, near Smithfield, the 2nd Maryland lost 26 men in a fight with the brigades of Custer and Devins. Color bearer John S.

Pendleton "was at the hottest places all the time. He held on to the colors though there were two bullet holes in the flag and several saber cuts on the staff."

2ND MARYLAND CAVALRY BATTLE FLAG. The field of red is bunting being 50-1/2" of the fly, 48-1/2" on the staff, and is edged on three sides with a 2-5/8" white border. The dark blue bunting cross is 5" wide and edged in 5/8" white cotton. The 13 white cotton five-pointed stars are 4-5/8" in diameter and are sewn on. The method of attachment is three whipped, equally spaced eyelets in the 2-3/4" wide white canvas. On the lower edge of the heading is penned in black ink "2nd Md Cav".

In this surprise attack at Moorefield following the burning of Chambersburg, Bradley T. Johnson also lost his headquarters flag. He would have become a prisoner had Lieutenant William H. Richardson of Company F, 2nd Maryland Cavalry, not dismounted and given the general his horse, only to be captured himself. This small 30-1/2" by 39" swallow tail flag of white cotton has a St. Andrews cross canton that was made of wool and cotton. The cross contains 12 white cotton stars with a large center star. There were three flags captured by Averell's 2nd Cavalry Division that day along with 420 of Johnson's troopers.

A tradition from the First War of Independence was the organization of Maryland commands into a single larger unit called the "Maryland Line." The manifestation of this concept was very important in southern service. The Marylanders tried unceasingly to rally as a single band of brothers. In the winter of 1863, after three different Confederate government sanctions to organize a brigade of Free Staters had failed, Bradley T. Johnson was finally able to establish the Maryland Line. The headquarters flag of the Maryland Line was a swallow tailed pennant. It was made of bunting and grosgrain, a composition of woolen and silk fabrics. The field of white is edged with 1/2" wide red bunting that is 41" on the fly to the end of the two tails and 19-1/2" on the staff. The center bears a bottony cross of red bunting with a red grosgrain binding. The cross bottony was the emblem not only for the Line, but was also used by many orphans of the black-and-gold state in all branches of Confederate service to proudly display their origin.

MARYLAND LINE HEADQUARTERS FLAG. It is bunting with grosgrain binding 41" on the fly to the end of each tail. The center of the V is 23-1/2" to the staff edge and 19-1/2" on the staff. The white field is edged on all sides with red 1/2" wide binding. The red bottony cross is 15" wide and 15-3/4" high and edged in the same 1/2" wide red binding that surrounds the field. The method of attachment is by a 3/4" wide sleeve formed by doubling back the leading edge, presumably to accept a rope. This pennant was placed on loan to the Richmond Confederate Museum by the Maryland Line commander.

Another standard graciously presented to the Confederate Maryland Line was a flag carried by patriots of the past who cherished their liberties. This heirloom was given to General George H. Steuart and was supposedly used in the Revolutionary War by the Maryland Line. According to the Richmond Confederate Museum catalog of 1905 it was on loan from Bradley T. Johnson and was carried during the Revolution. There is a question if any of the American Revolutionary flags are really of war vintage. The painted seal bears the inscription "Baltimore Independent Company". During this war with England units were designated by either the company or commander's name. There were so many independent companies from Baltimore they were designated 1st, 2nd and 3rd. In the second war with the British in 1812 there were also several Baltimore independent companies. This banner is possibly just the canton section of a flag that was presented to General

Steuart by Adelaide Pringle, daughter of Mark Pringle. He was a cornetist in Captain N.R. Moore's Baltimore Horse Troop in 1781. During the War of 1812, a Mark W. or N. Pringle was a private in Captain D. Warfield's Company of Baltimore United Volunteers in 1814. Whatever the provenance of this ancient banner, it was proudly saluted by the young sons who were mustering under the state's black-and-gold colors to fight for the same freedoms for which their forefathers had fought.

FORMER PATRIOTIC BANNER PRESENTED TO THE MARYLAND LINE. It is either a Revolutionary or War of 1812 flag. The crest in the center of the device is a lady, with her right arm extended upward and left arm down, within a frame painted "Baltimore Independent Company". It is not the 1794 state seal. Above is a cock holding an olive branch in its beak. The dexter supporter is a female with a shield and spear and the sinister supporter is a caveman with a club. The scroll at the bottom has a Latin motto in black block letters. This was probably the canton section of an earlier Maryland flag that was made of cotton and the existing seal is in six colors. The edges are hemmed and there is a sleeve for the attachment to the staff. It is framed and housed in the Richmond Confederate Museum.

During the winter of 1863-1864 at Camp Howard, the Maryland Line erected a church near Hanover Junction that seated 500 worshipers. Probably a church flag was constructed at this time. It is cotton with a field of white and red bearing a Christian cross in the center. Rev. Thomas Duncan was appointed chaplain of the camp. The Maryland Line also had its own hospital insignia. This piece is of an unusual proportion and is made of the same cotton texture as the church flag. The center emblem is in the shape of a hourglass. The department was under Medical Director Richard Potts Johnson, and Thomas Sargent Latimer was assistant medical director with a staff of five surgeons. The church and hospital flags are not as refined as the previously illustrated pieces and may have been roughly made and handstitched by one of the soldiers.

 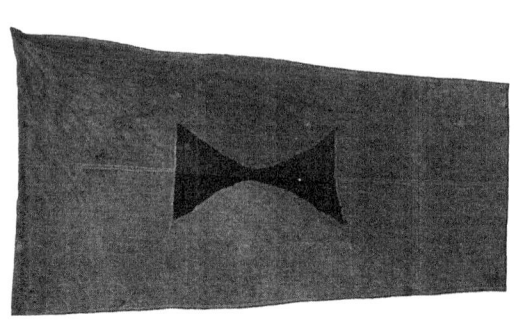

MARYLAND BATTALION CHURCH AND HOSPITAL FLAGS. The church flag is 40" on the fly, 30" on the staff and is white bunting which has faded yellow. It contains a large, cotton red cross which is centered. The hospital flag is 54-1/2" on the fly and 28-3/4" on the staff. It was originally white with a horizontal red and blue hour glass which is also of cotton.

Surviving flags seem to be abundant for some regiments because every company had at least one, but actually few banners have survived. George Pielert wrote in his diary on September 5, 1862, when the 2nd Maryland Artillery lead the Army of Northern Virginia across the Potomac "The women were almost crazy and the children all cheered us. A few asked if they could kiss the flag. Ours was the only Confederate flag that was here. The others only had their battle signs or markers." However, the 2nd Maryland Artillery flag remains unknown.

For those Marylanders who served in the Army of the West, homefolks were very far away. The opportunity to run the blockade to see loved ones was not available as it was to those in the Army of Northern Virginia. The large quantities of parcels and gifts could not be ferried to those far away from the Free State. This was one of the reasons Holbrook's Independent Maryland Light Artillery kept requesting reassignment back East. The 3rd Maryland Artillery was mustered into service on January 14, 1862, and on February 4 was sent to Knoxville, Tennessee. They were issued a small, artillery-sized, bunting quartermaster department produced battle flag in the early spring of 1864. The Army of Tennessee's battle flags had no border, instead the staff and fly edges are hemmed. The white cotton edging along the arm of the cross is wide. The intervals between the stars and the fabric ties are associated with flags of the western army. In black ink is inscribed "3rd Maryland Artillery" on the white lower edge of the upper staff arm of the cross. In small letters on the lower staff arms are the battle honors "Cumberland Gap, Tazwell, Baker's Creek, Vicksburg, Deer Creek and Jackson M". After the last mentioned battle they served with General Joseph E. Johnston around Atlanta and with General Hood in Tennessee.

3RD MARYLAND LIGHT ARTILLERY BATTLE FLAG. It is bunting, 40-1/2" on the fly and 29-1/2" on the staff. The field is red, the cross is dark blue, 5-1/8" in width edged in 1-5/8" white cotton with 13 white cotton five-pointed stars which are 3" in diameter. The distinct pattern of a 1-5/8" wide white edge with no border surrounding this piece and a 1/2" hem on the staff and fly conforms with the spring 1864 artillery issued flags of the Army of Tennessee. Inked in black is the unit designation and six battle honors along the white staff arms of the cross. The method of attachment is three pairs of red fabric ties, 1/2" wide and equally spaced in the hem's leading edge. This banner was given to the state by William Ritter.

Color bearers were usually men who had distinguished themselves in combat or were designated color sergeants. Flag bearers were favorite targets of the enemy in battle. As the men fell, the colors of the 4th Maryland Artillery would be planted between the cannon so the bearer could assist the gunners. Near Harrisonburg on June 6, 1862, when the 1st Maryland captured the Pennsylvania Bucktail Sharpshooter's, the Maryland colors fell twice but were caught each time before they touched the ground. When Color Sergeant Joseph T. Doyle went down it was seized by Private John H. Taylor and, when he was shot, by Private Daniel Shanks. Throughout the war the men proudly pointed to the fact that "It never felt the touch of hostile hands." At Gettysburg, five color bearers of the old bucktail flag of the 2nd Maryland Infantry were shot down until it was finally grabbed by William Jenkins as the boys rallied around him for their final charge up Culp's Hill. George D. Barnes of Company K, 9th Virginia Infantry, was the color sergeant for the regiment, and said "with joy I proudly waved it to the breeze." John William Lewis of Company I, 8th Virginia Cavalry, wrote "The beloved standard of the command was entrusted to my hands." The company flag of B Company, 1st Virginia Infantry, was born by John Hugh Figg, and more than one trusted bearer lost his life as the regiment rallied on the colors. About a mile below Sayler's Creek, Charles W. Lattimer of the 40th Virginia Infantry lost the flag to Sergeant William Morris of the 1st New York Cavalry. Morris received the congressional medal of honor for his capture. At the Battle of Frayzer's Farm on June

30, 1862, Pickett's Brigade had given way, when Captain W. Stuart Symington rushed at full speed on horseback to the 56th Virginia. He seized the flag from the color bearer, held it aloft and called for his men to rally. During Symington's advance Huger's Division responded and the enemy were overrun. At Gettysburg, courier H.W. Webb was wounded and did not want to be taken to the rear. "I know that I am going to die. Just carry me to the flag. I must die by my flag." But, he survived. On October 18, 1863, between Charles Town and Harpers Ferry the 2nd Maryland Cavalry overran the U.S. 9th Maryland. Lieutenant Polk Burke killed the Union color bearer with his own hand while he was in the act of tearing up his flag. They captured all the wagons, and three Federal flags were taken by Richard Gilmor, Ned Williams and Thomas Dobbs. On April 10, 1865, the 1st Maryland Confederate Cavalry was dismissed until April 25 when they would meet at the cattle scales in Augusta County, Virginia. The color bearer John Ridgley "stripped our beloved flag from its staff and placed it in his haversack. On April 25 about 10 a.m. Ridgley fastened our banner on a crude staff under which every Marylander present rallied and the little band moved through Waynesboro." On April 29, by order of General Thomas T. Mumford, their arms were relinquished. The flag, by vote of the command, was given to Colonel Dorsey and never surrendered.

In Baltimore in 1860 there were three firms who advertised as banner and regalia makers: Edward A. Gibbs, 23 N. Gay Street; A. Sisco, 95 W. Baltimore Street; and Peregrine T. Wilson, 43 N. Gay Street. During the war there was a buildup of militia suppliers, but by 1867 there were still only three businesses advertising as flag makers: Jabez W. Loane, 67 W. Pratt Street; Sisco Brothers, Charles and Fayette Streets; Emmart and Quartley, 2276 W. Baltimore Street. Thomas R. Jeffreys Jr. was an artist who handpainted banners for militia companies. He worked at 18 North Street in the 1850s and his signature can be found not only on militia flags, such as the Vansville flag pictured in the Militia chapter, but also on the C.S.A. banners of the Wilmington Light Infantry flag bearing the North Carolina coat of arms and a Virginia state seal canton on a stars and bars standard. After the war he was still painting at 106 N. Eden Street.

There were four naval flags associated with native born Maryland officers. At the 1897 centennial exhibition there was a display of Confederate memorabilia. Among the relics was the flag of rear admiral Raphael Semmes which was described in his book Service Afloat as a large silk battle flag made by Lady deHoghton of England that was presented to him after the sinking of the Alabama.

Those few officers who acheived the rank of commodore or admiral, were granted the privilege of using a distinctive command flag. Commodore James I. Lynch, commander of a squad of lightly armed gunboats in action around Roanoke Island, had his own flag. Captain William H. Parker referred to the flag at Lynch's masthead as resembling the French flag with the colors reversed, which was revered by the commodore.

All through the battle of Mobile Bay, Admiral Franklin Buchanan floated his command flag on the C.S. Tennessee. In addition to the ensign there was a 2nd National flag with a battle flag design in the canton. Buchanan's command color was of plain blue bunting measuring 51-1/2" on the fly and 36-1/2" on the hoist with a canvas heading for attachment. As the Union ships entered the bay, they were confronted by the smaller Confederate fleet. After the initial clash, the small surviving ships of the Southern squadron slipped under the protection of the guns of Fort Morgan. The admiral steered the flag ship after the damaged Federal fleet. The C.S. Tennessee challenged the entire Union fleet of three ironclad monitors and 14 wooden vessels by herself. The old admiral, lame from a previous wound received aboard the Virginia, had his leg broken when a shot from the monitor U.S. Chickasaw pierced the ram, the only shot to do so. After an hour of this unequal contest, in which the ship's steering chains were shot away and the gun deck exposed, the Tennessee was compelled to strike her colors. These two flags were sent to the war department and in 1869 the admiral's personal flag was given to the Massachusetts Historical Society.

The 1st National flag brought home by Lieutenant John W. Bennett was used to drape his casket when he was buried at Springfield Cemetery. It was purchased from his granddaughter's estate sale along with a sea trunk containing over 30 pieces of naval memorabilia. It has "Lieut. Bennett" stamped in black on the cotton heading. The stamping is 1-1/4" overall and located 4-1/2" from the bottom

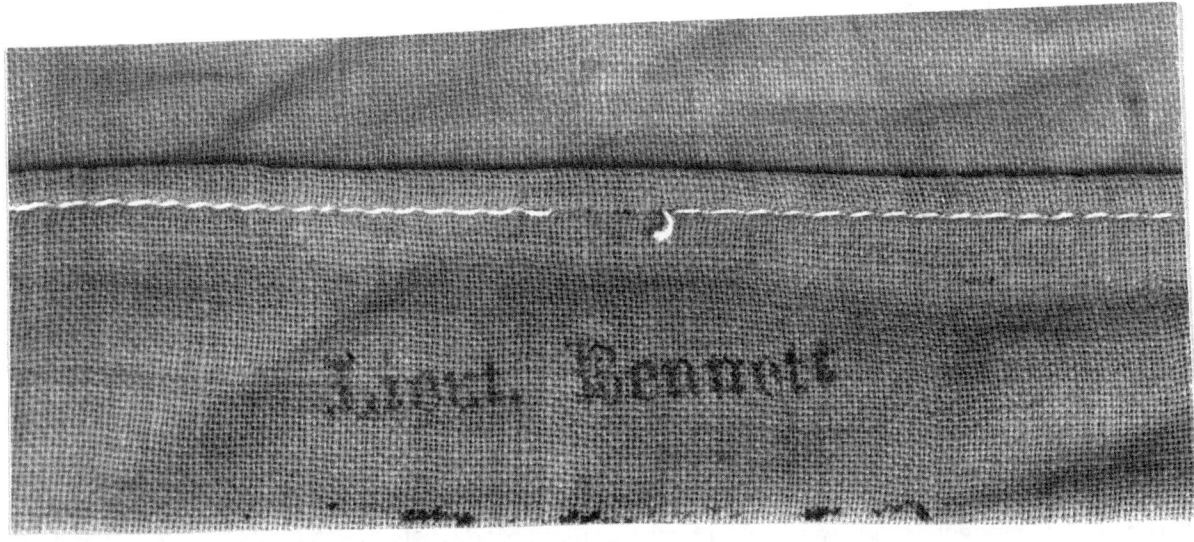

NAVAL 1ST NATIONAL FLAG OF LIEUTENANT JOHN W. BENNETT. It was made of cotton, 84" on the fly and 50" on the lanyard. The dark blue canton is 33" by 34" with 10 white five-pointed stars set in a 27" diameter circle around a central star. The field has red, white and red horizontal bars. "Lieut. Bennett" is stamped in 1-1/4" black letters which is 4-1/2" from the bottom on the heading on the obverse and reverse. The method of attachment is seven whipped eyelets pierced through the 7/8" doubled-over leading edge.

on both sides. It was probably not from the steamer Nashville, the gunboat Gaines, or the later Nashville, on which Bennett served, unless they had several flags. On March 17, 1862, the cruiser Nashville ran into Georgetown. Her name was changed and with a new crew she became a blockade runner. The Gaines went down on August 5, 1864, with a 1st National ensign at her masthead still partially above water. Bennett took command of a new sidewheeler, also called Nashville, that was surrendered on the Tombigbee River. Bennett wrote in the Confederate Veteran Magazine about a flag presented to the last Confederate ship Nashville by the ladies of that city. To keep it from becoming a trophy of war it was burned in the ship's furnace on the eve of the surrender of the Confederacy in May of 1865. These three ships were of sufficient size to have carried several ensigns. The author sent the Bennett's 1st National flag to H. Michael Madaus, assistant curator of the Milwaukee Public Museum, who is a Civil War flag authority and has seen more Southern banners than anyone since the war. He concluded after examining the flag that is was contemporary to the Civil War. The method of attachment was by hand whipped eyelets worked into the leading hem. The large size, the stamping of the names and several other characteristics pointed to naval use. In Madaus' opinion it could have been an ensign of one of the smaller boats upon which the crew escaped from the Gaines at Mobile Bay. Madaus felt the only way to reinforce his opinion was that the flag should be given a thorough fabric analysis. Complete testing by the Textile Preservation Association of Sharpsburg, Maryland, was completed using microscopic examination and chemical testing of fabric and thread. The microscope revealed dirt stains which would be consistent with sea service. Selvage edges were found at the top of the first red stripe and the top of the white stripe and the bottom of the lower red stripe in the field. The dark blue canton indicates that the warp side of the loom was cotton and the weft side wool. The white cotton thread was machine stitched with a lock stitch on most of the pieces. However, the stars on each side were first whip stitched by hand then machine sewn for strength by catching the stars in 1/4" on both sides. The eyelets were hand stitched in blue and red thread and the hem in blue. The findings of the chemical procedure substantiate the flag's authenticity. However, due to unethical alterations that are attempted by some today, it was requested by the examiner, Fonda G. Thompson, that the procedures not be disclosed. The analysis revealed that the materials used in the construction are consistent with war-period Confederate flags.

The relic list of memorabilia that was housed in the Maryland Line Confederate Soldiers Home contained 392 lots. Some of the individually numbered lots contained six different items loaned to the Pikesville home. This magnificent collection contained 22 southern flags, along with three different pieces of C.S.A. banners. Those flag remnants were of a flag from Fort Hatteras, a piece of a hospital flag and a piece of a flag sent by Maryland women to soldiers in the Confederate army. Some of these cherished banners, to which reference has not been made, include the 8th Virginia Cavalry regimental flag which is a 2nd National flag of cotton material. It is embroidered in the white field with the unit designation and battle honor "White Sulphur Springs August 26 & 27, 1863". It was captured at Moorefield on August 7, 1864, by Captain Thomas Kerr of the 14th Pennsylvania Cavalry, who later received a medal of honor for its capture. A 12-star silk battle flag of General Fitzhugh Lee is almost in shreds and was made by Miss Hattie Carrie. A bunting 13-star battle flag of William McIntosh was also on loan to the Maryland Line Confederate Soldiers Home by his wife. It bears 3-1/4" wide felt letters "Pegram Battalion 1861-186 ", with the later year never filled in. Another earlier flag associated with McIntosh was that of the Pee Dee Battery. While at Camp Suffolk Virginia in 1861 they were presented this piece made by the commander's sister, Miss Louisa McIntosh, and other ladies from Society Hill. It bore the design of the palmetto tree and crescent in the blue field and was marked "Presented to the Pee Dee Rifles Under This Standard We Will Conquer". When the guns were surrendered at Greensboro this faded, bullet sheared banner was placed under the jacket of R. Clark Nettles and returned to Miss McIntoch. The unusual standard of Company B, 6th Virginia Cavalry, was on display by Mrs. William H. Stewart. The white cotton field on the obverse has a truncated blue cross with 13 silk stars. The reverse bears a large 14-pointed star made of silk that is now faded pink. It was presented to Company B by the ladies of Gordonsville as they went into battle at Cedarville on May 23, 1862.

The banner carried by Lieutenant Robert Brand in the Red River expedition by General Joseph Lancaster Brent when he captured the U.S. iron clad Indianola on March 24, 1863, was on exhibition. It is recorded that the means of communication by signaling between the three southerners in the expedition was accomplished with lanterns because the only flag available was this Confederate flag. This piece was on loan to the Pikesville soldiers home from the flagbearer's father, the Rev. William Francis Brand, who left the state during the war and was in charge of the education of Jefferson Davis' two sons. A number of the flags from the fine collection in the Pikesville home are not identifiable. A small Confederate flag carried from Manassas to Appomattox was on loan by Mrs. Mary Severs Hughes. A Confederate flag, whose history today remains unknown, was loaned by Miss Caughy. A Georgia regimental flag was loaned by Mrs. Robert Atkinson. The last Confederate flag to fly over Fort Sumter was on loan from Mrs. Robert H. Coleman. There was also a miniature flag presented by General Beauregard to Mrs. Claudia Johnson about June 1, 1861. The last is a piece of a battle flag which has no donor or provenance.

In the Maryland Line Confederate Soldiers Home were three flag staffs. A portion of a flag staff from Fort Sumter that was shattered during the first seige was presented by some of the Baltimore secessionists of Ritz Artillery who participated in the action. Another portion of a staff from Fort Sumter was taken home as a souvenir by Captain Francis T. Miles. The last was a flag staff that was presented by the ladies of Baltimore to Company A, 2nd Maryland Infantry, which was shot in half on the breast works at Cold Harbour.

There are a number of other banners which have Maryland origin and association. A superb 2nd National flag was carried by Stuart's Horse Artillery. On May 1, 1863, the 2nd National flag was adopted by the Confederate congress. This new National flag was white with a St. Andrews cross in the canton and became known as the stainless banner. This flag was returned to R. Preston Chew from the family of the last flag bearer after his death in China. The white bunting field has two painted 19-1/2" crossed cannons. A bronze tube overlaps an iron black tube with the embroidered inscription "From The Ladies Of Charlottesville To Stuart's Horse Artillery Our Brave Defenders" in dark blue. This St. Andrews cotton canton had 13 cotton stars, but only 12 remain. This unit contained 10 commissioned officers and many enlisted men from Maryland.

In the museum of the Confederacy in Richmond, there are also a 1st National flag of 11 stars belonging to the 1st Maryland Infantry, and a state seal flag of the 2nd Maryland Infantry. They are made of silk and are deteriorating from being in a furled/rolled position. Also in the Maryland Department are pieces of the St. Nicholas flag captured on June 28, 1861, the Virginia flag, a banner that floated over Jackson Hospital, and the U.S.A. 1st Maryland Infantry flag captured by the C.S.A. 1st Maryland Infantry on May 24, 1862.

There were other Southern banners that were sent by Maryland sympathizers to Confederate units. Company H, 5th Louisiana Infantry, carried a beautiful silk 1st National flag that is painted in the canton on the reverse "Presented By The Ladies Of Baltimore To The Perrott Guards Of New Orleans".

The large military collection of Richard D. Steuart of Baltimore was donated to the Virginia Historical Society and is displayed in the Battle Abbey in Richmond. There are four Confederate flags contained in this collection, one of which he wrote about in the Confederate Veteran Magazine. "This banner was made by a Baltimore flag maker whose loyalty was above reproach." However, he did not leave us his documentation as to which of the flags he was referring.

The flag of the 43rd Virginia Cavalry was made in the area called Mosby's Confederacy by the ladies of Northern Virginia. Bunting was a scarce commodity and the blue field was cut from the blouse of a Union soldier. In 1927 it was conveyed by a son of one of the four Dorsey's in Company D to a few remaining rangers at a reunion in Arlington National Cemetery.

A war department order of June 7, 1887, to return captured flags was approved by President Cleveland and raised wide spread protest in the North and so was revoked a week later. By an act of Congress on February 28, 1905, the identified southern flags were to be returned to the states from which they had come. Most of the flags turned over were from the war department but some in private hands were never returned. A.H. Huber of Westminster wrote to the <u>Confederate Veteran</u> in regards to the U.S. flag taken from the Westminster courthouse during the Gettysburg campaign. "This flag says Mr. Huber was a handy work of a number of our resident union ladies, one of whom was my wife, now deceased. Each star bore the name of a lady engaged in the work. Until removed from the staff and placed in the fire proof vault, the flag had floated from the cupola of the courthouse. The surviving desire to say that, as the survivors on both sides are returning captured banners to their original owners, it is no more than fair that the banner taken from the ladies of Westminster Md, be returned to them."

On May 7, 1909, Confederate veterans met at Annapolis and ovations were given when the Confederate states banners were given to Governor Warfield. These banners were no longer national flags or political symbols but emblems of a heroic epic. These sacred momentos are embodied in memories that will forever be tender and holy. When the home at Pikesville was closed the 10 remaining camps of the Maryland Line Confederate Veteran Association presented the flags to the state of Maryland.

The flag staffs which held the Confederate banners in the state house, before they were moved to the Hall of Records, were new, large diameter poles. They were fastened to these banners with tacks when they were presented to the state, and each bore a brass bottony cross at the top. A plaque was attached midway on the staff giving the unit designation and they were cataloged by number by the state adjutant general in 1928. Many of the flags presented to the states were from the Maryland Line Confederate Soldiers Home in 1807 by a committee of James R. Wheeler and Spencer C. Jones under Governor J.W. Smith who received them.

Chapter 12

UNIFORMS

Prior to the war, generations passed down guns, powder horns and other personal items which had been proudly carried by kin. Clothing was something that was rarely passed down only for more than one generation because of the limited life of the garments. However, Major Thomas E. Rowland presented a sash to the the Maryland Line Confederate Soldiers Home which had been worn during three wars: the War of 1812, the Mexican War and the War between the States. The relic room of the Pikesville home displayed 14 identified uniforms. When the home closed most of the clothing was inherited by the Maryland Historical Society. Unfortunately, over the years the names of the former donners were lost.

During the early part of the war, units were clothed in a variety of colors. A photograph of David Gregg McIntosh and one of his five brothers depicts them in March of 1861 wearing two different shades of blue. The cut and the color was determined by the company or the seamstress, not the War Department. The June 1861 regulations called for cadet gray with facings of the branch color on the collar and cuffs: red for artillery, yellow for cavalry, blue for infantry, buff for staff, and black for medical. Sky blue trousers were authorized for enlisted men and regimental officers with dark blue for staff and higher ranks. Gray forage caps were copied from the French kepi, with a band of the branch color. Captured Union stock furnished many Southern soldiers with sky blue trousers. Single breast frock coats, instead of double breasted, were worn by many junior officers. The increased use of inferior dyes, and prolonged wear, caused many of the uniforms to fade to a butternut color. Every tailor knew, and soon every seamstress had learned, how to make an enlisted man's shell jacket and the short jackets that required the least amount of cloth. The shell jacket became the standard upper garment for the rank and file, and was initially made of wool and shortly after, a variety of mixtures of wool and cotton. Military insignias were sparingly used in Confederate service, and were usually limited to officer collar devices and gold sleeve braid.

The uniforms worn by the two Maryland infantry regiments can be defined by surviving examples. The 1st and 2nd Maryland Infantry Battalions were never clad in the butternut brown or rag-tag collage as were many Confederate units. They were imbued with an esprit-de-corps of uniform appearance.

On June 21, 1861, orders were issued that the companies of Weston's Maryland Battalion would be transferred to other commands. Weston's Battalion got their uniforms from the Richmond firm of Kent-Paine and Company. On June 29, Weston's troops also received 500 blankets, 500 shirts, 500 pairs of drawers, 500 pairs of socks, 500 pairs of shoes and 500 fatique caps. Dorsey and Murray's companies, when sent to the 1st Maryland, and Clarke's Company, when sent to the 21st Virginia, were completely clothed. Robertson's Company was held in Richmond on guard duty because their complete alotment of clothing had not been received. James S. Sterett, who was discharged on May 30, 1861, in order to receive a naval commission, had to reimburse $25 for clothing. An example of the uniform worn by J. Alden Weston's men can be found in the trousers and jacket of Private E. Courtney Jenkins Jr. He only remained with the Maryland Guard in Company B, 21st Virginia Infantry, until November of 1861 when he also received a naval commission and laid his infantry uniform aside. It is of gray color and is made of heavy satinet woolen fill twill which is woven to show the wool on the cloth face. The matching suit was hand sewn and lined in whitish cotton sheeting. The trouser side seams have 1/2" black tape as does the jacket on the collar and shoulder tabs. The jacket was made in a 6-button front with button shoulder tabs.

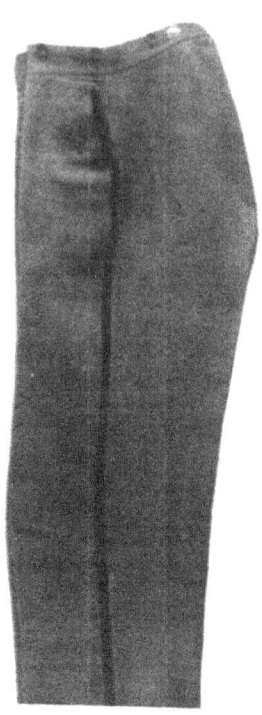

EARLY JACKET AND PANTS MADE BY KENT-PAINE COMPANY, RICHMOND. Private E. Courtney Jenkins Jr.'s uniform which was issued and worn in Weston's Maryland Battalion for six months before he received a naval commission as a flag officer's secretary. The matching jacket and pants are made of satinet woolen fill twill. The wide black tape on the collar and buttoned shoulder tabs along with the half-inch stripe on the trousers are the outstanding features of this period of Kent-Paine uniforms.

The Harpers Ferry companies which originally made up the 1st Maryland, were armed by Mrs. Jane Claudia Johnson, wife of Bradley T. Johnson. Mrs. Johnson, a native North Carolinian, went to Raleigh, N.C., to obtain guns and munitions for her husband's regiment, while Bradley returned to Richmond for clothes and tents. She secured cloth by purchasing it from the mills that manufactured it for the state of Virginia, and paid for making it up into uniforms. These Harpers Ferry companies had uniforms very similar to those of Weston's companies, except that the black braid tape pattern was slightly different. In the spring of 1862 the 1st Maryland's clothing was used up, and the four quartermasters requested pants, jackets, drawers and caps from the ordnance department. But they drew more shoes than any other item. The type of uniforms that were issued were the Richmond Depot type I jacket. When the 1st Maryland was mustered out of service, Company B went to North Carolina and Captain Charles C. Edelin stated to the ordnance department that "the company had lost all their clothing in the Battle of Newborn and had received none since."

Most Maryland troops were issued quartermaster clothing made in the capital city. The Richmond Depot jacket was made with a six-piece body, two-piece sleeve, nine-button front and contained an unbleached cotton osnaburg lining. The Richmond Depot type I jacket had shoulder straps with a button on each. The shoulder straps and collar edges had taped or piped trim, and the cuffs raised piping decoration. The Richmond Depot type II jackets had top-stitched edges on the shoulder straps. There are interior pockets, and a belt loop on each hip. The type III style were made almost exclusively of Kersey material. These late-war enlisted man jackets bear no decoration on the shoulder straps. They also exhibit a less tailored appearance.

FIRST MARYLAND INFANTRY UNIFORM received in August of 1861 and worn by Francis Leonard Higdon (1835/1896). He was born at Pisgah in Charles County. His father died when he was very young and he was raised at Newport, becoming a school teacher. He enlisted on June 15, 1861, at Richmond in a Charles County company. The enlistees were designated Company I of the 1st Maryland Infantry. By September, Higdon was a corporal, and by November 4th a sergeant. He was mustered out on June 13, 1862, after his 12-month term of service, and was entitled to a $15 balance for clothing not drawn. He and his cousin, John H. Stone, left Richmond on July 3, 1862, to return to Charles County. A Federal company came to the area where they were visiting, which forced the two relatives to return to Dixie by separate routes of travel. On August 27 Higdon re-enlisted at Richmond for three years or the war in Company B, 2nd Maryland Infantry, and soon became a sergeant. In 1863 he was appointed ordnance sergeant of the 2nd Maryland. His parole was signed on April 10, 1865, at Appomattox. Returning to his home, he immediately took the oath of allegiance on April 18. Higdon was a farmer in Charles County until October 1, 1885, when he entered the Maryland Line Confederate Soldiers Home.

When the 2nd Maryland Infantry was formed, they received on September 21, 1862, jackets at a cost of $10.75 each, pants at $7, $6 and $4.50 per pair. They also received some shoes for $3 per pair, and others for $1. On October 1 Quartermaster Charles R. Harding received more gray uniforms at a cost of $12.50 a piece. Shoes during this period were also shown at $3, $4.50 and $5. On November 2 the $5 shoes that were received were referred to as English shoes. The enlisted man's uniform of the 2nd Maryland Infantry had matching jacket and pants of blue-gray wool. They were the Richmond Depot type II. This unit kept up a neat appearance and is referred to as being dressed much finer than most of the southerners.

With the formation of the Maryland Line, the 2nd Maryland was again in top condition. General John C. Breckenridge in the spring of 1864 was pleased to have them assigned to his command, and complimented them highly upon their neat soldierly appearance. They were clad in the type III Richmond Depot uniforms of blue-gray kersey that were made without shoulder tabs and collar base stitching. Private John C. Henry, upon donating his coat to the Confederate Memorial Hall in New Orleans, wrote "Confederate jacket drawn from quartermaster department Richmond, Virginia in September 1864 by Mrs. Kluff a refugee from Maryland and given to me. I had it altered by a tailor in Richmond at a cost of $50. After the surrender I wore it to my home in Cambridge, Maryland, and the buttons were cut off as soveniers by the young ladies of that place."

SECOND MARYLAND INFANTRY RICHMOND DEPOT I UNIFORM with piped collar, shoulder straps and cuff trim shown on John Alexander Hayden (1828/1863). Hayden became a member of Richard Thomas Zarvona's Company in his native St. Mary's County, Oakville district, where he farmed. While traveling to Richmond, Colonel Zarvona was captured and the Maryland Zouave Regiment was not formed. The first company to which Hayden belonged to was sent to the 47th Virginia Infantry as Company H, and later to the 2nd Battalion, Arkansas Infantry. After his 12-month term of enlistment expired, he returned to Richmond and enlisted in the 2nd Maryland Infantry, Company B. At Gettysburg he was wounded in the shoulder outside of the log breast works near Rock Creek. Hayden died from this wound on July 7, 1863. His brother, William S., rode with the Marylanders in the 1st Virginia Cavalry.

SECOND MARYLAND INFANTRY DRUMMER'S UNIFORM worn by John Thomas Bond and featured black tape across the front which matches the tape around the standing collar. The collar tape was used on the first uniforms issued to the company. Bond (1840/1925) was born and raised in Calvert County and enlisted as a private on June 18, 1861, for one year the 2nd Company H, 1st Maryland Infantry. He was a drummer under Chief Musician Alexander Hubbard in Drum Major Hosea Pitt's unit. On October 6 he was ill with remittant fever and was sent to Manassas Infirmary. Upon completion of his term of service he re-enlisted for two years but was mustered out with the entire regiment.

SECOND MARYLAND INFANTRY ENLISTED MAN'S SHOULDER TABBED, HIGH COLLAR COAT worn by William Thomas Bailey (1840/). Born in St. Mary's County he enlisted for two years or the war on August 25, 1862, at Richmond in Company A, 2nd Maryland Infantry. Bailey's last recorded draw for clothing was made in the fourth quarter of 1863. On October 1, 1864, at Squirrel Level Road, he was wounded in the left eye and was admitted to the Brigade Hospital on October 3. He received a 60-day furlough on November 14 but never reported back to the command. After the war he returned to the family farm in the St. Clemens Bay area and was a member of the Murray Confederate Association of Maryland.

MID-WAR RICHMOND DEPOT II JACKET, featuring a low collar and should tabs with top-stitched edges, pictured on John Craig Lake (1845/1864). He left his ancestral home in Cambridge to enlist on March 9, 1862, in Company A, 2nd Maryland Infantry. Severely wounded in the right leg on Culp's Hill during the Gettysburg Campaign, he retired with the Army of Northern Virginia through the rain and mud and was left with the seriously wounded at Hagerstown. The 2nd Maryland recrossed the Potomac on July 14, leaving behind 300 dead, wounded and missing. Lake was taken to the General Hospital in Baltimore and exchanged. While recuperating from his wounds, he contracted smallpox and died on March 9, 1864.

140 - Uniforms

RICHMOND DEPOT II 2ND MARYLAND INFANTRY UNIFORM. It was worn by Alexander Murray (1843/1925) who was born at West River in Anne Arundel County, and came to Baltimore where he was a member of the Maryland Guard Militia. At the age of 18 he joined the army with his two brothers, Captain William H. and Clapham Murray. He enlisted for three years or the war at Richmond on August 20, 1862, in his brother's Company A of the 2nd Maryland Infantry. He was captured at Stroudsburg on December 21, 1862, and was immediately paroled and sent back within the southern lines. As the 2nd Maryland advanced at Gettysburg, while being led by his brother William, Alexander stepped forward to catch his brother as he was killed. Alexander was wounded by the many fragments which were piercing the ground and the men at the time. He continued service with Company A until they reached Appomattox where he was paroled on April 10, 1865. Returning to Baltimore, he was made to take the oath on May 2. He resided at the family home called Woodstock where he farmed as generations had done before him. He was a member of the Murray Confederate Association.

LATE WAR RICHMOND DEPOT III UNADORNED SHELL JACKET of Edward L. Claggett (1836/) After leaving the Buckeystown area of Frederick County, Federal enrollment officials recorded him as gone south and his name was stricken from the draft. Claggett enlisted for the war at Richmond in September of 1862 in Company F, 2nd Maryland Infantry. At Gettysburg he was detailed to regimental surgeon Dr. Richard Potts Johnson, also from Frederick. Both were taken prisoner on July 5 and sent to the West Building Hospital at Baltimore, arriving on July 28. Medical personnel were to be immediately exchanged but after this battle Federal authorities refused to adhere to the agreement. Claggett was sent to prison at Elmira, arriving on August 16. He was exchanged on February 13, 1865, and reported to his unit in the trenches at Petersburg. Wounded in the right hand, he was sent to Chimborazo Hospital in Richmond and then returned to duty on March 27. Claggett was captured as the army retreated toward Appomattox and was sent to Point Lookout. With the release of Confederate prisoners on June 1, and after taking the oath, he returned to the Buckeystown area. He was a member of the Alexander Young United Confederate Veterans Camp of Frederick. Going to Washington, he worked as a machinist and on April 6, 1915, became a resident of the Maryland Line Confederate Soldiers Home.

Uniforms - 141

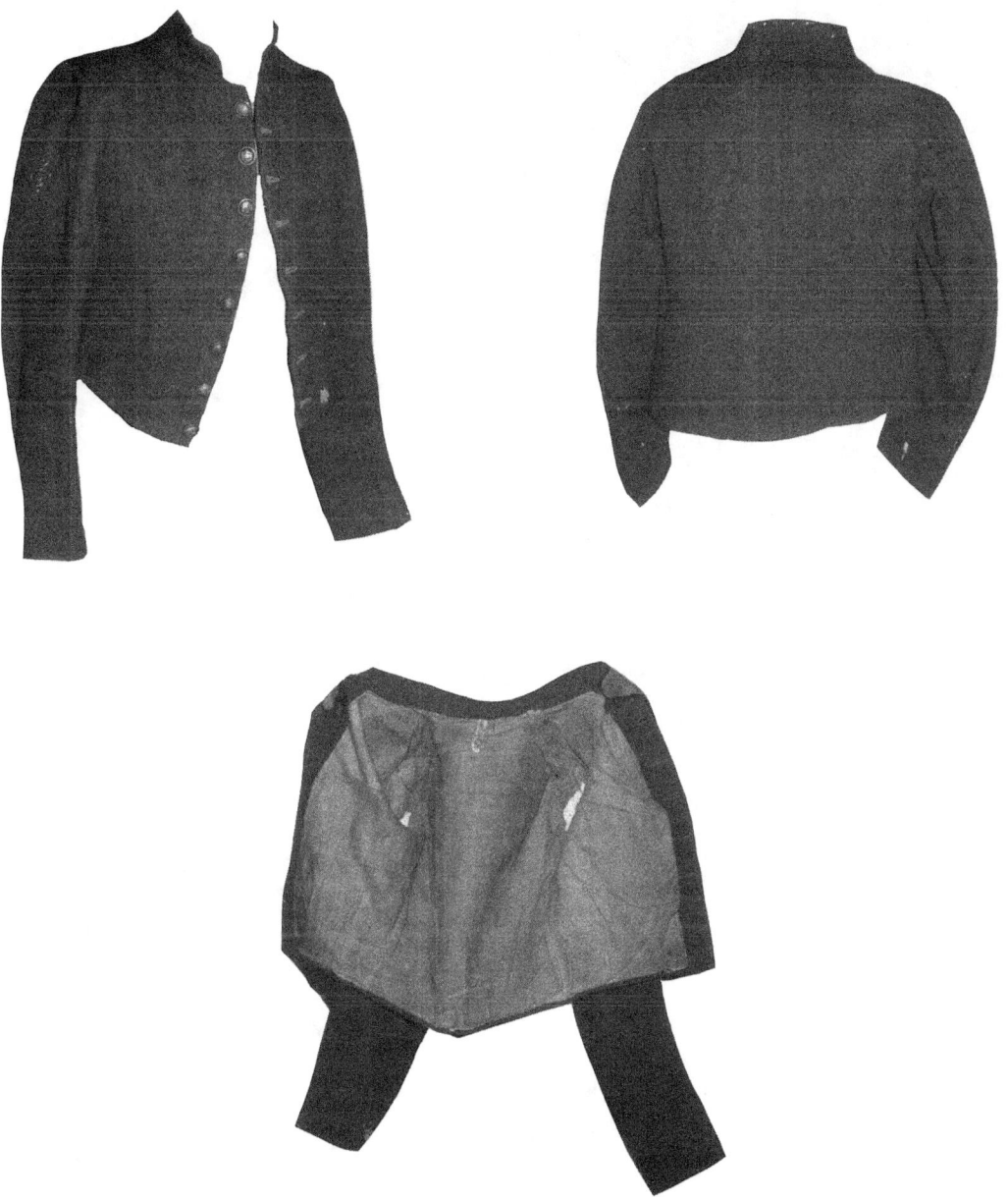

TAIT-TYPE CONFEDERATE 2ND MARYLAND INFANTRY JACKET. This gray-blue jacket was worn by Private William H. Harrison (/1907). It was produced by Peter Tait in Limerick, Ireland, and is of blue-gray kersey wool and was machine stitched with white thread. The jacket is trimmed in blue with a hook and eye on the collar and has two Federal eagle buttons and six state seal buttons, five which are marked "Scovill MFG Co * Waterbury *" and one marked "Extra Quality." He enlisted in Company C, 2nd Maryland Infantry, on September 15, 1862, and four months later was transferred to Company A. In December of 1863 he was a patient at Robertson Hospital in Richmond. He drew clothing in the fourth quarter of 1863 and the fourth quarter of 1864. During the last days of the defense of Petersburg, he belonged to a picked band called "Dale's Sharpshooters," and was captured during the evacuation at Hatcher's Run on April 2. He was imprisoned at Point Lookout until being released on June 13, after which he returned to Baltimore.

RICHMOND DEPOT III SHORT JACKET of John C. Henry (1840/1910) that was "drawn from the Quartermaster Dept Richmond in December of 1864 by Mrs. Huff, a refugee from Maryland and given to me. I had it altered by a tailor in Richmond at a cost of $50. After the surrender I wore it to my home in Cambridge, Md, and the buttons were cut off as souvenirs by the young ladies of that place." This is taken from a donation card when Henry donated the jacket to the Confederate Memorial Hall in New Orleans. The gray-blue jacket has one inner pocket. The vest has three small Maryland state seal buttons marked "Scovill MFG Co * Waterbury *". The lining of both the jacket and vest is of polished white cotton material.

JOHN C. HENRY FROCK COAT bearing a label of "C.D. Carr & Co, Charleston S.C." It is decorated with large eagle staff buttons.

In the Petersburg trenches the uniforms of the 2nd Maryland Infantry were completely worn out. Colonel George Proctor Kane, who had recruited Marylanders from other states and funnelled them into Maryland commands, was inspector of the Maryland Line. Upon visiting the troops on February 20, 1865, "He was shocked at the condition of the men and was moreover surprised at their cheerfulness under such trying circumstances. When he left the boys he promised them each a new uniform and a change of under clothes. He kept his promise, and on the 4th of March, 1865, they arrived. Many a God-bless-you, Colonel Kane, went up from those poor boys as they threw aside the miserable rags in which they were clad and donned their comfortable suits." The new clothes that were worn by the men as they abandoned their Petersburg line were made of twill jeans in a light gray color with white cotton lining. The fatigue-blouse jacket with a standing collar was hand stitched, and the pants with narrow legs were made of a coarser twill. As they moved toward Appomattox and the dreary end, the 2nd Maryland Infantry was better clad then most Confederate units.

 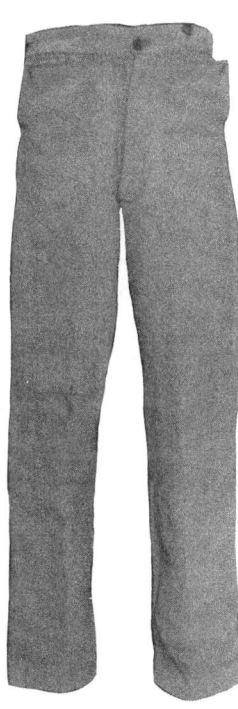

LAST 2ND MARYLAND INFANTRY UNIFORM issued to Private Henry Hollyday Sr. (1836/1921), and later purchased in 1865 by Colonel George P. Kane. The jacket is made of a fine twill jean with white cotton lining. It was made with a four-piece body and one-piece sleeves. It is cut like a fatigue blouse, only shorter, with a standing collar. This single-breasted coat has six state seal buttons marked "SUPERIOR QUALITY" and a small state seal cuff button on each sleeve. The trousers are of a coarser twill jean, cut narrow in the legs with one patch on the knee. Hollyday was born in Baltimore and reared in Queen Anne's County until being sent to St. James College at Hagerstown. In 1852 he entered the mercantile business in Philadelphia for several years, and then went to Centerville in the same line of work. He left his home and family in early September, 1862. On September 15, Hollyday enlisted for three years or the war as a private in Company A, 2nd Maryland Infantry. In July of 1864 he was in Robertson's Hospital in Richmond and received a 30-day furlough. The rolls show that he received his clothing allotment for the third quarter on August 15, 1864, prior to receiving this uniform. He was paroled at Appomattox on April 9, 1865. He resided in Queen Anne's County until 1869 when he moved to Easton to become a banker. He was a member of the Murray Confederate Association.

144 - Uniforms

Unlike the 1st and 2nd Maryland Infantry, the Maryland cavalry units were often partially clad in captured Federal clothing. Quartermaster Ignatius W. Dorsey of the 1st Maryland Cavalry, and Nicholas Owings of the 2nd Maryland Cavalry attempted to outfit their battalions through the quartermaster department. Most of their requests were for pants, shirts, drawers, socks and shoes. The need for jackets was supplanted in the summer with cotton shirts. Shoes were issued, but boots were more desirable and could be obtained from captured stores or soldiers. Colonel Harry Gilmor, in a raid on Alpine Depot on the Baltimore and Ohio Railroad, wrote, "Such quantities of stores at one view I have never before seen. There was case after case loaded with shoes, and clothing of all kinds; sugar, coffee, whiskey, molasses, and stores of every description, besides haversacks, knapsacks, canteens, and two cases of Enfield-rifles the aggregate value not less than half a million dollars. We hastened back to camp, each one loaded down with plunder, and then to inform Captain James L. Clark, whose Company of Maryland boys were in very bad condition, of our good luck. I told Captian C. that he might equip his whole command at the depot and off we started, I acting as guide."

With the exception of some ships, most of the supplies that are documented as having crossed the borders of Maryland into the Confederacy were small packages. Bradley T. Johnson, in writing about the formation of Company F, 1st Maryland Cavalry, states it "was recruited by three rich young Baltimoreans - Augustus F. Schwartz, Captain; C. Irving Ditty, First Lieutenant, and Fielder C. Slinghoff, 2nd Lietenant. They furnished uniforms, horses accoutrements and arms for their company at an immense expense, for everything except horses had to be smuggled through the blockade from Baltimore." Davis' Maryland Cavalry at Camp Maryland on September 9, 1862, received 50 jackets, 50 pants, 100 flannel shirts, 100 drawers, 100 socks, 30 caps and 50 blankets. Six days later they received 33 more complete uniforms. Quartermaster Henry D. Brewer in the summer of 1863 requested "clothing for new recruits who were without clothing fit for soldiers." On August 15 he received 22 complete uniforms and on August 30, 25 jackets, 25 pants and 25 pairs of shoes only for newly mustered recruits. In the spring of 1864, General Imboden sent Thomas B. Gatch, whose command was on picket at Woodstock, to remount his broken down troopers saying these Baltimore roughs can steal horses and arms to equip a company. Captain Gatch wrote "Scouts reported that Confederate gray cloth was being manufactured at a factory near Charleston for uniforms for Jessie Scouts who were a group of Freemont's men that impersonated Confederates. The battalion was badly in need of clothes so six men made a raid and returned with four bolts of gray cloth. A tailor measured and cut it to fit the troopers who were most in want and the ladies about this park made the uniforms." This may have referred to the firm of Kelly, Tackett & Ford of Manchester, Virginia.

WAR SHIRT UNDER THE SERGEANT'S JACKET worn by John Eager Howard Post prior to July of 1863. He was a clerk in Baltimore prior to the war where he was a member of Company D, Maryland Guard Militia. He enlisted on October 6, 1861, with many of his pre-war militiamen in Company H, 1st Maryland Infantry. He served in the rank and file as a private until his company was mustered out. He re-enlisted in Company C, 1st Maryland Cavalry as a private for three years or the war, and soon became sergeant. On July 1, 1863, Post was appointed sergeant major of the battalion. When George W. Booth was promoted to assistant adjutant general on December 1, 1863, Post was appointed to fill his vacancy as adjutant with the rank of 2nd lieutenant. Although he was not wounded during the rebellion, he was twice hospitalized with scabies. Being paroled at Mechanicsville on March 24, 1865, he remained in Virginia for about a year before returning to his native city. At the formation of the 5th Regiment Maryland National Guard in 1867, Post was elected 2nd lieutenant of Company K and became its captain in 1870.

ENLISTED MAN'S FINE QUALITY CAVALRY JACKET worn by Private Edward Howard Hall (1844/1917). It has what appears to be yellow piping on the front and around the cuffs. Hall left his home in Harford County to enlist as a private in Company A, 1st Maryland Cavalry, on July 15, 1862. The last receipt rolls signed by him for the issue of clothing was on March 31, 1864. He was taken prisoner in a flank movement at Pollard's Farm on May 21, 1864. The 1st Maryland lost between 50-60 men in the dreadful hand-to-hand combat before they were given the order to retreat. Hall was exchanged on February 18, 1865, and returned to his company. He was again captured at Hanover Courthouse on March 13 in an all-day skirmish. He was held at Point Lookout until released on April 20, 1865.

PLAIN 1862 UNIFORM, with round bottom and front closure, of Gresham Hough (1844/1894). There exists another picture of Hough showing him much older, sporting a beard and wearing a later cavalry uniform. Upon leaving his Baltimore home he enlisted on June 18, 1861, in Company H, 1st Maryland Infantry, and served with them until the expiration of his 12-month term of service. He re-enlisted as a private for two years in the 1st Maryland Cavalry, Company A, on June 15, 1862. In the spring of 1863 he endeavored to secure a position in the Marine Corps. His widowed mother, because of her seccessist sympathies, was banished from Baltimore to the South. With the expiration of his enlistment, he joined John S. Mosby in Company D, 43rd Virgiia Cavalry, in the fall of 1864. Hough surrendered and received his parole on April 25, 1865, at Harpers Ferry.

146 - Uniforms

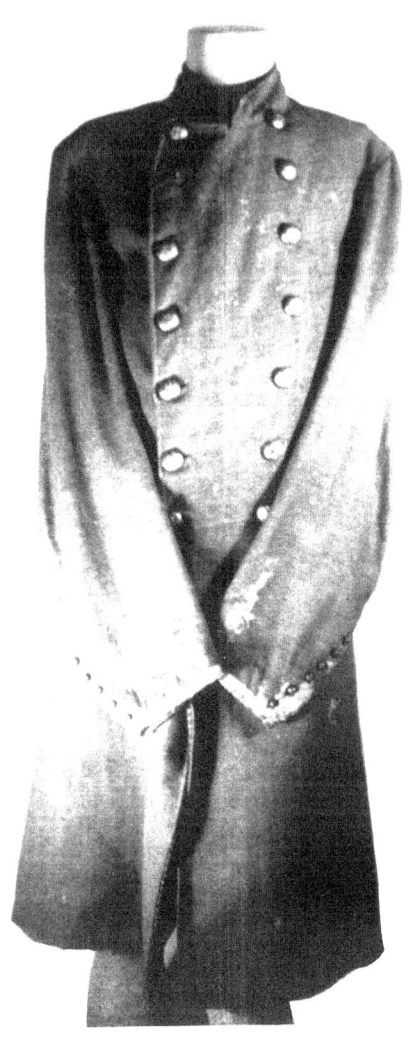

HOMEMADE FROCK COAT worn by Private Jacob Smallwood Barnes of Baltimore in Company A, 7th Virginia Cavalry. Surviving information from the Maryland Line Confederate Soldiers Home states "It was made from wool of sheep raised on a Southern plantation which was carded, spun and woven into cloth and made by the women of the plantation." The double-breasted coat has 13 Federal army large buttons and 5 brass studs on each sleeve. It is gray, cotton wrapped wool with a brown standup collar. The bottom edge of the sleeves are bound by white rawhide.

SHELL JACKET WITH OUTSIDE PATCH POCKET on Frederick S. Wilson (1847/) shown in this carte de viste by Jacob Bierley of Frederick, Maryland. Wilson was a student at Georgetown University in the class of 1864. Returning to his home in Frederick County during the summer break of 1863, he enlisted at Boonsboro on June 16 in Company D, 1st Maryland Cavalry. This unit was composed of men from Carroll and Frederick counties and he was enrolled as a private for three years or the war. On December 28, 1863, Wilson was sent to Chimborazo Hospital in Richmond with camp itch, and on January 15 received a furlough of 30 days. On March 1, 1865, he was in General Hospital No. 9 at Richmond. Returning to his unit, he surrendered at Winchester on April 19, 1865, and took the oath of parole again at Harpers Ferry on April 26. Wilson returned to his home and was required to go before the provost marshal of the 4rd District in Maryland on July 6 to again affirm his allegiance.

RECRUITS DURING THE BALTIMORE-WASHINGTON RAID. Hoffman Gilmor (seated), wearing hunting leggings and holding a Mississippi rifle, and Joshua Frederick Cocky Talbot (standing), in a long sack coat, both of Baltimore County joined Harry Gilmor's Band during his ride around Baltimore. They had this photograph taken during the Baltimore-Washington raid. They are clothed in their frontier hunting-pattern clothing as they accompanied the 2nd Maryland Cavalry. On July 27, 1864, at Big Springs, Virginia, these volunteers were enrolled in Company F by Bradley T. Johnson. Hoffman was wounded in August of 1864. His cousin Harry removed a piece of bone from his upper arm. The next night, February 5, 1865, Hoffman and his commander were captured while sleeping at Moorefield. He was confined at Fort McHenry on February 8 and was listed as a guerrilla not to be exchanged. J.F.C. Talbot surrendered on May 16, 1865, at Danville. He took the oath at Marietta on August 26 so he could return to his Lutherville home.

OFFICERS DURING THE BALTIMORE-WASHINGTON RAID. Taken in the same studio is James Louis Clark (1841/1920), right, and Richard T. Gilmor (1840/) James Louis Clark was appointed a captain in the quartermaster department on November 20, 1861. Assigned to the 1st Maryland Regiment, he resigned on June 28, 1862. During the Antietam Campaign, Clark organized a cavalry company of 100 men from the state but he was unable to furnish horses. He carried these men into Stuart's Horse Artillery, where he served as a volunteer aide on the staff of General J.E.B. Stuart. On June 16, 1863, he was appointed commander of Company F, 12th Virginia Cavalry, to fill the vacancy of Harry W. Gilmor, who was raising a battalion of partisan rangers. Clark was captured at Moorefield on August 7, 1864, in the surprise Federal attack that cost the regiment many men. He was sent to Camp Chase Prison and on February 12, 1865, was transferred to Point Lookout until the end of the war. Returning to Baltimore, he became an attorney and on July 23, 1911, a resident of the Maryland Line Confederate Soldier's Home. Richard T. Gilmor was born at Glen Ellen. To avoid a bench warrant arrest he went south in May of 1861. After serving 12 months in Company H, 1st Maryland Infantry, he re-enlisted in August of 1862 in Company F, 12th Virginia Cavalry. He assisted in organizing Company C of his brother's 2nd Maryland Cavalry and was elected 1st lieutenant. After the capture of his brother he commanded the 2nd Maryland Cavalry and was paroled in June of 1865 and returned to Baltimore on August 9.

CAVALRY SHELL JACKET AND LIGHT GRAY MILITARY VEST WITH KEPI belonging to James Louis Clark. The kepi is blue, has two rows of gold braid, a leather chin strap and visor and has gold braid on the top. The gray vest has nine state seal cuff buttons marked "extra quality". The gray jacket is tailored with piping, two rows of braid on the sleeves and three rows on the collar. It has four Maryland state seal buttons, two "Scovill MFG Co * Waterbury *" and two "Extra Quality"

MILITARY CADET GRAY VEST of John Miffin Hood (1843/1906) with four pockets, and seven state seal cuff buttons marked "Canfield Bro & Co Bal". Born at Bowling Green in Howard County, Hood became an engineer. Returning to Baltimore from Brazil in 1862, he went south. Hood enlisted as a private in Company C, 2nd Maryland Infantry and was wounded at Spotsylvania. In the early part of 1864 he accepted a commission as 2nd lieutenant in the 2nd Regiment, Engineer Corps. After the war he became superintendent of the Western Maryland Railroad, and later president and general manager.

150 - Uniforms

The Maryland Flying Light Artillery, the Baltimore Light Artillery and the Chesapeake Light Artillery were supplied by the Richmond Quartermaster Department. A request for replacement clothing was more readily filled when requested by the brigade to which they were attached. When organized, the 1st Maryland Artillery drew 50 uniforms, 50 caps, and 50 pairs of shoes on July 2, 1861. They were mustered in on July 10 and on the 18th received 102 shirts and 54 caps. On March 21, 1862, they drew 100 pairs of shoes sizes 6, 7 and 8 but had requested 140 pairs. On August 10, 1862, at Bunker Hill, the 2nd Maryland Artillery was resupplied with the following clothing: 5 suits gray, 3 cotton shirts, 4 flannel shirts, 2 jackets, 4 pair Manchester gray pants, 5 pair Manchester blue pants, 2 suits, tuscaroro jeans, 2 suits jeans, and 11 pairs of shoes. Corporal George Pielert wrote that a full uniform for review consisted of knapsack, canteen, haversack and saber. He also wore a pair of steel spurs and a Bowie knife which he made for himself. He purchased a Yankee shin bone from a camp of the New York Zouaves near the Manassas battlefield, which he then used to make the handles for his Bowie knife and several others. Quartermaster John P. Hickey was able to reuniform most of the 4th Maryland Artillery in the summer of 1864. The last two small field issues of clothing were made on November 17 and December 8, 1864, to only those who were present. The jacket of Private George Wilson of the Flying Artillery is in the Smithsonian and is of blue-gray kersey. This jacket is of the Richmond Depot type, in the transition between types II and III. It has collar based stitching, with no shoulder tabs, and a nine-button front. His last two receipt rolls for clothing were on July 22 and October 4 of 1864. One of these may have been the issue for this jacket.

ENLISTED MAN'S 1ST MARYLAND ARTILLERY UNIFORM trimmed in red and worn by John Hanson Briscoe (/1894). He was born and raised in Baltimore and enlisted for the war in the Maryland Flying Artillery on August 10, 1861, at Richmond. In the summer of 1862 Briscoe served with that section of the 1st Maryland Artillery that became Company B of Hampton Legion Battery of Artillery. On September 14, 1864, Briscoe was in Chimborazo Hospital in Richmond. He was discharged by writ of habeas corpus in the Confederate states in District Court by Judge Gally Burton in October of 1864. His last issue of clothing was on September 15.

ENLISTED MAN'S SHELL JACKET of Louis W. Knight (1844/). It is a Richmond Depot III made of blue-gray kersey wool. The eight Maryland buttons on the front have the skanks piercing the cloth and are secured with ribbon. This was a more secure type of attachment than just using thread. The cuffs have Louisiana State buttons. He was born in Baltimore and enlisted on August 5, 1863, in Company D, 2nd Maryland Cavalry. In April of 1864 he was transferred out of Gilmor's Battalion to the 2nd Maryland Artillery. After being captured in the Valley in the fall of 1864 he was sent to Point Lookout Prison. In 1866 he graduated from the University of Maryland Medical College and practiced as a physician in Baltimore.

ENLISTED MAN'S LATE-WAR 1ST MARYLAND ARTILLERY VEST AND COAT on George Addison Cooke. He enlisted for the war on July 20, 1861, at Richmond in the Maryland Flying Artillery. Private Cooke was one of the artificer's who was sent to Hampton Legion as Company B, Light Artillery, on June 21, 1862. After being transferred back to the 1st Maryland Artillery they were in Lieutenant Colonel McIntosh's Battalion. After the narrow escape from the explosion of Burnside's Mine they proceeded to the fortifications around Petersburg. It was at this time that Cooke was marked on the rolls, "Not present - deserted."

152 - Uniforms

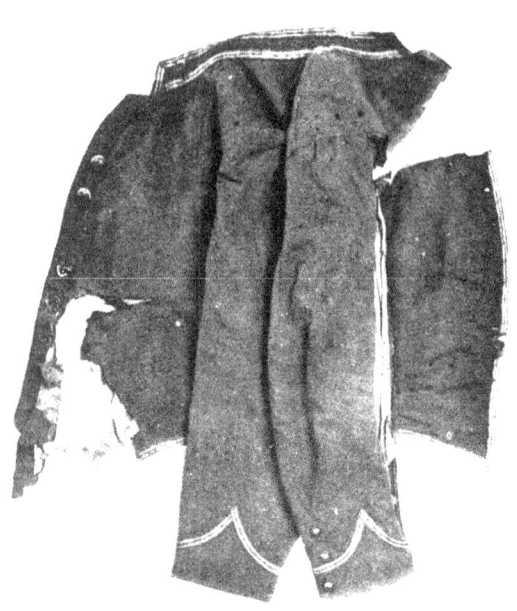

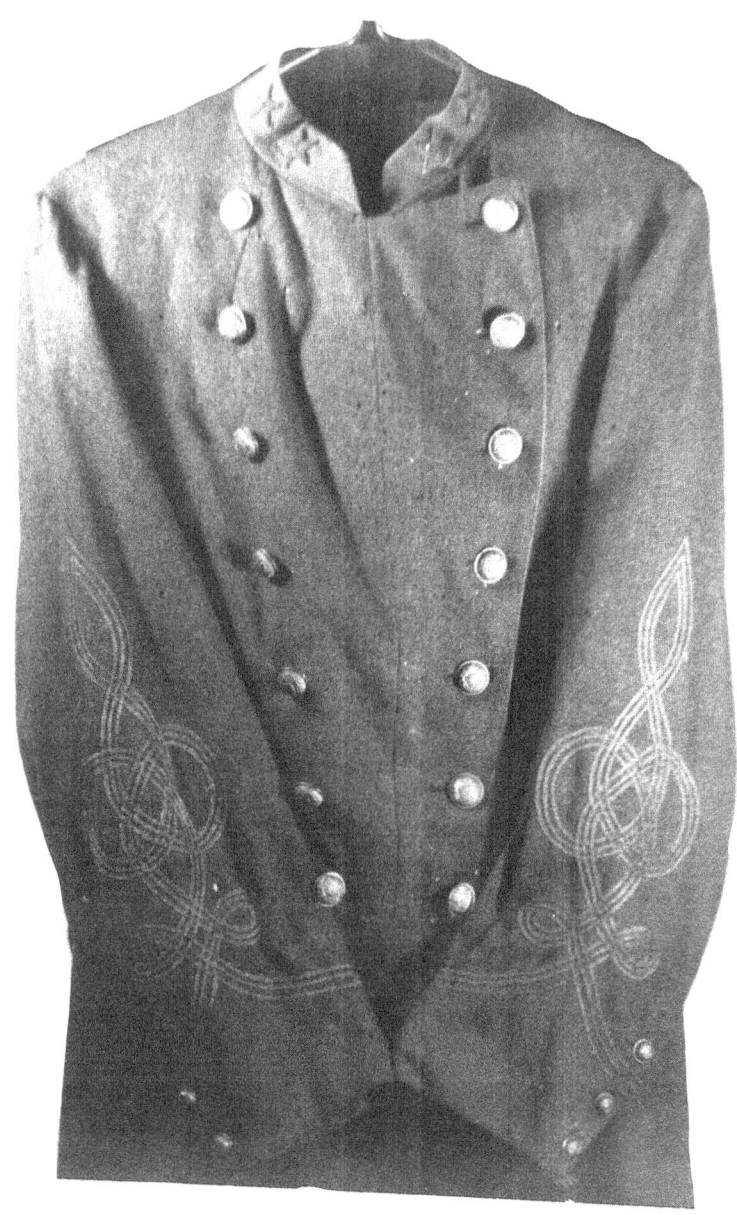

SHELL JACKET AND FROCK COAT. Colonel Richard Snowden Andrews shell jacket is the one he was wearing when wounded by a shell at Cedar Run. It has two Maryland seal buttons "Scovill MFG Co * Waterbury *", two buttons with only the backs remaining which are marked the same way, and three state seal cuff buttons. Also pictured is his frock coat of gray wool broadcloth with metallic braid. It has a double-breasted standing collar of red wool and lower sleeve with three silver gilt braids forming loops with red cuff lining. The coat contains seven Maryland state seal buttons "Extra Quality", three state seal cuff buttons "Extra Quality."

The 3rd Maryland Artillery, after being mustered and drilled, was sent to the Army of the West. They served in the Army of Tennesse and the Army of Mississippi. In September of 1863 they were sent to Demopolis, Alabama, for repairs, and the entire battery received new uniforms. On January 31 they received 40 jackets, 108 shirts, 121 pairs of pants and 11 pairs shoes. Most of the command were wearing boots. During the retreat from Nashville in December of 1864, the 3rd Maryland Artillery had been issued demons boots. Captain William L. Ritter wrote that the half naked "shoeless men marched all the way from Nashville to Mississippi without any protection whatsoever to their feet".

Officers were required to furnish their own clothes. Randolph H. McKim, who received a commission on the staff of General George H. Steuart on June 8, 1862, reveals that fine uniform cloth cost $13.75 per yard. At the Battle of Cross Keys he had to wear a jacket with the chevrons of a color sergeant. He also had to use a borrowed horse, and General R. Ewell made fun of him and called him a courier without any spurs. Three weeks later at Staunton, McKim was pleased when he "purchased a horse and other equipment - uniform, sword, pistol, spurs, etc. - suitable to my rank as a staff officer." In April of 1861, a Marylander's letter reveals that clothes were out of sight: cap $10, coat $125, pants $50, vests $20, boots $50, shoes $15-$30, wool shirts $20, Maryland buttons $1, drawers $5. McHenry Howard received a staff appointment to General Charles S. Winder's staff on March 24, 1862. He wore a plain, ready-made gray coat without any sign of rank. On May 28 he sewed on a pair of Federal 1st lieutenant's epaulettes. Finally, at the end of July in Richmond he wrote "my uniform being made." In a letter from his sister Liz, dated October 11, 1864, she talks about a coat she had made for their brother, Assistant Surgeon Edward Lloyd Howard. "I tried on Eddie's new uniform coat. It is a beauty and will go directly to him." Surviving uniforms of enlisted men are rare. Many of them only had one while officers may have had several. There are three uniforms of Elliott Johnston which are still in existence today. All three bear Maryland state seal buttons and all are of superior quality wool blend material and were tailor made. They bear the buff staff color of the rank of captain, and consist of a waist coat, a shell jacket, and a frock coat. The probability for their survival is that on January 1 of 1865 he travelled to Europe to obtain an artificial leg. By mid war officers were allowed to wear fatigue uniforms. These often consisted of a single-breasted, plain frock coat or a plain jacket with embroidery only on the collar. George W. Booth was in Richmond on April 2, 1865, the day before the lines broke at Petersburg. "I called upon my tailor and paid him for an undress uniform coat $1200, giving him in payment a $20 gold piece."

SILVER BULLION-FRINGED EPAULETTE captured from an enemy officer by Charles Columbus Edelin during the charge which won the day at Manassas. The pair of epaulettes proudly became a part of his own uniform. When the regiment went into camp at Fairfax they were inscribed, "Capt Edelin Maryland Volunteers taken at Bull Run July 21, 1861 left at Sagars Fort Centerville Virginia." Edelin was one of 15,000 volunteers who enrolled and began to drill. He was chosen captain of Company A, 2nd Battalion of the Maryland Line. With the disbanding of the militia, Edelin became one of the first to move with a group of his men by foot through Frederick to Point of Rocks where, on May 21, 1861, they were mustered in as Company B, 1st Maryland Infantry, with Edelin chosen as commander. In January of 1862 a large portion of his Company B re-enlisted. They received a furlough but offered to forgo their well-deserved leave and consequently were ordered by the war department from Gordansville to detached service at Goldsboro, North Carolina. They served as infantry at the Battle of Newburn, then in scouting service and, at Brunswick Point, as heavy artillerists.

BRIGADIER GENERAL'S FROCK COAT of Bradley T. Johnson. This dark gray, double-breasted coat has 16 state seal buttons with 11 of them "extra quality", 2 "Scovill MFG & Co * Waterbury *", and 3 are "Canfield Bro & Co Baltimore." There are 6 small state seal cuff buttons, 4 are "extra quality", 1 is "Scovill MFG Co * Waterburg *" and 1 "Canfield Bro & Co Bal".

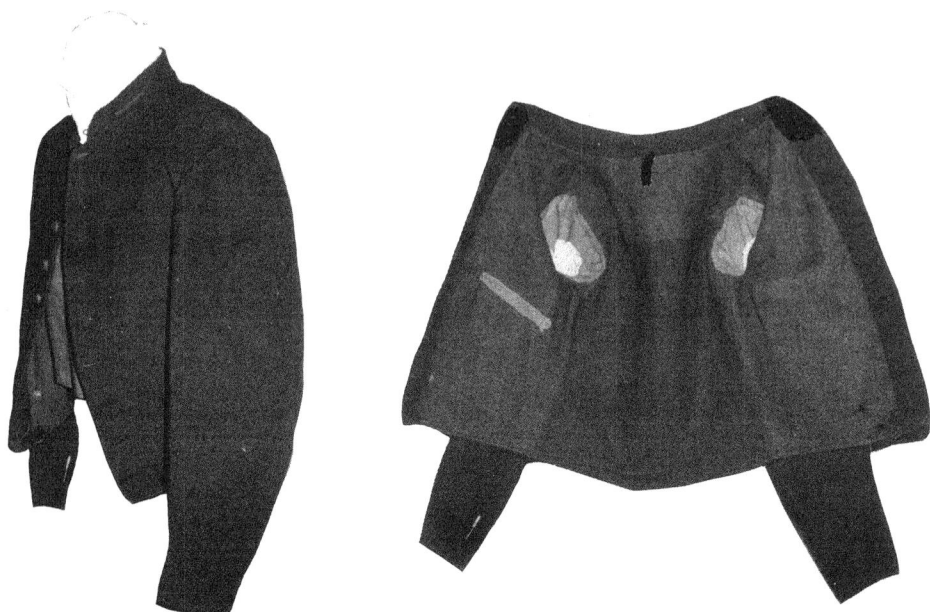

ENLISTED MAN'S SINGLE-BREASTED JACKET WORN BY AN OFFICER of gray-blue wool belonging to 2nd Lieutenant Thomas H. Tolson (1840/) of C Company, 2nd Maryland Infantry. It has a round standing collar with a gilt braid bar on each side. It is a Richmond Depot III, which were made of a coarser kersey wool, and it had the lieutenant bars added on the collar. The lining is crudely sewn patchwork. Tolson's diary entry of February 10, 1865, states "paid $100 to have my jacket and pants fixed in Petersburg. The weather wet and cold." He was captured with a 32-man picket detail on April 2, 1865.

SUPERBLY TAILORED OFFICER'S SHELL JACKET belonging to John Donnell Smith. It is slate gray and the collar is accented in red with captain's bars and the sleeve decorations contain three rows of gold braid. It is beautifully piped in red along the nine large Maryland state seal buttons that were made by "Scoville MFG Co * Waterbury *". The cuffs contain three state seal buttons on the right and two on the left marked "Canfield Bro & Co Bal".

CHARLES HOWARD JR. WEARING THE ILLUSTRATED FROCK COAT in soft gray with no branch color. Howard (1836/) lived in Baltimore and was one of four brothers who served in the C.S.A. He enlisted on May 22, 1861, in Company D, 1st Maryland Infantry, as a private. Charles was discharged on October 26, 1861, and served in the quartermaster department of the 4th Brigade. After being joined by his wife and children he served under General J.H. Winder in Richmond. On May 8, 1862, he was promoted to major in the commissary department under General Arnold Elzey in the defense of Richmond. Relieved as chief commissary of troops on August 16, 1864, Howard served as quartermaster of General Lomax's Cavalry from September 10, 1864, until the conclusion of the war. The double-breasted frock coat is deep brown wool with a standup collar and has gold gilt on each side of the lower sleeve, two rows of 13 state seal buttons marked "extra quality" and 5 small state seal cuff buttons also marked "extra quality."

BLOOD-STAINED, HOME-SPUN FROCK COAT of Charles Grogan that is now butternut brown in color and trimmed in blue. When it was given to the Maryland Line Confederate Soldiers Home it was cataloged as "Spun, woven and made in Jefferson County, Virginia. Stained with blood of the wearer Lt. Charles Grogan, aide-de-camp to General Trimble at Chancellorsville and torn by a shell at Gettysburg."

OFFICER'S DOUBLE-BREASTED SHELL JACKET on James Thomas Bussey (1838/) which he wore when sent to Richmond to offer Bradley T. Johnson command of the 2nd Maryland Infantry. Bussey was reared in Cecil County and at the outbreak of war was in Baltimore. He enlisted and was elected a lieutenant in the Winan's Guard in April of 1861. He ran the blockade, and on September 11, 1862, joined the 2nd Maryland Infantry and was chosen 2nd lieutenant in Company D. On January 27, 1864, Bussey was elected captain of Company H. He was wounded in the left hip at Weldon Railroad on August 19, and was sent to General Hospital No. 4, and then to No. 7, both in Richmond. After recuperating, he returned to his company and surrendered on April 9, 1865. He was released on parole on April 19 and returned to his home in Baltimore. Bussey was a member of the Society of the Army and Navy of the Confederate States in the State of Maryland.

ELLIOTT JOHNSTON WEARING THE ILLUSTRATED SHELL JACKET with Maryland buttons and a two-piece buckle. A native of Baltimore, Johnston resigned from the United States Navy after seven years of service to follow the Southern banner. In December of 1861 he served as a volunteer aide to General R.B. Garrett and was commissioned lieutenant as his aide-de-camp on June 30, 1862. At Sharpsburg, Johnston was severely wounded and had a leg amputated. By August of 1863 he had recovered enough to serve on the staff of General R. Ewell. On November 19, 1863, Johnston was promoted to captain and assistant adjutant general of Stafford's Brigade. By September of 1864 he was unfit for field duty and served in General Preston's Conscript Bureau. He applied for a four-month furlough on January 1, 1865, to to go Europe to get another artificial leg. Johnston wore this blue-gray wool, single-breasted captain's jacket. The donation card stated that this jacket was worn during 28 battles and skirmishes. It has a round, standing collar of cream-colored ribbed cotton, which is also found on the lower sleeves. It is decorated with two rows of gold metallic braid. There are three surviving buttons, one federal and two Maryland seal marked "Scovill MFG Co * Waterbury *" and three small cuff buttons with the state seal and marked "Extra Quality." The military vest is of matching color and has nine state seal cuff buttons marked "Extra quality."

DRESS FROCK COAT of Elliott Johnston is made of medium color gray wool. It is double-breasted, has a rounded standing collar and cuffs trimmed in buff wool flannel and contains two rows of gold gilt braid. It bears 18 large Maryland state seal buttons on the front, 6 small buttons on the cuffs and 6 large state seal buttons on the tails.

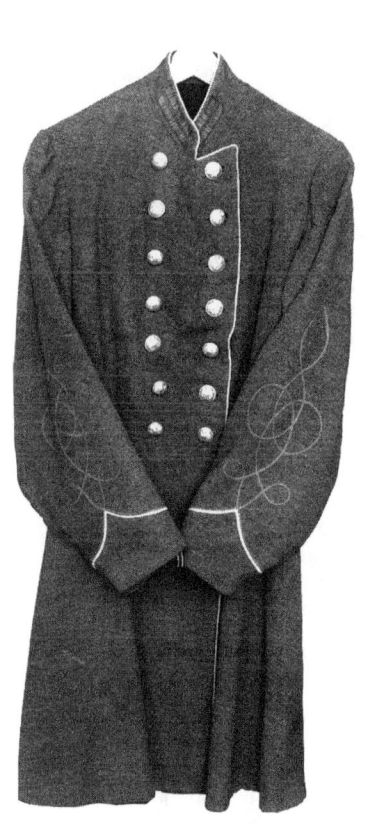

JUNIOR OFFICER'S FROCK COAT belonging to McHenry Howard made of woolen, weft-faced, cotton wrapped twill fabric in medium gray color. It is piped in buff with thin gold bullion galloons on the sleeve and collar. The collar also contains two gold bars signifying a 1st lieutenant. The body lining is black while the sleeve lining is a light-weight white cotton. There are pockets in the rear skirt which are accessible externally and show his wallet and Confederate money that was sent to him by his father. The coat bears U.S. staff buttons.

FIRST LIEUTENANT'S UNIFORM AND KEPI of George W. Howard. This light-gray frock coat was made from six pieces of material, called French tailoring, and contains the single black braid of a lieutenant on the sleeves and standing collar. The 14 front double-breasted buttons are state seal and marked "Canfield Bro & Company Bal" with three small cuff buttons from the same maker. This uniform is either late war of demonstrates his inability to afford a better one. His lieutenant's dress kepi is wool and has one row of gold bullion trim. It is accented in dark blue wool with a patent leather viser and chin strap. George was a member of his native Howard County Dragoons. A 1st lieutenant of Company K, 1st Virginia Cavalry, he resigned in July, 1861. After helping organize Company C, 1st Maryland Cavalry, Howard was elected 1st lieutenant on August 4, 1862, and then promoted to captain on August 25, 1863. He was hospitalized at General Hospital No. 4 at Richmond for just over a month, returning to duty on April 12, 1864. Howard was taken prisoner at Pollard's Farm on May 27 and confined at Point Lookout and later Fort Delaware. Exchanged on December 3, 1864, he returned to his company and was paroled on April 30 at Manchester, Virginia.

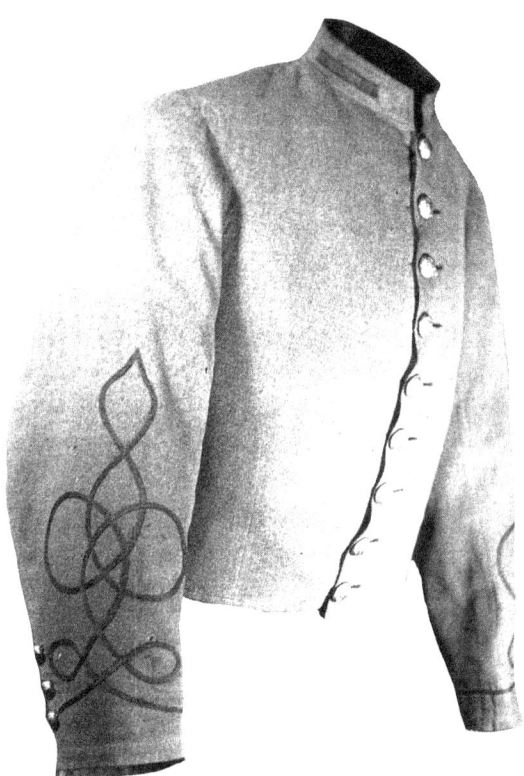

SECOND LIEUTENANT'S SHELL JACKET, in a soft mouse-gray wool broadcloth, of Andrew Cross Trippe (1839/1918). It is single-breasted with nine large Maryland buttons "Extra Quality" and three state seal cuff buttons "Canfield Bro & Company Bal." It is fully lined in a quilted type material with sleeves of polished cotton. It contains an inside pocket in the left breast and a patch pocket was added to the inside of the right breast. This coat was altered after he was wounded at Gettysburg because the left arm is shorter than the right. After receiving his informal education in Baltimore, his place of birth, Trippe was graduated from Lafayette College in Easton, Pennsylvania, in 1857. Three years later he was admitted to the bar in Baltimore where he began to practice. He went south in the fall of 1861. With the organization of the 2nd Maryland Infantry, he became a private in the ranks of Company A. He was wounded in the left shoulder on Culp's Hill at Gettysburg. Trippe remained near the battlefield convalescing in a small cottage with Colonel Herbert and Major Goldsborough. On October 6 he was sent to the West Buildings Hospital in Baltimore. Upon being exchanged he reported to the Maryland Line then being formed and on December 3, 1863, was commissioned 2nd lieutenant and ordnance officer ranking from November 28. In the fall of 1864, Trippe was sent to Danville, Virginia, on ordnance duty. His surrender was consummated at Burkittsville on May 12, 1865, and he returned to Baltimore. Continuing his law practice he was active in politics and served on the city council from 1869-1871. He was a member of the Society of the Army and Navy. In 1894 he was on the board of governors of the Association of Maryland Line and in 1896 he was one of the founders of the Franklin Buchanan Camp of Confederate Veterans. In 1900 he was commander of the Isaac R. Trimble Camp, chairman of the State Commission that erected the Confederate Woman's Memorial in Baltimore and in 1910, General Trippe was elected commander of the Maryland Division Confederate Veterans of the State. In a military capacity he was also colonel on the staffs of Generals McLane and Lloyd.

By 1862, C.S. Navy regulations prescribed colors of gray or steel gray, but white jumpers were worn in warm weather. Actually, any shade of gray was acceptable, and up until this time, Confederate naval officers often wore the blue of the old Navy, with the new Confederate system of rank insignias on the full-sleeve style cuff. The insignias included encircled cuff braids with top or bottom loops, to shoulder strap devices and a cap device with braid. In addition to the frock coats, officers were permitted to wear jackets of gray or white linen which were cut off at the waist line. Vests were also of gray wool or white linen.

Seamen were issued gray cloth jackets and trousers. Frock jumpers were to be of gray wool with white duck cuffs, and collars lined with blue cotton cloth. Thick gray caps without visors, or black hats and neckerchiefs were worn with white clothing, although straw hats were very common. Most seaman's clothes were made of goods that were manufactured in the South. There were many complaints about the quality of Southern material and workmanship. Seaman John Thomas Gatelry, desperately in need of shoes, bitterly wrote about the canvas shoes issued to him at Mobile. George Pielert wrote extensively about his war experiences. He began writing upon leaving Catonsville for Richmond on August 15, 1860, until May 7, 1875, when he was returning home, filling six diaries. He worked in the Tredagar Iron Works and served in the Tredagar Cannon Works Artillery Company. In addition, he served in the 3rd Virginia Artillery, 2nd Maryland Infantry and the navy. He ran the blockade to his home and was captured on February 5, 1863, and exchanged at City Point on March 18. Pielert re-enlisted in the navy seven days later in submarine service in the James River Squadron aboard the iron tug tender C.S.S. Torpedo. His diary illustrates the severe lack of supplies. --March 25, 1863, "Today I enlisted in the navy service and sent aboard the Torpedo."

--April 8, 1863, "I drew a pair of shoes and a coarse cotton shirt."

--May 2, 1863, "Today I drew a pair of pants and a shirt."

--June 6, 1863, "... went to the Ship Richmond to draw clothes and money. I drew 30 Dr NO CLOTHING."

--July 1, 1863, "This morning we drew clothes and small stores from the "Richmond". I drew 2 pairs of duck pants, two Froks, one over shirt, one pair of shoes and 20 Dr in money."

--December 22, 1863, "... rated me 2nd class fireman and provided a blacksmith shop with 75 Dr a month."

--December 23, 1863, "Today I went up to the steamer Richmond and drew Forty dollars, 2 pair of drawers, 2 under shirts, 1 pair of shoes, one pair of pants and one coat."

--January 6, 1864, "I had my daguerrotype taken 8 Dr."

NAVAL ENLISTED MAN'S UNIFORM on George Pielert (1840/1928). In this rare naval photo he is wearing a gray color tarpaulin hat, gray double-breasted jacket with long, wide lapels, 12 large brass buttons and four small cuff buttons on each of the slashed sleeves. He is wearing a white blouse with a silk neckerchief and belt over the gray trousers. Born in Germany, he emigrated to Catonsville with his parents. On June 2, 1861, he enlisted in the Washington Artillery composed of employees of the Tredagar Iron Works which became the 3rd Virginia Artillery. On June 18, 1862, he was transferred to the 2nd Maryland Artillery and was captured in Baltimore on February 5, 1863. Exchanged from Fort Delaware he joined the navy on March 25, 1863. After the evacuation of Richmond, Pielert went to Greensboro where he surrendered. He worked as a farrier in Baltimore County and, on November 6, 1916, he entered the Maryland Line Confederate Soldiers Home.

NAVAL PETTY OFFICER'S UNIFORM. It is steel gray with large cuffs and sleeve buttons. The naval hat has a gold braid cap device of laurel leaves with an E centered above it. They are pictured on Eugene H. Browne (1837/) who entered the Southern Army on April 19, 1861, in the 16th Virginia Infantry, Company C, and soon became corporal. His skills being needed at the Tredegar Iron Works he was called to work on the Merrimac at the Norfolk Naval Yard. On March 24, 1862, he was commissioned a 3rd Assistant Engineer in the navy. Sent to Memphis, he was assigned to the ironclad steamer, Arkansas. He later served aboard the cruiser, C.S.S. Florida, as 2nd Assistant Engineer and in May of 1863 was aboard the captured ship, Clarance. The guns and crew of 22 transferred to the captured Tacony and, on June 24, he again changed his ship to the schooner, Archer, another captured vessel. Taken by the Federal Navy off the Portland, Maine, coastline he was not exchanged until October of 1864. His next assignment was the C.S.S. Chickamauga until it sank off North Carolina. He was next assigned to Drewry's Bluff for a month and then aboard the ironclad Richmond in the James River Squadron. After the evacuation of Richmond, Browne joined Semmes' Naval Brigade and was paroled at Greensboro on May 1, 1865. He proceeded to Portsmouth where he resided for a year until returning to Baltimore. Engineeer Browne became a member of Camp No. 747, Franklin Buchanan United Confederate Veterans.

NAVAL PAYMASTER'S UNIFORM in steel gray with a single sleeve stripe and naval buckle worn by Douglas French Forrest (1837/1902) - Forrest was born and raised in Baltimore. In 1851 the family moved outside Alexandria and three years later he entered Yale College. After attending law school at the University of Virginia he was just admitted to the bar when he joined the 17th Virginia Infantry, Company H, on April 17, 1861. He was soon elected a 2nd lieutenant and served for one year. At the conclusion of his term of enlistment he was a volunteer aide on the staff of General Isaac R. Trimble as a quartermaster. With the wounding of General Trimble he became a volunteer aide to Admiral Franklin Buchanan. Desiring service in the navy, he received a position on March 15, 1862, through the influence of his father, French Forrest, in the Provisional Navy as an assistant quartermaster and was stationed aboard the C.S.S. Virginia. Going to the Wilmington Naval Station, Forrest was next assigned to the C.S.S. Arctic for nearly a year and then the Richmond Naval Station. As paymaster, he sailed to England on May 27, 1863, and next served aboard the C.S.S. Rappahannock. He was in Havana when he learned of Appomattox and slipped into Galveston on May 31, 1865 and was paroled on June 26 in Galveston. After an unsuccessful attempt to move to Mexico, Douglas became an attorney in Baltimore. In 1873 he was awarded the degree of Bachelor of Divinity and became a minister of the Gospel for the Episcopal Church in Ellicott City. He was a member of the Society of the Army and Navy of the Confederate States in the State of Maryland

NAVAL SECOND LIEUTENANT'S DRESS UNIFORM.
This full picture shows the complete uniform of Henry H. Marmaduke. It is a double-breasted, open collared steel gray naval uniform which has a shoulder strap bearing one star and a large looped cuff insignia. Henry Hungerford Marmaduke (1842/) entered the Naval Acadmey on September 21, 1858, and resigned on April 24, 1861, as a 2nd class cadet. On May 8 he entered the Southern navy as an acting midshipman. After serving in torpedo service and aboard the C.S.S. Chicora, he was promoted to 2nd lieutenant in the summer of 1863 and sent to Europe on special duty. In 1864, Marmaduke returned to the U.S. along with another Marylander, Midshipman Henry H. Tyson, but was not assigned to a vessel. After the evacuation of the Charleston Naval Station, Marmaduke was assigned to the big gun batteries at Dreury's Bluff. He was captured at Saylor's Creek while commanding a company in the Naval Brigade, and was released from Johnson's Island on June 20, 1865.

NAVAL SENIOR OFFICER'S DOUBLE-BREASTED FROCK COAT. It is a cadet gray, English manufactured, open collared coat pictured on Joseph Nicholas Barney (1818/1899). It has a shoulder device with two stars and cuff insignia of two gold braids that encircle the cuff with a single small loop at the top. Barney was born in Baltimore and was appointed a midshipman from Maryland in the Navy on June 30, 1835. Resigning in June of 1861 while on a Mediterranean cruise, he proceeded to Richmond and received a commission of 1st lieutenant. He was given command of the C.S.S. Jamestown on July 4. This two-gun converted river boat participated in the naval battle at Hampton Roads during March 8-9, 1862. He also engaged the enemy off Drewry's Bluff. During that summer the Jamestown's guns were placed in a battery on shore and she was sunk to form an obstruction just off the bluff. In December, Barney was ordered to Mobile to relieve Captain Morfitt in command of the Florida, but the order was revoked and he was sent to Texas instead to command the cutter Harriet Lane. That vessel, however, was found unsuitable as a cruiser and he returned to Richmond. Lieutenant Commander Barney was sent on special duty to Europe and after a few months was again ordered to relieve Captain Morfitt, whose health was broken. He never took the Florida to sea due to illness forcing him to relinquish command on January 4, 1864. Commander Barney returned to his country on Séptember 29, 1865, and took the oath of allegiance. He was listed as a member of the Society of the Army and Navy of the Confederate States in the State of Maryland but he resided in Powhatan County, Virginia, until 1874 when he moved to Fredericksburg.

TAILOR-MADE NAVAL DOUBLE-BREASTED FROCK COAT of Admiral Franklin Buchanan. In steel gray, its rolling collar can be buttoned up or turned back. The shoulder straps contain four 5-pointed stars. There are two rows of 18 double-breasted buttons which bear the Maryland state seal and are marked "Scovill MFG Co * Waterbury *". There are four Virginia cuff buttons and the cuffs are slashed so they could be opened or closed. There are five 1/2" wide gold braid stripes on the sleeves. It is lined with gray-brown sateen.

Marine Corps uniforms were also gray. Enlisted mens' dress consisted of gray cloth jackets, blue pants and gray flannel shirts. For summer wear, fatigue white cottonade pantaloons and white tunic blouses were issued. Their caps were also of the French kepi pattern. In 1861 the Marine complement aboard the C.S.S. Sumter wore fatigue suits that cost $9.70, and a dress uniform at $11.50. Toward the end of the war, Captain James Waddell, on the C.S.S. Shenandoah, provided captured infantry pants for Marine wear. The infrequency of proper pay at the Mobile Marine Barracks caused Captain J.E. Meiere to write to Commandant Beall on December 1, 1862 "for pay to be sent for my men are entirely out of money, in consequence of which they sell their clothes and report them stolen." This remained a problem, and on December 7, 1863, Corps Quartermaster A.S. Taylor wrote a general order that Marine clothing "found in the possession of any person not in the corps will be seized and such person, if belonging to any military organization, will be reported to his commanding officer." Again, on November 5, 1864, Colonel Beall issued a general order calling for strict economy in the use of clothing.

Uniform regulations for Marine officers required four types of dress: a dress uniform, an undress uniform, and two fatigue uniforms, one of gray and one of white. Rank insignia was shoulder knots of double gold cord, and braided sleeves. There were, however, variations in the corps. Paymaster Richard T. Allison's war memorabilia, left to his family, consisted of two 5-pointed plain gold stars which were collar insignias. Vests could be of steel gray or white. During the second quarter of 1864, 1st Lieutenant James R.Y. Fendall, at Mobile, received 10 yards of gray flannel cloth for a uniform for $3.56 a yard. At the Marine barracks in Savannah, material could not be had. Second Lieutenant Thomas St. George Pratt, son of ex-governor Thomas George Pratt, wrote to a friend on April 24, 1864, "Could you not draw a pair of Grey pants and dark jacket and let me have them."

MARINE GRAY KEPI AND DOUBLE-BREASTED FROCK COAT. This coat of James Cambell Murdoch has a medium standing collar and two rows of 14 buttons which widen over the chest. It is decorated with a pair of gold-colored lace shoulder knots which were regulation for marines and gold sleeve braid which was not.

Overcoats for enlisted men were of the union army pattern except the color was to be cadet gray. Free Staters who made their way into the Confederacy during the spring, summer or fall would not have had an overcoat because the few personal bags of clothes did not allow room for bulky items. English manufactured overcoats were much darker than the U.S. sky blue issues. These overcoats, secured by successful blockade running ships, were also of warmer material than the Federal ones. The first company of Zarvona's Maryland Zouaves received a box of 57 overcoats at Brooke Station on January 8, 1862. This was one of the largest number of overcoats which can be found in one draw for a company. In requests for an equal number of shoes and overcoats, Company A of the 1st Maryland received three overcoats and 66 pairs of shoes. Company G received five overcoats and 56 pairs of shoes.

For many, it was far easier to obtain an overcoat from one of Uncle Sam's boys. Oilcloth ponchos, which entirely concealed gray uniforms, were often used by partisan rangers. In February of 1864, Harry Gilmor selected six men donned in blue overcoats, and set off to examine the camp of the enemy near Middletown. They went into the camp of the 21st New York Cavalry without any problem. Upon returning, "They came up with four men belonging to Blazer's Scouts having on a Federal overcoat and we had no difficulty in making them believe we belonged to Torbert's Cavalry. They were on their way to vote in the presidential elections. Capturing them the band took their tickets and papers. I proceeded to camp where I voted for Lincoln and gained information requested by General Early."

The colored cabinet card of William H.H. Raleigh shows him in a flannel shirt with a pocket in the front under a shell jacket. The open cape with military buttons is not part of an overcoat. This long cape was just thrown across the shoulders. Eight inches from the center seam on both sides appears to be reinforced at the top and the bottom for the arms to come through. For additional warmth and protection, capes were many times added to overcoats. They could be permanently attached to the overcoat or detachable. D. Schacleford has on a cape with no slits for arms. It has 4 buttons on the bottom, one being just below the waist. At the top the small collar could be turned down or up.

In October of 1863, the quartermaster general listed material for overcoats along with blankets and shoes, as being the most needed articles. The 2nd Maryland Artillery received 13 overcoats that showed a cost of $13 each. There were no overcoats prescribed for officers in Confederate regulations. Two types of topcoats are found: a loosely fitted overcoat, and a tailored style made similar to, but larger than, a frock coat. Either could be made with hooks and eyes for capes under the collar.

Mason Morfit's finely-made frock coat appears to match the gray color of his well-made double-breasted overcoat. The topcoat has a long cape hanging down on the back of a chair showing the quilted innerlining. Doctor N.G. West, shown holding a kepi with an oilskin, waterproof cover, is wearing a military vest, along with a piped, single-breasted frock coat with a laid down collar. It has large coin-type buttons under a heavy knap overcoat with brass military buttons. The short cape appears to be permanently attached and is also adorned with military buttons. George Thomas' first lieutenant's uniform was worn prior to his promotion at Gettysburg. It has a dark blue overcoat, most probably British. The overcoat is single-breasted and has an outside row of two large buttons and one small top button for the long cape which could probably be removed. The detachable cape overcoats would have five to seven buttons under the collar to be used for attaching the cape.

McHenry Howard wrote that General Richard Taylor "wore a black hat and overcoat (a mounted officer who so conveniently carried his overcoat bundled up and strapped behind his saddle, wore it often even in summer for protection from chill or rain) while Gen. [Charles S.] Winder's overcoat was white or light drab, and riding just behind the two I used to think of them as the black and white generals. Gen. Winder's overcoat had nothing military about it, although he looked very soldierly in it, as in everything. Not long before the war, it had become suddenly discovered on the Eastern Shore of Maryland that the thick and strong white or light drab cloth which was bought in large quantities for the 'servants' (they were seldom called slaves there), was excellent material for overcoats and nearly every young gentlemen in Miles River Neck [Talbot County], had one made. A long cape came down to the waists."

DOUBLE-BREASTED OVERCOAT WITH CAPE worn by John Emory Scott. He enlisted as a private in Company E, 12th Virginia Infantry. After capture, he was imprisoned at Point Lookout where this photo was taken. It bears the backmark J.C. Spaulding, Army Photographer, Point Lookout, MD. After being paroled, Scott returned to his native Baltimore and graduated from the Baltimore College of Dental Surgery, becoming a dentist.

OPENED FULL BODY CAPE worn here by William H.H. Raleigh (1839/1924) - Dorchester County was the place of his birth and after his collegiate education he was in the Midwest when the difficulties of the time led him to affiliate with the Southern cause. Making his way to Richmond, he enlisted on March 20, 1862, in Captain Fry's Company. They were known as the "Orange Artillery" and he was appointed 4th sergeant. By April 1, 1863, he was a sergeant major. Raleigh received a promotion and served as adjutant until he was badly wounded during the Seven Days Battle around Richmond. He later received a commission as a 2nd lieutenant in the Engineering Corps. He was assigned to Carter's Battalion until paroled at Appomattox Courthouse on April 9, 1865. After the war he made his home in Baltimore. He was presented a cross of honor on June 3, 1923, through the Maryland Division United Daughters of the Confederacy, Baltimore Chapter No. 8.

FULL BODY CAPE with turned down collar shown here on Durand Schacleford (1848/) - On July 28, 1864, at Upperville, Durand and his cousin, Elzey D. Schacleford, enlisted in Company E, 43rd Virginia Cavalry. Durand continued to ride with Mosby's Rangers until May 8, 1865, when he was paroled.

REGULATION, DOUBLE-BREASTED OVERCOAT beside Mason Morfit (1836/1921) - Born and educated in Baltimore, he left a lucrative legal practice to go to the aid of the South. Serving from the beginning of hostilities as a private, his poor health and exposure caused him to be removed from the field. In June of 1861, he became transportation officer in Weldin, North Carolina. He also acted as an agent in October at Petersburg. Going into the Quartermaster Department, he received an appointment as captain on January 5, 1862, and on November 26, received the star of a major. Detailed to the railroad commissioner, Morfit served at Richmond and then Wilmington, North Carolina. In December of 1863 he was in charge of Federal prisoners at Danville. On October 14, 1864, he became prison quartermaster at the Military Prison Hospital, formerly General Hospital No. 9, at Salisbury, North Carolina. Morfit was paroled on May 1, 1865, at Salisbury and returned to Richmond where he took the amnesty oath on June 8. On July 1 he reported to the provost marshal at Baltimore where he was again made to swear his allegiance. The ironclad oath made it impossible for him to resume his legal practice as an attorney so he went to St. Louis, Missouri, where he passed the bar and practiced his profession. Morfit was a member of Baltimore's Franklin Buchanan United Confederate Veterans Camp but made his home at Webster Groves, Missouri.

NON-REGULATION, DARK, DOUBLE-BREASTED ENGLISH OVERCOAT worn by George Thomas (1835/1903) - He was born at Mattaphany in St. Mary's County and was one of three brothers devoted to the Southern cause. His brothers were Richard Thomas, known as Colonel Zarvona, and James William Thomas. George was educated at Charlotte Hall and the University of Virginia. Enlisting as a private in Company H, 1st Maryland Infantry, he was elected 1st lieutenant on June 18, 1861. At the conclusion of one year of service, he assisted his commander, William H. Murray, in forming Company A, 2nd Maryland Infantry, and was again elected 1st lieutenant. Thomas was appointed acting adjutant of this regiment until July 3, 1863, when he was promoted to a captain. He was severely wounded in the left thigh at Gettysburg and could not return to his company until the spring of 1864. At Pegram's Farm on September 30 he was severely wounded in the face as they advanced upon the enemy, fracturing his inferior mandible. As a result, he always wore a heavy beard to hide the scars of his facial injury. Being unfit for field service, he was detailed to the ordnance department in Richmond until paroled on April 25, 1865. He returned to the mansion at Mattaphany where he farmed and conducted a school. On October 26, 1871, the surviving members of Company A, 2nd Maryland Infantry, formed the Murray Confederate Association for the purpose of keeping alive and preserving the friendships and memories. Thomas was elected president of this United Confederate Veterans Group and in 1874 the surviving members of Company H, 1st Maryland Infantry, were admitted to the association.

OVERCOAT AND LAYERED CLOTHING of Dr. Nelson Grey West (1832/1915) - Dr. West was educated privately in Frederick County and received a medical degree from the Jefferson Medical College in Philadelphia in 1854. Forsaking his practice in his birthplace of Frederick County, he followed his convictions into the Confederacy. On February 5, 1862, he was commissioned an assistant surgeon and saw field duty with the 1st Virginia Cavalry. Upon reorganization on March 18, 1862, they became the 9th Virginia Cavalry. By that fall, Assistant Surgeon West was with the 7th Georgia Infantry and was later transferred to the 2nd Georgia Regiment. He was stationed successively at Warrenton Hospital and Lovington Hospital. On July 21, 1864, he was administering in General Hospital No. 2 at Danville where, on November 4, he was advanced to the rank of surgeon. He was assigned to the capital city in General Hospital No. 10 after a short field service with Longstreet's Corps. After receiving a valid parole he returned home immediately but was not allowed to practice his profession within his home state, so he made Leesburg, Virginia, his new home. As a prominent physician in northern Virginia he belonged to many state organizations and societies but also held membership in the Alexander Young Confederate Veterans Camp No. 55 of Frederick.

In winter weather it was essential for sailors to have warm outer garments. Lieutenant John T. Wood reveals that during the 1864 winter naval expedition in North Carolina waters, his 150 naval raiders were well clothed in pea-jackets. Franklin Buchanan's soft gray colored heavy wool overcoat is extremely thick. It is double-breasted with five South Carolina buttons marked "extra gold" with what appears to have been a lion. It is long, going below the knee, with hooks and eyes under the laid down collar for the use of a cape. There are four exterior pockets with flaps that could be worn inside or out.

NAVAL, SLATE GRAY, HEAVY WOOLEN OVERCOAT of Admiral Franklin Buchanan.

Chapter 13

WEAPONS

When hostilities arose there was a terrible lack of ability to produce weapons on the part of the South. The agricultural orientation of this section of the country meant that the South had neither the material nor the machinery for weapons production. The most accessible markets were immediately tapped for all types of arms and munitions. Arsenals and armories within the seceding states were stripped of all serviceable firearms. These were distributed to awaiting troops. Seized naval yards and forts provided some artillery, but this was just a drop in the bucket. Raphael Semmes was dispatched to New York, and then London to purchase available guns and ammunition. For a more indepth commentary on Confederate-made weapons, see Confederate Presentation and Inscribed Swords and Revolvers.

The vast European markets would slowly be closed to the South by the blockading Federal fleet. In addition, the flow of weapons through the Old Line State would gradually became a mere trickle as security and arrests became more prevalent.

There were two manufacturers of military arms in Baltimore during the war, James H. Merrill and Poultney & Trimble. Merrill manufactured .54 caliber breech loading carbines and rifles, of which the U.S. Government purchased 14,695, plus another 770 that were termed navy rifles. The American Machine Works produced Smith patent .50 caliber breech loading carbines for Poultney & Trimble, who in turn sold 30,060 to the Federal Government during the war. These firms advertised their products to the Baltimore public, but it isn't known if any of the Confederate units were able to tap this resource.

Richard Snowden Andrews, recruiter of the Maryland Flying Artillery, wrote a full description of the light, 12-pound brass Napoleon guns at the Pikesville Armory. He took these papers with him when he travelled to Richmond. These papers, after being endorsed by the Virginia chief of ordnance, were given to the Tredegar Iron Works for production under Andrew's supervision. The first two guns completed were given to the Washington Artillery of New Orleans. They had recently arrived at Richmond and were completely equipped with the exception of two guns. Next, the 1st Maryland Artillery was supplied with four Napoleons and four Parrot rifles. The Maryland Flying Artillery was invincible in the field and one of the few batteries in the Army of Northern Virginia to never lose a gun in battle. No battery saw more hard fighting or lost more men. In January of 1865 these conspicuous artificers were ordered to relinquish their four original issue brass Napoleons, in order that they could be used to bolster the defenses at Drury's Bluff as heavy artillery. When General Lee evacuated Petersburg the 1st Maryland artillerymen shouldered muskets and followed in the wake of the tattered remnant of this once proud army toward Saylor's Creek.

When the Baltimore Light Artillery was mustered into the Confederate service, subsequently becoming the 2nd Maryland Artillery, they were issued four English guns known as "bellowing, loud-mouth Blakely's." On July 13, 1863, the Baltimore Light Artillery dueled effectively with Alexander's Federal Baltimore Battery. Their precise fire drove the enemy below Kernstown resulting in their being awarded a section of the captured guns. J.E.B. Stuart lost his life at Yellow Tavern while defending the Baltimore Light Artillery. He had borrowed the battery from the Maryland Line at 2:30 a.m. on May 11, 1864. Hour after hour they created havoc among General George Armstrong Custer's ranks. Finally, with the supporting cavalry giving way, the battery was left to the mercy of the enemy. In a vain attempt, Stuart rallied his horsemen and rode forward exclaiming "Charge Virginians and save those brave Marylanders." This was Stuart's last order. The 2nd Maryland was wrecked and lost two of its four guns. Returning from the burning of Chambersburg in 1864, they were surprised at Moorefield and lost two more pieces. On October 8, 1864, the 2nd Maryland Artillery lost 23 men and four guns in the battle at Fisher's Hill. The following spring they were ordered

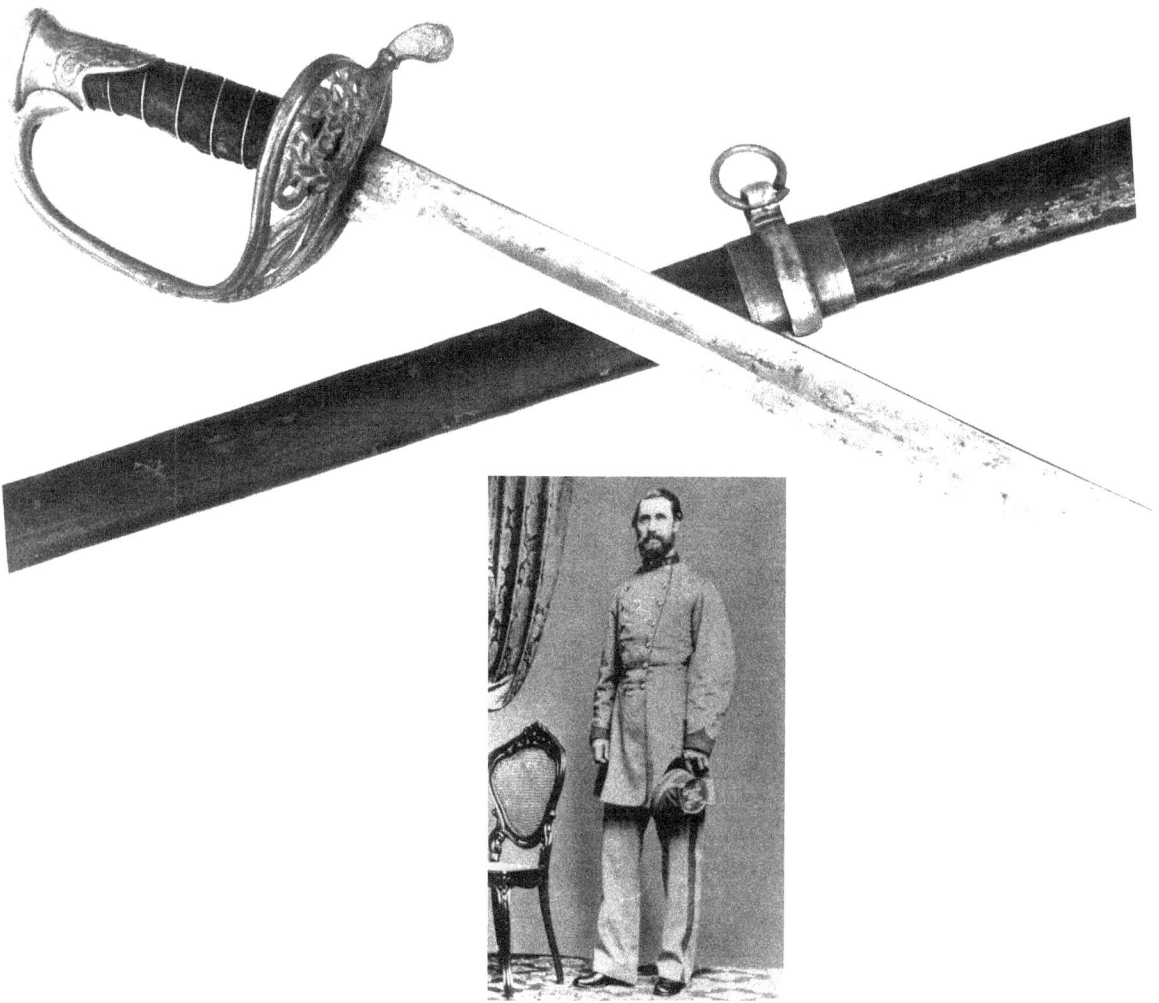

ARTILLERY OFFICER'S BOYLE & GAMBLE SWORD. This unmarked field and staff officer's sword has a brass hilt with "T.S. Rhett" engraved between the ivy leaf decoration on the mushroom-style cap. The counterguard is decoraged with a 4-petaled flower, an ear of corn with fodder, a wreath of laurel leaves with a star at the apex and a ribbon bearing "CS". The grips are leather covered with a slight center swell and wound with a single strand of brass wire. The single edged blade is almost straight with a rounded back and a single, unstopped fuller on each side. The blade is etched with decorations of leaves, berries, flags, flowing ribbons and "C.S.A." in plain, non-styled modern spurred Gothic letters. The leather scabbard is top stitched with two parallel tooled lines and brass mountings. Thomas Smith Rhett (1827/1893), born in South Carolina, was a graduate of the Military Academy, class of 1848. Commissioned a second lieutenant, he served on the frontier in the artillery until 1855, when he resigned and came to Baltimore County. By the fall of 1861, Rhett was in the Confederate capital and on November 19, was appointed a captain in artillery. On May 10, 1862, he was promoted to colonel and by July had assumed command of the Richmond defenses. Soon he was in charge of the Ordnance Bureau. In December of that year he was made chief of artillery. Major General Arnold Elzey recommended he be made a brigadier general on October 31, 1863. President Davis requested General Lee to send two artillery officers abroad to inspect and purchase guns for the South. Colonel Richard Snowden Andrews of the 1st Maryland Artillery and Rhett were chosen. They ran the blockade in January of 1864 from Wilmington to Europe by way of Nassau. They travelled the European continent, visiting foundries, arsenals, workshops and observed military actions, forwarding the results to their government. In the spring of 1865, while returning to America to report the results of their investigations, they heard of General Lee's surrender upon arriving in Cuba. The cannons they were delivering were sent back to England to be sold and the proceeds returned to those who had supplied the money. In 1866 Rhett returned to Baltimore. In 1877 he again went into active service organizing and drilling the state artillery during the Baltimore & Ohio Railroad riots.

to help man the trenches around Petersburg from which very few were left to surrender at Appomattox.

Recruited and drilled near Richmond, the 3rd Maryland Artillery was issued two 6-pound, smooth bore pieces and two 12-pound howitzers. They were ordered to Knoxville, Tennessee. That spring they acquired two 3-inch iron rifled pieces from Richmond along with 75 new recruits. Near Nashville, General John Bell Hood lost over half of his men, arms and munitions between November 20 and December 20, 1864. Thus began one of the most disastrous retreats of the war. The 3rd Maryland Battery suffered 4 killed, 8 wounded and 16 captured plus the loss of all their artillery. Many of the Marylanders were shoeless during the march to Columbia where the battery obtained an iron howitzer before continuing their march toward Mississippi. At Mobile they manned Battery D, which contained two 12-pound siege pieces, four 32-pound naval guns and one 32-pound field cannon. They continued here until November 11, 1864, whereupon they were conveyed to Meridian and surrendered with General Richard Taylor's army.

Joseph Forrest's Battery became the second company of David G. McIntosh's Artillery Battalion and was known as the Chesapeake Battery. At Camp Lee, near Richmond, they received instruction and were issued four inferior caliber smooth bore cannons. Becoming the 4th Maryland Artillery, they won distinction at Cedar Run in August of 1862, and were presented four 10-pound Parrot rifles captured from Cushing's Battery by General Early, which enabled them to discard their old smooth bores. At Gettysburg, the 4th Maryland, under Major Joseph White Latimer, opened fire at 4 p.m. and had three pieces silenced resulting in 8 killed, 8 wounded and the loss of half their horses. At Fort Gregg on April 2, 1865, the 4th Maryland showered destruction with its superb accurate fire. Upon exhausting their ammunition, Lieutenant Walter S. Chew's coat was used to pick up projectiles from the field to refire, but he lost his life before the return of his coat. Private William Culver was killed fighting with a clubbed musket when the battery was overrun by Michigan men. Only 13 gunners of the 4th Maryland Artillery reached Appomattox.

SPILLER & BURR REVOLVER. The firm of Edward N. Spiller and David J. Burr produced this revolver carried by Thomas W. Hall. It is unmarked except for serial no. 493, which is not unusual. Many pistols by Spiller and Burr did not bear their name, but there can be no doubt this is a product of the Atlanta, Georgia, factory. The barrel is octagonal, six inches in length, .36 caliber, and is rifled with five bands and grooves with a right grain twist. The small trigger is also brass and both show superior casting with no faults. The Colt-type rammer latch is on one end of the loading lever while the other end attaches to the cylinder pin that is not threaded. Thomas William Hall (1833/1901) was editor of the South Newspaper in Baltimore. He was arrested at his home on September 12, 1861. He was incarcerated at Fort McHenry as a political offender. The following day he was transferred to Fort Monroe, then to Fort LaFayette and finally to Fort Warren. Unconditionally released in November of 1862, he ran the interior blockade south. He was commissioned a captain on the staff of General John Gregg as assistant adjutant general. Late in 1864, Hall was promoted to major and assigned to special duty under the direction of the secretary of war. By direct order of President Davis, he was enroute to Louisiana when he learned of the surrender of Lee's army. He reported to President Davis at Washington, Georgia, where he was later paroled. Hall resided in Marengo County, Alabama, until the ironclad oath system in Maryland was removed in 1867. He returned to Baltimore to practice law and later served as city solicitor.

BRITISH LONDON ARMOURY REVOLVER. This Kerr Patent pistol belonged to Captain John Donnell Smith (1829/1928) of Alexander's Battalion in Lee's Baltimore Artillery. It is a six-shot, single-action revolver made in 1862 under a contract issued by the Confederate government in May of 1861.

3RD MARYLAND ARTILLERY CAISSON AND LIMBER. These relics were recovered from Big Black Water River near Edwards, Mississippi, in 1965-1966 by the U.S. Park Service. The weight of the ammunition it contained was over 3,000 pounds. Recovered with the caisson was 139 3-inch, 7 1/2-pound shells, along with a pick, a Dutch oven and a wooden canteen. At the battle around Vicksburg on May 16, 1863, the 3rd Maryland Artillery was ordered to proceed, leaving one caisson to replenish its supply and catch up with the column. While the enemy passed over the river at Bridgeport, the Southern Army, a mile and one half below, used a light pontoon bridge. After two regiments and the artillery had passed over, this caisson, overloaded with shells, came upon the bridge. The caisson broke through when the bridge gave way and carried its horses along to the bottom. That portion of the bridge was cut away and it was not until 3 o'clock in the morning on the 17th that the entire command could be passed over.

Corporal Eugene H. Browne, an early member of the 16th Virginia Infantry, preserved three flints he received for his old flintlock musket in the spring of 1861 and donated them to the relic room in the Maryland Line Confederate Soldier's Home. He stated "So many changes and improvements have been made in firearms that few of our younger generation have any idea how heavy and clumsy were the old muzzle loading muskets with which we were first armed. Many of these old weapons were originally flintlock guns and some had been changed to be exploded with a percussion cap. They had seen service in other wars before our time. They were dangerous at both ends, with a kick like a young mule. The day after a battle a commrade opened his shirt and showed me his shoulder beaten black by the pounding he got every time his gun was discharged. Mine kicked me 10 feet out of the ranks and laid me flat on my back with a broken nose and blood streaming from my mouth. They threw a round ball and three buckshot and were effective at a range of 200 yards. Every man in the regiment who was disposed to do so now cast aside his old gun and picked up a new Enfield or Springfield rifle as the ground everywhere was strewn with them."

During past wars, Maryland gunsmiths were used as armorers or articifers to repair arms. With the drastic need for weapons during this period, Dennis McCool was detailed from the 2nd Maryland Cavalry to perform this task. Amasa W. King, son of John H. King of Hagerstown, who was superintendent of Hall's Rifle Works, was appointed a captain in the Confederacy and placed in charge of producing weapons at Fayetteville Arsenal, utilizing machinery salvaged from Harpers Ferry. William Stewart Polk, an Old Navy man, was commissioned in the Confederate Engineering Corps. His first nine months were spent converting flintlock muskets to percussion. Captain Polk then became superintendent of cartridge production.

Robert Breckenridge McKim wished to join his cousin in Weston's Maryland Battalion after their formation, only to be informed that he would have to furnish his own musket since they had already been armed. Unable to accomplish this he enlisted in the Rockridge Artillery. William E. Colston, of J. Lyle Clarke's Company of Weston's men, wrote "My musket being the only one brought from Baltimore that I know of it is still an object of attention. Our company is armed with flintlocks altered to percussion." George Wilson Booth records that Captain Dorsey and Murray's companies, mustered in at Richmond, "were armed with the improved Springfield musket, well uniformed and otherwise equipped ... with bayonets - Our Grenadiers, as we term them." Actually, these two companies of Weston's men were issued model 1842 Springfield smooth bore muskets, not the 1861 rifled Springfield .58 caliber musket that was considered the new and improved. This fact was revealed by the issue of .69 caliber buck and ball ammunition.

The Harpers Ferry companies of the 1st Maryland Infantry were armed with Mississippi rifles. Mrs. Jane Claudia Johnson, wife of Bradley T. Johnson and a native North Carolinian, travelled to Raleigh and implored Governor Ellis to furnish weapons for her husband's men. The governor ordered 500 Mississippi rifles and 10,000 .54 caliber cartridges turned over to her on May 28, 1861. An invoice of the Ordnance Department shows "500 rifles made at Herkimer NY without bayonets" were issued to Mrs. Johnson. These were Model 1841 rifles manufactured by E. Remington & Sons. With the acquisition of these rifles the Frederick Volunteers were able to discard the 60 Hall carbines they had obtained during the subjugation of the John Brown conspiracy at Harpers Ferry.

With the disbandment of the 1st Maryland Infantry and the formation of the 2nd, it is believed that the Marylanders retained Mrs. Johnson's Mississippi's since the new battalion was still drawing .54 caliber ammunition. For a number of months they were still referred to as the 1st Maryland. On April 20, 1863, Company C received 4 saddles, 15 sabers and an additional 5 Mississippi rifles plus 1,000 Mississippi, 600 army and 600 navy cartridges.

INSCRIBED BRITISH TOWER MUSKET. This musket is dated 1862 and is engraved on the trigger bow "Richard H. Shepard, 2nd Maryland Infantry Co D C.S.A." Shepard, from Anne Arundel County, enlisted at Richmond on August 29, 1862, and served in all his regiment's campaigns except for 18 days during the summer of 1864 when he was in Chimborazo Hospital. He was paroled at Appomattox on April 10, 1865, and was one of only four men present from Company D. The entire regiment could only muster 63 men.

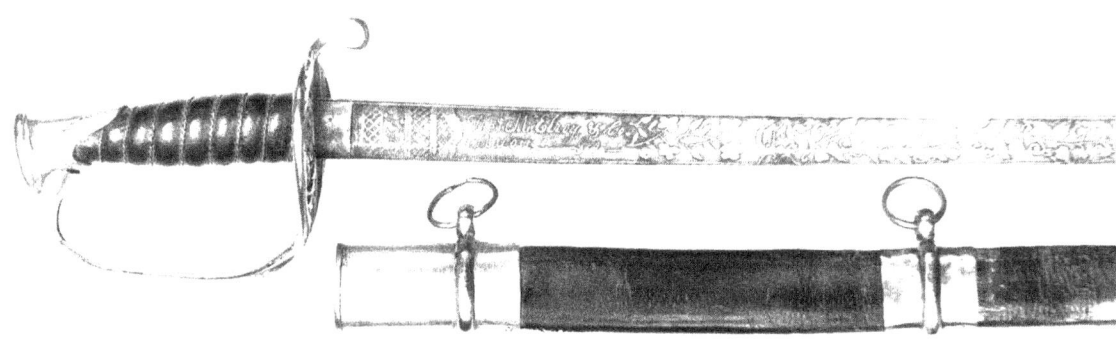

INSCRIBED WILLIAM J. McELROY INFANTRY OFFICER'S SWORD. This brass-hilted sword has a rose pattern design, pierced counterguard that has superb relief flowers, leaves and scrolls. The knuckle bow originates one-quarter inch from the posterior inferior position of the rounded pommel. It is slotted for a knot and has two lines on each side which flow into the outer edges of the counterguard. The reverse cone grip is covered with thick leather wound with twisted copper that slants from the back toward the front and returns into the grip on the obverse side at the junction of the guard. The single fuller, stopped, square-backed, slightly curved blade is etched by one of the three etchers of the firm. The firm's name is incorporated in the design of the blade and the old German lettering, "C.S." The obverse is etched with lattice, "W. J. M.cElroy & Co. Macon Geo", stems, flowers with four petals, "C.S.", stem of plain leaves and leaves with veins. The reverse bears cross hatching, vine, drums, two national flags, "D. McDonald", stem with acorn and small leaves. The soft, flexible, brown leather scabbard is backstitched with two wide parallel lines. The throat of plate stock is in the top of the first, nickel-silvered, sheet stock mount and the reverse is scratched, "Co B 56 NC Vol". Daniel M. McDonald (1837/1891) enlisted in April, 1861, as a corporal in Company F, 11th North Carolina Infantry. After serving two six-month terms and being promoted to sergeant, he joined the Cape Fear Guards as a 2nd lieutenant on July 2, 1862. This unit subsequently became Company B, 56th North Carolina Infantry. McDonald was captured on May 22, 1863, at Gum Swamp near Kinston and imprisoned at Fort Delaware until exchanged on February 24, 1865. Suffering from acute rheumatism, he was admitted to Stuart's Hospital in Richmond and took the oath on May 25, 1865. His father and Dr. Tilghman Biser went down and removed him to their farm in Frederick County. The doctor had two sons who served in the Army of the West, Captain Charles Tilghman Biser and Lieutenant William Doddridge Biser, who was killed at Pines Bluff, Arkansas.

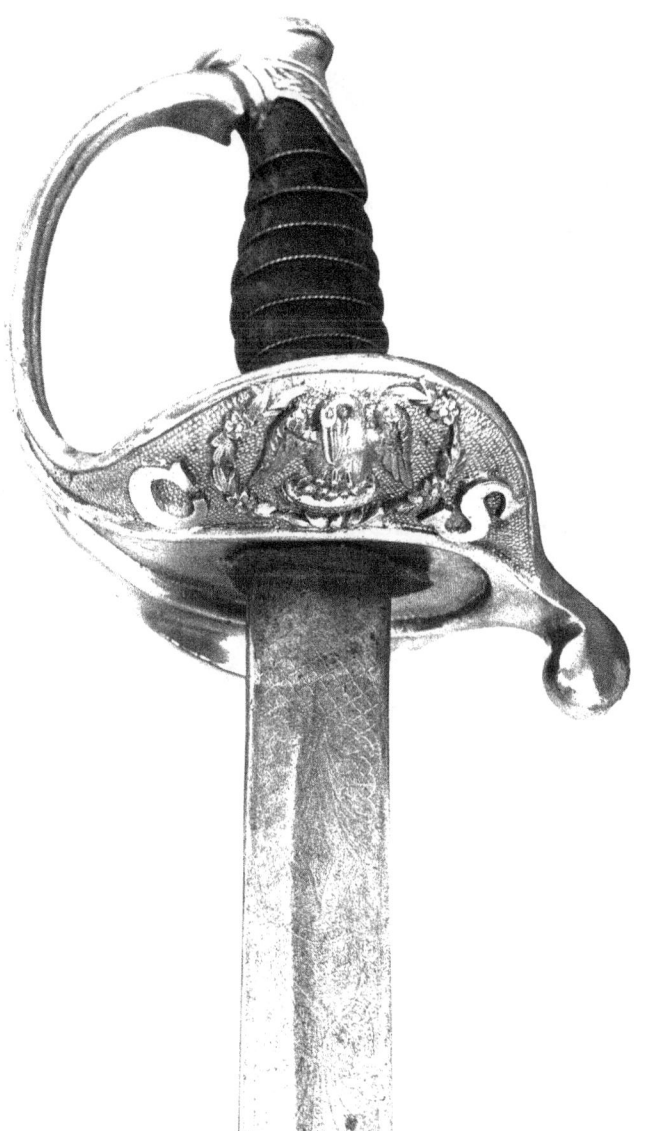
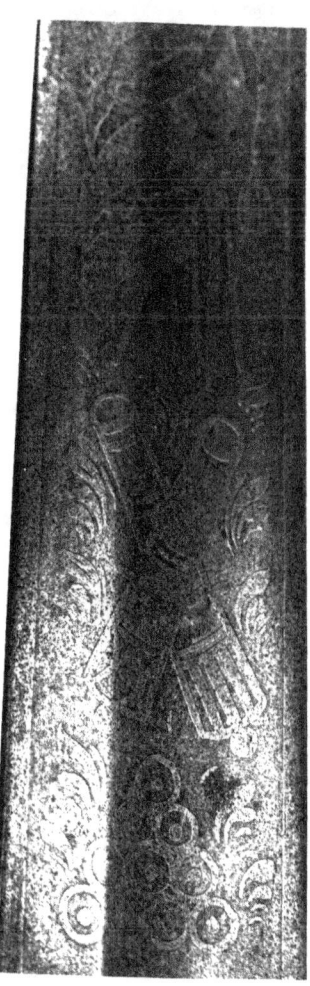

PRESENTATION A.H. DUFILHO INFANTRY OFFICER'S SWORD. This solid brass counterguard has high relief letters "C.S." separated by a laurel wreath with petaled flowers and a pelican with a closed beak on the nest feeding her young, which is also in high relief. This sword by Dufilho of New Orleans contains two letters that are smooth but the entire background of the device has punch marks. The front edge of the pommel is decorated with laurel leaves that are curved back to form a blank center and the top has a two-step build up. The grips are of leather with a swell in the center, wound with delicate thread-like brass, twisted wire which returns into the back of the grips. The straight blade, with a single unstopped fuller and a square back, is finely etched with ornamental, vaulting, interlacing lines of superb tracery and, the etcher's name, "Zimmerman" is marked on the back of the blade with a chisel. The obverse is superiorly etched with hatch marks, a diamond-shaped design going into the plumage, cannon balls, cannon, stand of flags, ivy leaf-type decoration with a ribbon, "C.S." in Old English and more elaborate leaf work. The reverse is in a completely different pattern of stylized leaf and scrolls and reads from the foible to the forte on the broken blade, (Present is broken off) "ed by Jefferson Fire Guards to Captain G. Geiger of the Confederate States of America March 24, 1862", in Old English letters and more ornate scrolls and leaves. George Geiger (1818/) was born in Hesse, Germany, Coming to America, he migrated from Baltimore to New Windsor, in Carroll County, then on to New Orleans. In the fall of 1861, 24 fire companies organized the Fire Battalion of the Louisiana Militia. Geiger was elected commander of Company C, a zouave unit known as the Jefferson Fire Guard. New Orleans was evacuated on April 25, 1862, and the Fire Battalion probably dissolved in the general collapse of the militia. In 1866, he closed the doors of his masonry and coffee business and returned to Carroll County.

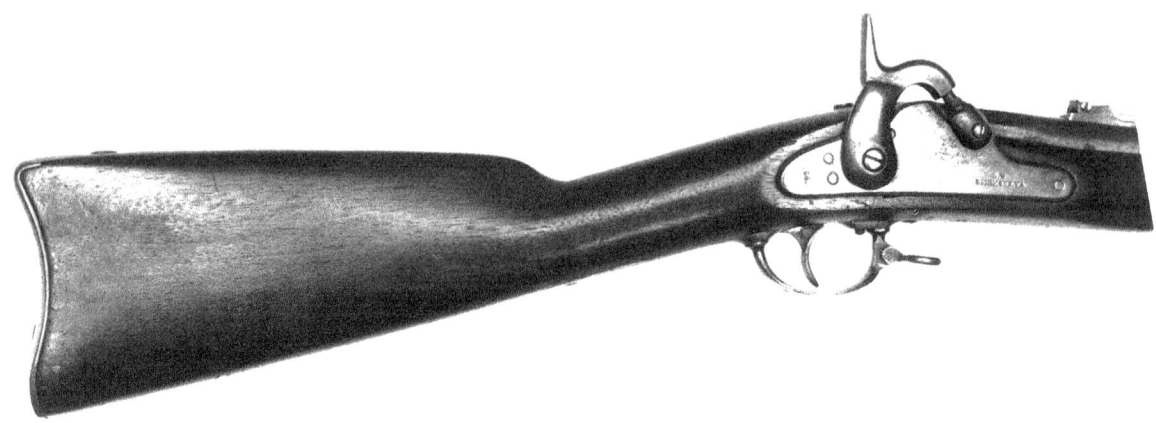

1862 RICHMOND INFANTRY MUSKET. It was carried by Charles F. Hitzelberger. The musket is dated on the lock and has a brass butt plate and brass nose cap. The remainder of the furniture is iron. Charles Francis Hitzelberger (1829/1899) was born in Baltimore and resided in Libertytown. Leaving with Bradley T. Johnson on May 8, 1861, he enlisted in the 1st Maryland Infantry, Company A. At the end of his 12-month enlistment he was discharged and went to see his uncle who had a sugar plantation in Louisiana where he met his wife. His father was a sugar merchant in Baltimore and was supplied by his brother in Louisiana. Charles obtained a transfer for his cousin, Stephen V. Hitzelberger, from the Richmond Howitzers to the Maryland Line. In April of 1864, they both joined Barry's Maryland Volunteers under Elias Griswold, provost marshal of Richmond. After the war he returned to Libertytown.

Company A, 1st Maryland Cavalry, was apparently armed with Sharps carbines. An ordnance department report shows them in receipt of 400 Sharps carbine cartridges, 400 Sharps carbine caps, 100 Colt army pistol cartridges, 100 Colt navy cartridges, and 300 pistol caps. Theophalius Tunis, of Company B, 1st Maryland Cavalry, wrote "We found our own cavalry horses, our Colt revolvers made in Hartford, Connecticut, and our Chicopee sabers made in the town by that name in Massachusetts, and were paid for by Maryland money shipped to Cuba, then to Nassau and on to Wilmington in a blockade runner. These were received during their 1-month training at Charlottesville which afterward made them full-fledged troopers." Captain George Emack's sister wrote that he received his commission as a lieutenant in the Confederate service and had secured his uniform and other equipment in Baltimore before safely going to Virginia. His sword came too late, so she smuggled it south for him. "The Howard County Dragoons brought with them their militia arms from the state of Maryland which were the best cavalry sabers and Colt revolvers."

Confederate cavalry sabers received the most punishment of all swords. Although the guards containing the letters C.S.A. were most desirable many times a Yankee saber was more suited. John Gill, of the 1st Company, 2nd Virginia Cavalry which would later become the 1st Maryland, wrote "In his first mounted action they were ordered to draw sabers and charged against the 6th Michigan. The two regiments locked sabers as dust and confusion became so great it was hard to distinguish friend from foe. His saber of Confederate iron was bent and quite useless as he engaged three Yankees. Kindly aid was received from Trooper Rawling W. Nelson, who cut down two of his opponents. The third Gill made a right cut with his bent saber which missed and nearly unhorsed him. Gathering his thoughts in a brief moment his pistol was drawn and bellowed at a Michigan officer and yelled surrender or die. He is now well mounted with a Yankee horse, a Yankee saddle, a Yankee saber and Yankee boots." On September 17, 1863, Nicholas W. Owings, Gilmor's Battalion quartermaster, received and issued to Company A, 11 Mississippi .54 caliber rifles, 15 Enfield .58 caliber rifles, 5 .69 caliber muskatoons, 500 Mississippi rifle cartridges, 560 Enfield rifle cartridges, 2,000 musket cartridges, 1,000 shotgun, 600 Colt army .44, 600 Colt navy .33, and 1,000 sporting caps. On October 15, Company C received 90 Mississippi .54 caliber rifles, 2,100 Mississippi

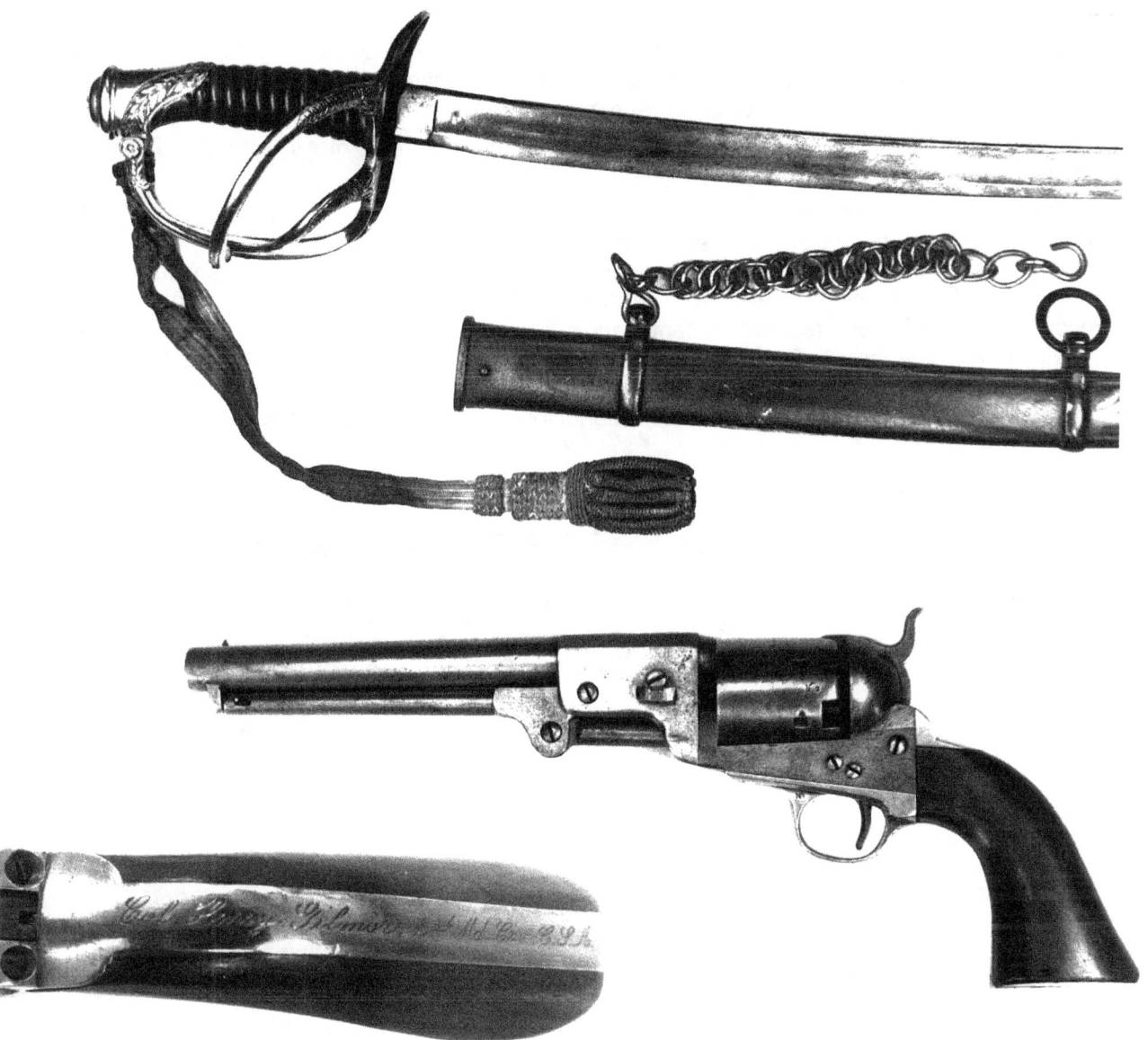

INSCRIBED LEECH & RIGDON REVOLVER AND FRENCH CAVALRY SABER. Lt. Col. Harry W. Gilmor, commander of the 2nd Maryland Cavalry, carried this revolver and sword. The revolver, produced by Leech and Rigdon, is often referred to as the original Confederate Colt. The top of the rifled barrel has seven bands, seven grooves going to the left and is stamped, "Leech & Rigdon C.S.A." The brass backstrap is engraved "Col. Harry Gilmor, 2nd Md. Cav., C.S.A." This officer's French light cavalry saber has a brass hilt with two branches joining the knuckle guard. Both sides of both branches, the back top of the counterguard, the forward edge of the pommel and front of the hilt are ornamented in floral relief. The front of the pommel cap is engraved with a five pointed star and on the back side of the knuckle bow is engraved, "Harry Gilmor". The grip is polished wood. This French cavalry officer's sword was the pattern of the U.S. 1840 model and Confederate sabers. The iron scabbard is painted black and the top ring has been replaced with a brass horse chin strap that hooks in the pierced knuckle bow of the sword hilt.

cartridges, 1,000 Enfield rifle cartridges, 600 Colt army cartridges, 500 sporting caps, 3 ammunition boxes, 60 rounds Gallagier carbine cartridges, 100 rounds Sharp's carbine cartridges, 228 rounds Colt army, 72 rounds Colt navy, 200 musket caps and 200 sporting caps.

Ordnance reports reveal that Davis' Maryland Cavalry were armed mostly with Sharp's carbines and Colt army and navy revolvers.

Cavalrymen were indifferently armed, many with long muskets which were terribly unwieldly on horseback. Some civilian weapons were altered to a uniform length with their barrels bored out and, on occasion, rifled to the regulation Confederate caliber of .577, but the enemy's weapons were most desired. The favored personal weapons of Confederate cavalrymen and officers were revolvers. Many early enlisted men in infantry and artillery regiments went to war with personal pistols on their belts. After March of 1862 the ordnance states "infantrymen should carry only muskets as weapons and the artillerymen to rely solely on their field guns. Pistols and revolvers were to be turned in to be purchased by the government, be reconditioned and reissued to mounted commands."

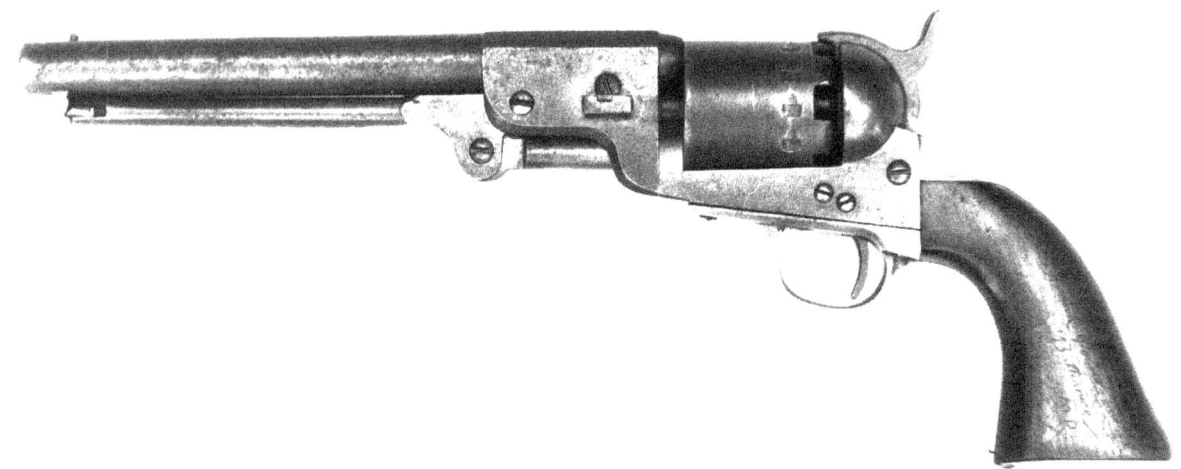

PERSONALLY INSCRIBED RIGDON & ANSLEY REVOLVER. This piece followed very similarly the Leech and Rigdons. Under the serial number is stamped with the same small die, but the brass trigger guard and brass backstrap along with this serial number have an "O" below. There is also a "W" on the obverse side of the trigger guard. The top flat of the barrel is stamped only "CSA". The cylinder has 12 stops. The Colt-style loading lever latch was adopted. The one-piece, finished walnut grips also have this number penciled in the backstrap channel. The obverse side of the grips is carved "Frank Severe Baltimore Md". Francis M. Severe (1841/) was raised in Talbot County. Running the blockade, he joined Company I, 12th Alabama of Northern Virginia, and after an enlistment of 12 months, he joined the C.S. Navy for a year. In July of 1863 he re-enlisted in an independent unit of partisan rangers composed of men who were born under the black and gold flag. Severe rode in Company A, 2nd Maryland Cavalry, until the tattered battle flag was furled forever, and then made his home in Baltimore. After he retired as a seaman he entered the Maryland Line Confederate Soldiers Home in Pikesville on July 6, 1909. There he joined his brother, John O. Severe, who had been in Company I, 59th Virginia Infantry, and who had been a sail maker until entering the home in 1890.

BRASS HILTED LANYARD KNIFE. This five inch, cast brass grip and guard has an encircling ring at the pommel, an oval, a thong for a lanyard strap and the tang is square but not riveted. Under the front of the guard is found "1XX". The heavy, single-edged blade is 11-1/2 inches in length with a long ricasso and could have been made by a factory or a blacksmith who had some knowledge of casting. The blade was roughly forged, then flat ground; it was probably set in a mold with the brass being poured around which keyed in the tang. It was carried by James J. Williamson of Company A, 43rd Virginia Cavalry.

INSCRIBED CAPTURED WILHELM CLAUBERG AND COMPANY SWORD. This brass-hilted, infantry officer's sword which is gilded. The leather-bodied scabbard has gilded brass mounts, the upper mount being stamped on the reverse, "Ames Mfg Co. Chicopee Mass", while the obverse is engraved, "Captured at Battle of Winchester from 1st Lieutenant 5th Rhode Island Battery by John C. Carroll 1st Maryland Cav C.S.A." Under the red washer between the blade and the hilt is scratched, "1st Lt Thortin Charles", from whom he captured the sword. John C. Carroll of Baltimore crossed the Potomac on September 5, 1862, with three other Baltimoreans, joining Utterback's Dragoons. On July 24, 1863, he transferred to Company F, 1st Maryland Cavalry. Carroll deserted to go home for Christmas and was captured in Baltimore on Christmas Day in 1864. He had been back in his state during the Gettysburg Campaign and the Baltimore-Washington Raid.

WILLIAM GLAZE & COMPANY ENLISTED MAN'S CAVALRY SABER. It was made seven to eight years prior to the rebellion for use by South Carolina militia. The half basket-type guard is made of brass. Under the leather washer on the obverse side of the convex oval where the tang inserts into the hilt is stamped "P.F.C.K." The cone shaped wood grips are wrapped with light cord which is covered with leather and wrapped with twisted brass wire. The curved flat-backed blade has a single edge with a rudimentary false edge and two fullers. The reverse side of the ricasso is stamped "Columbia S.C." The scabbard is entirely made of iron and this palmetto armory sword was carried by Frank Louis Hering. He was a private in Company D, 1st Maryland Cavalry, and probably obtained this sword from a South Carolina trooper while riding with Gilmor's Band.

182 - Weapons

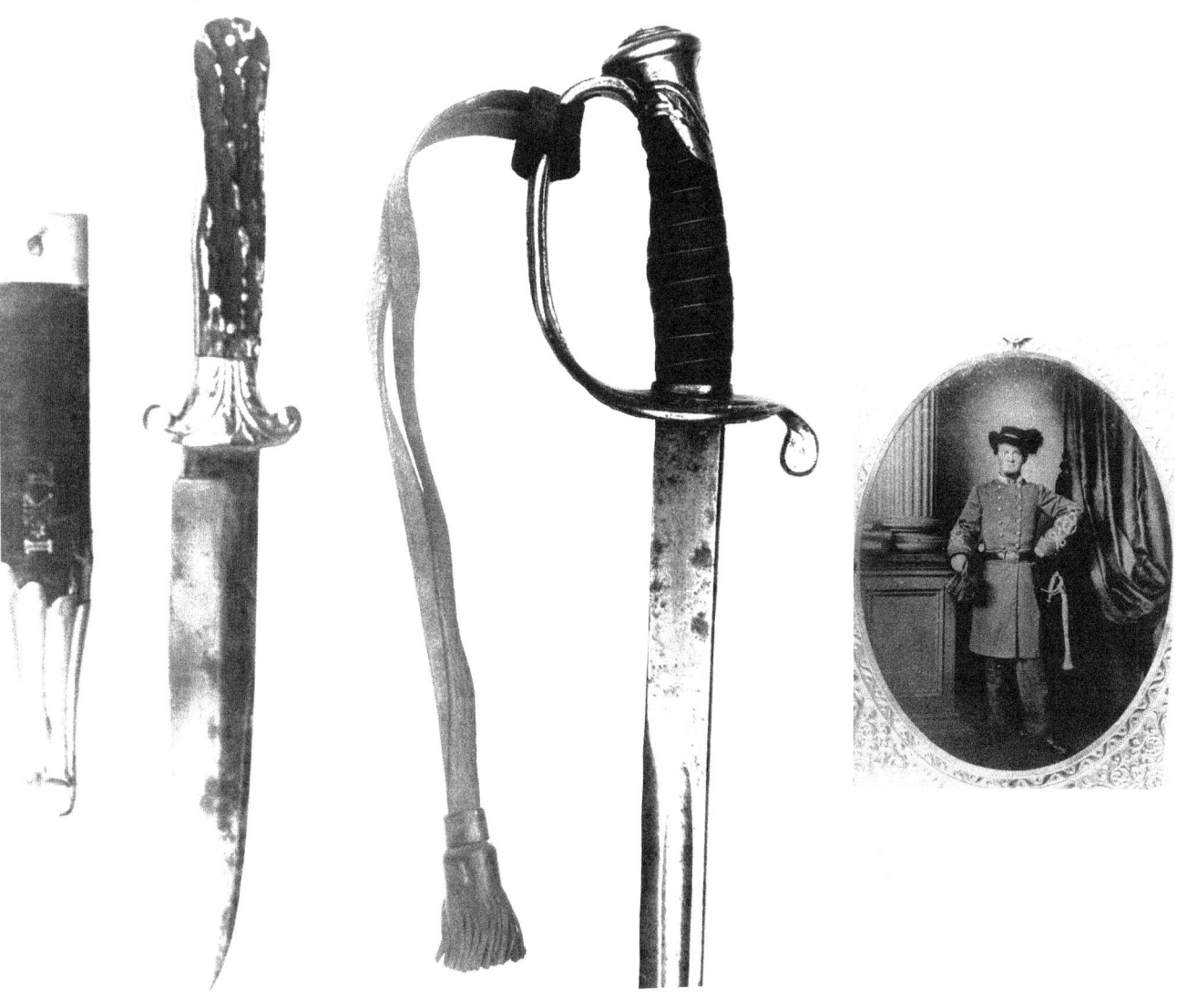

ENGLISH DIRK AND BOYLE & GAMBLE OFFICER'S SWORD. This stag-handled, single-edged, spear-shaped side knife has a silver escutcheon plate and is trimmed in German silver that was moulded. The reverse ricasso of the knife is engraved, "I* XL", and is stamped opposite the true edge, "G. Wostenholm and Son Washington Works Sheffield", in three lines. The leather sheath, with two tooled lines, bears the same Roman numerals which are stamped upside down on the obverse side and is also decorated with German silver. This Boyle & Gamble sword has a pommel ornamented with laurel leaves on the forward edges and a flower in the center. The brass counterguard is pierced and bears flowers, leaves and scrolls. The single-edged blade has a single unstopped fuller on each side and a very, very long ricasso area. William Independence Rasin (1841/1916) was born at Still Pond in Kent County and, at the age of 15, moved to St. Louis. Rasin entered the struggle early in Price's army without formal enlistment and served until after the battle of Lexington. He returned to his native county and found the state shackled under Federal control. On February 1, 1862, he was arrested, court-martialed as a spy and sentenced to Fort Warren for the duration of the war. Notice was given him on April 23 to be ready to go the next day to his permanent imprisonment. At 9 p.m. that night, three other Maryland captives assisted in his escape from the Old Capitol Prison. He crossed the Potomac under disguise in a fishing schooner but in King George County he was pursued by a squad of Union soldiers. Hurrying to the Rappahannock, an avarice ferryman saw his plight and demanded $100 in gold for his services. Rasin offered him $20 in gold; as the cavalry approached he drew out his pistol and the ferryman was compelled to push out into the stream as random shots were exchanged. At the opposite side he dismissed the ferryman with the gift of $20. Proceeding to Richmond, he raised Winder's cavalry who were assigned to the 1st Maryland Cavalry as Company E on January 20, 1863. Captain Rasin was slightly wounded in the shoulder at Greenland Gap. At Winchester he was seriously wounded and taken a prisoner but was recaptured by the Southern army three days later. His command did not surrender at Appomattox, but was disbanded on April 28, 1865, and they were paroled as individuals. He was engaged in the mercantile business in Virginia for a few months, then moved to Baltimore. After eight years he returned to his homestead in Kent County, but after three years was again in Baltimore with the Internal Revenue.

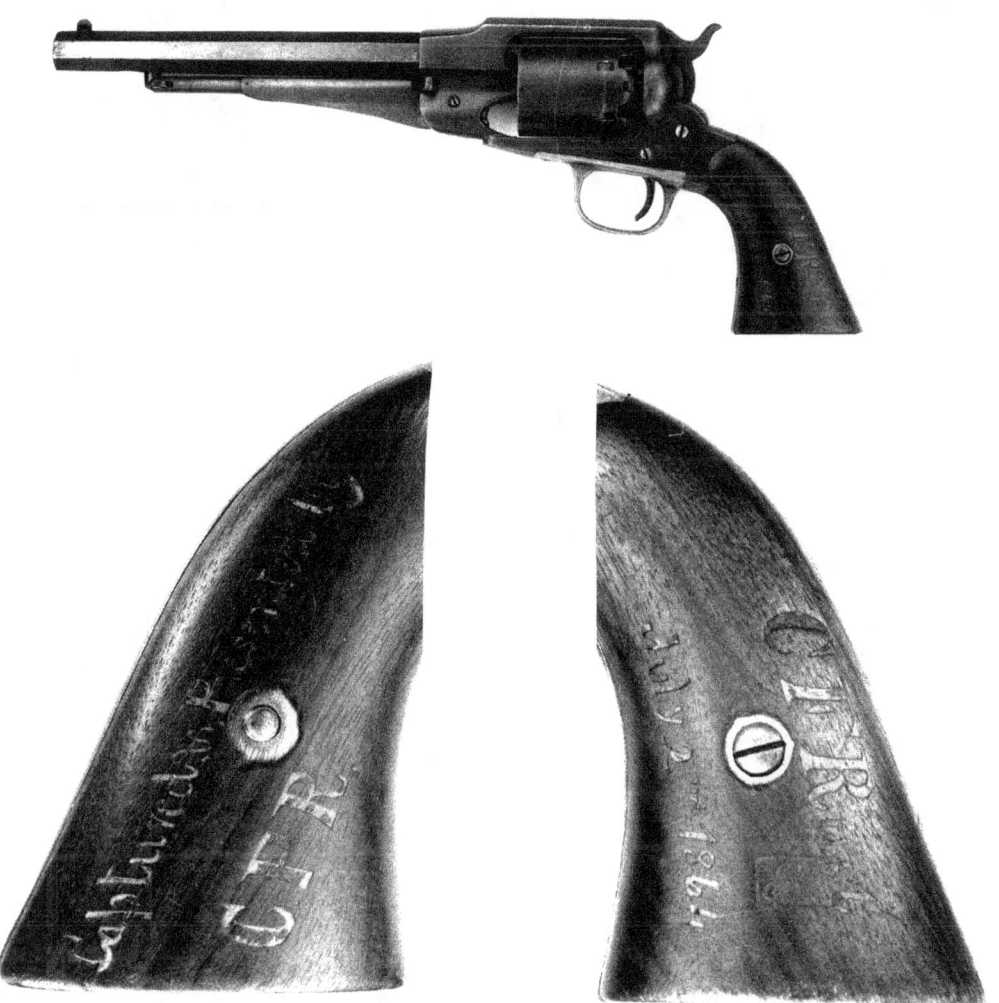

CAPTURED AND INSCRIBED REMINGTON REVOLVER. This New Model revolver has the right grip carved "C.F. Rust July 2, 1864." The documentation states that it was captured by Charles P. Rust from a Northern Delaware soldier about 18 years of age and was presented to his brother C.F. Rust. Charles P. Rust lived on the eastern shore of Maryland and enlisted on June 27, 1861, at Mathian Point for one year in Beale's Cavalry Company of Lee's Legion. In January of 1862, the battalion became Company H, 9th Virginia Cavalry. Charles re-enlisted again as a private for two more years; in June of 1862 he was detailed to General Stonewall Jackson's headquarters as a courier. Returning to his company in the fall, he served until mustered out in August of 1864. Discharges in the Southern army were only given because of expired enlistment or physical disabilities, but Charles obtained a discharge because he was not a resident of a seceded state.

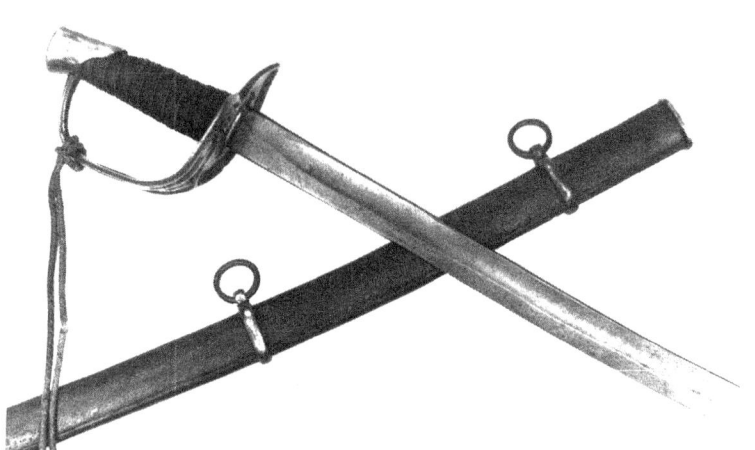

DOCUMENTED CAVALRY SABER ATTRIBUTED TO LOUIS FROELICH. This unmarked, brass-hilted, cavalry saber was made at Froelich's sword factory in Kenansville, North Carolina. The pommel cap is made of plate brass and it is knob-like and plain. The knuckle bow comes out of the reverse lower side where it apparently forms a T-connection; it goes into two branches forming a half basket. The branches are rounded and they are heavy; they appear to be perhaps of sheet brass but they definitely are not. The reverse side of the counterguard is just as broad as is the obverse side and it comes to a definite tapering point. Just ahead of where the branch terminates on the obverse side is chiseled "XVIII". The grips are leather with a seam in the back. They are wound with iron wire which returns into the grip on the obverse side and they are slanting from the front towards the knuckle bow. The blade is unstopped with a modified rounded back and it is curved. The iron scabbard body is made from sheet iron that was formed by being wrapped around a standard core with the edges lapped and then soldered. The bottom portion is slightly separated. This firm then coated their scabbards with red lacquer which is still evident on this piece. Charles E. Grogan (1841/1922) was born in Clarke County, Virginia, and was a clerk in Baltimore prior to the war. Crossing the Potomac, he mustered in H Company, 1st Maryland Infantry, on July 20, 1861, as a private for 12 months. After the expiration of his service, he became an aide to General Isaac Ridgeway Trimble and he received his first wound at Chancellorsville when the staff remained mounted during the battle. At Gettysburg, he was twice wounded and was left in Seminary Hospital. After several weeks he was taken to Fort McHenry and, later, to Johnson's Island. He was one of only three officers to escape from the prison on Lake Erie during the war. Returning to his home on Monument Street, he then spent a few pleasant days in Howard County where he purchased a young mare and, being joined by some local new recruits, again entered the Confederacy. Meeting John Singleton Mosby, he served as a volunteer and was frequently entrusted to lead small detachments. On March 28, 1864, at Paris, Company D of the 43rd Virginia Cavalry was organized and Grogan was chosen 2nd lieutenant. Mosby's Partisans contained an amazing number of Marylanders. He was among the rangers that went to Winchester on April 22, 1865, to accept the terms of surrender. By 1867 he was back in Baltimore as a commerce merchant until the mid 1880s when he went from grocery to fertilizer. By the 1890s he was the bailiff in the City Court in the Baltimore City Courthouse.

DOCUMENTED CONFEDERATE CAVALRY SABER. By an unknown maker, this large, brass-hilted saber, carried by Warner Griffith Welsh, captain of Company D, 1st Maryland Cavalry, has a plain mushroom-style pommel that is made from heavy plate stock. The reverse side is flat and bears the number "7" while the bottom is open for the attachment of the knuckle bow which is in a T-beam shape. The half basket has two branches on the obverse side and a small one on the reverse. The quillon is almost straight, terminating in a disk that is almost pear-shaped. The grips are in the shape of a reverse cone, leather-covered, with a seam in the back, wound with heavy iron wire that terminates at the back of the grips a quarter-inch above the hilt. The broad, curved, square-backed blade has a single unstopped fuller on each side. Fissure lines can be seen two inches from the hilt where the iron of the tang and the steel of the blade were forged together. The iron-bodied scabbard was made of heavy sheet or plate stock. It was made by wrapping around a standard core, hammered into place, the edges being lapped. It was then soldered with a tin-lead type material.

Most of E.V. White's first company of the 35th Virginia Cavalry, nicknamed the Comanches, were riding with double barreled shotguns and civilian saddles. After the capture of the U.S. 1st Maryland Cavalry on May 23, 1862, they were able to secure sabers, revolvers, bridles, halters, saddles and blankets. General R. Ewell furnished the Comanches with Merrill carbines. The main breechloading carbine made in the South was the Richmond Sharps manufactured by C.S. Robbins. The main problem was obtaining ammunition of the proper caliber. As the southerners picked up Federal carbines there was a variety of calibers and special cartridges required for these breechloaders that the Confederacy had a problem providing. Colonel Elijah V. White was issued Richmond Sharps carbines. General Rosser tells the amusing story that an overdue ordnance report caused an officer to come to his headquarters and ask Colonel White about the 340 guns that were issued to his command. White's men refused to carry these carbines. Col. White's adjutant jokingly replied that these were "drotted Richmond carbines and they like to have killed all the men in the West Virginia Raid. The ordnance officer wrote that 260 burst in western Virginia."

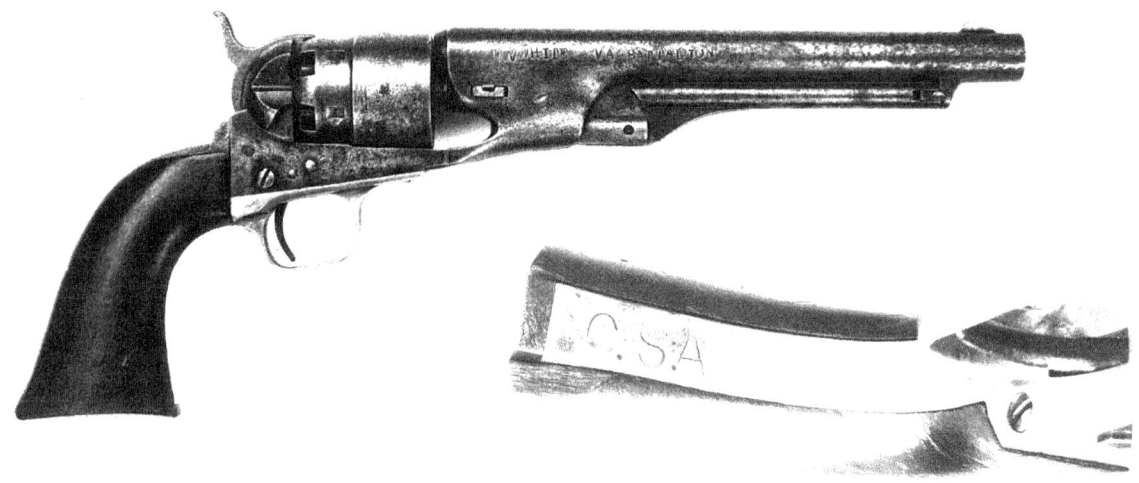

INSCRIBED 1860 COLT REVOLVER. This 4-screw Army revolver has stamped on the obverse side of the round barrel "E.V. WHITE VA. BATTALION". The right side of the frame and the brass trigger strap are stamped "C.S.A." The left side of the muzzle of Elijah Veirs White's pistol is split for about one inch and the pistol had to be put aside. After being a trooper in Company G, 7th Virginia Cavalry, he organized a battalion of partisan rangers known as the "Comanches," and were designated the 35th Virginia Cavalry.

There were many types of sharpshooters during the war. Some were strictly the best shots in the regiment, and these dozen men were sent forward early in a skirmish. Others were the best shots in a company that were called upon when a single shot was needed, while still others formed a special unit equipped with long firing guns. Sharpshooters created havoc by picking off the enemy with long range shots. Samuel D. Buck recorded "I took an Enfield rifle from my orderly sergeant and started in the direction of the fire coming out to the right of our lines some distance and immediately in front of a sharpshooter who was picking off our men at long range, five to six hundred yards. He was behind the hill in a plowed field. Selecting a big tree I opened fire on him. My first shot fell short so I raised my sight to three hundred yards, this shot fell short about fifty yards so I put her up to four hundred yards and saw at once I had his range. In the mean time, he saw smoke from my gun and returned the fire promptly. I was determined to kill him and he seemed to have a similar thought in mind about me. For a full half hour we shot at each other, he dodged my shots by falling behind the brow of the hill while at the smoke of his gun I would step behind the tree and his ball would whiz by me or strike squarely into the tree. He had an elegant shooting gun and could have struck me easily but for the protection of the tree and I could have killed him could I have kept him from dodging behind the hill. In the midst of this duel Charlie Seevers, who was with me at the time of the bridge burning, came up to my left. He had come up to see the 'fun' and see where I was. As soon as he saw me he asked if he could have a 'crack' at the fellow. Consenting and telling him to get a tree first, he asked me what I was holding my range at. 'Four hundred yards.' He laid his rifle on the fence and fired and my enemy fell either killed or wounded. The poor fellow was watching the smoke from my gun but was not prepared for Severs."

The diary of James William Thomas, on April 9, 1862, states "On this morning amid the Yankee force across the river, on a white horse, was seen an officer, evidently one of rank. Col. Johnson turned to Willmington Blakiston (known by his favorite expression as By Ganna) and asked him if he could pick the officer off. By Ganna turned to several of us and asked how much we thought the distance. All agreed at about one mile. His Enfield rifle sight was gauged at 1,700 yards. Putting it to its full and aiming high he pulled the trigger and the officer fell."

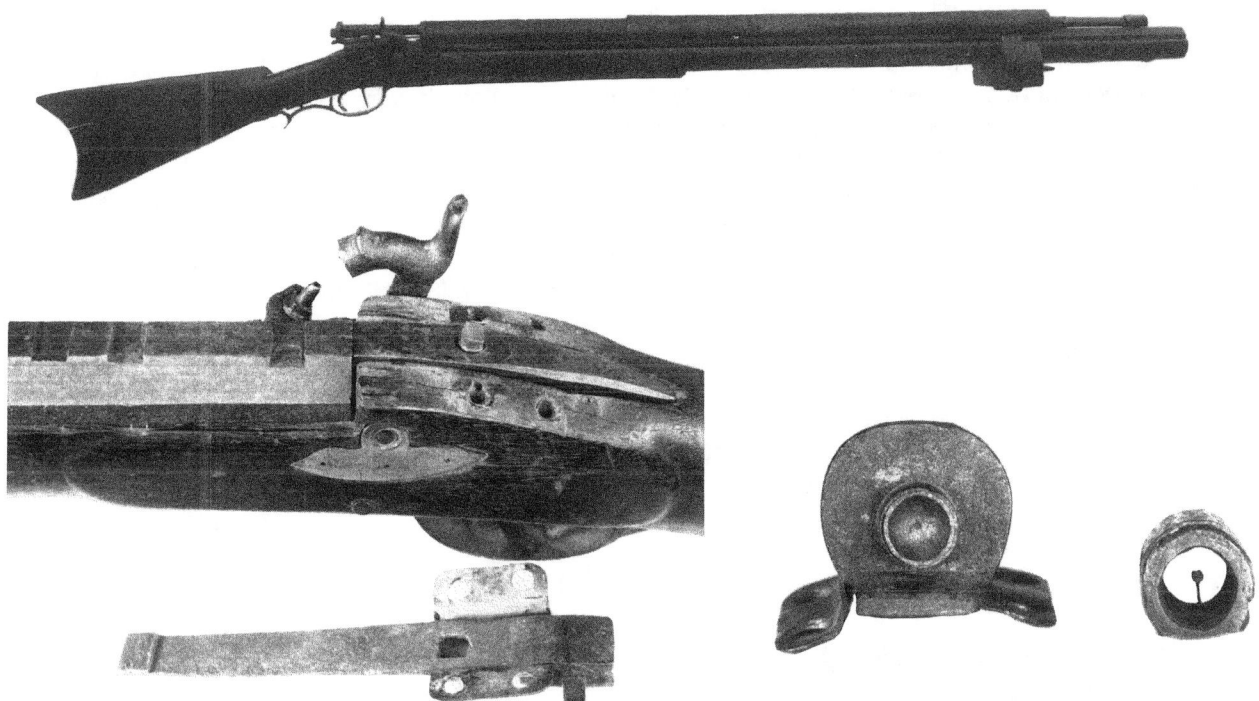

SHARPSHOOTER'S KENTUCKY-STYLE LONGRIFLE. This unmarked Kentucky-style rifle, used to pick off Yankee officers, is .52 caliber, has an octagonal rifled barrel, the butt plate was removed and the comb of the wooden stock was made higher for long range shooting. The stock fore end near the muzzle cap, originally rounded, was planed flat for use as a rest. Attached behind this area is a wooden block with embedded prongs, and appears to be a device to help steady the rifle. The barrel was further enhanced with a long sun shade and later a tube was added. The tang screw head is square to stabilize the rear sight. There are three grooves in the top facet of the barrel for three sight placements for varying distances. The rear sight is a peep sight with a small hole, and the front sight has a fine, narrow post surrounded by a brass housing. It was carried by George W. Dodd (1845/) of Marston. He served in Company H, 2nd Virginia Infantry, Local Defense Troops. In the fall of 1864, he was detailed to the C.S. government shoe depot for a short period, then returned to the line as a sharpshooter. That winter, he was in the Receiving and Wayside Hospital, and later in Chimbarazo Hospital. After the war, he returned to Carroll County.

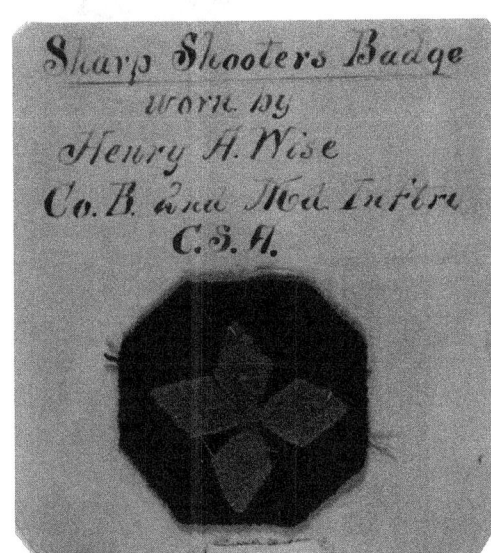

SHARPSHOOTER'S BADGE. This is on the original card from the Maryland Line Confederate Soldier's Home. It was worn by Henry A. Wise of Company B, 2nd Maryland Infantry. It has a blue woolen background cut from a piece of broad cloth. The unfamiliar design of the insignia is made of red, tightly woven wool. He and his brother, Charles B. Wise of Great Mills in St. Mary's County, both enlisted on August 27, 1862. His brother was made a lieutenant and Henry served as a private. He was wounded and captured at Gettysburg and sent to Point Lookout Prison. He was exhcanged on March 17, 1864, and returned to his company. Henry was again captured at Petersburg on April 2, 1865, and was again sent to Point Lookout until being released on August 5.

188 - Weapons

The most popular Confederate naval sword was made in England exclusively for the Southern trade. It was of superior quality with Confederate devices, dolphin head pommel and a counterguard of flowers, tobacco leaves, cotton leaves, stems and bolls. The blade was nicely etched with various southern motifs and was retailed by Philip and Samuel Firmin in London or imported by Courtney & Tennent of Charleston with slight variations. Midshipman Lodge Colton carried one which bears the name Courtney & Tennent of Charleston while Midshipman James Morris Morgan's bears the name Firmin & Sons. Franklin Buchanan had two 1852 model naval swords. The one used in Confederate service was altered on the ribbon and had the raised letters U.S.A. completely ground down and then engraved in script C.S.N. Due to the scarcity of weapons and the desire for adornment, some old service weapons were altered to reflect the C.S.A. of the south. General John Henry Winder was presented an 1850 staff officer's sword which had the "U" in the guard altered to a "C" which then read C.S. It was rehilted on a Boyle & Gamble blade and is etched with crossed flags, one bearing the Maryland state seal and the other the Confederate St. Andrew's emblem. Thomas Sappington Davis stated "I did not mind using the Yankee product because my interpretation is that the U.S. stood for United South."

CAPTAIN FRENCH FORREST CRADLING THIS ENGLISH NAVAL SWORD. This superb sword has a gold-plated hilt. The dolphin's head comprises the entire pommel and the convex backstrap runs down the top of the large white-beaded sharkskin grips that are round with triple strands of bronze colored wire. The knuckle bow originates from the mouth of the mammal, is D-guard in shape, which is a Firmin characteristic, rectangularly pierced and flows into a solid counterguard of relief tobacco leaves, cotton leaves, flowers, cotton bolls and a Confederate naval coat-of-arms, which again Firmin varies. The straight, rounded back blade has a stopped, single fuller on each side and is etched on the reverse ricasso, "Firmin and Sons 153 Strand and 13 Conduit St., London". The flag bears a St. Andrews cross in the canton as well as what appears to be three bars in the field. The leather on the scabbard is brown in color, but appears to originally have been darker. The long tip is also gracefully sculptured, line decorated with a drag formed by two twisted snakes going in reverse directions.

French Forrest (1796/1866), of St. Mary's County, was appointed a midshipman in the old navy on June 19, 1811. His older brother was also in this branch of service but was killed during the War of 1812. On March 5, 1817, French became a lieutenant, February 9, 1837, commander and captain on March 30, 1844. Like the majority of Maryland military men, he resigned his commission on April 19, 1861, after the first blood of the war was shed in the streets of Baltimore. His marriage to Emily Semmes, sister of Raphael Semmes, produced a son Douglas French Forrest, who was a paymaster in the Southern navy. French Forrest was not officially appointed until June 10 and then it was from the state of Louisiana. Captain Forrest was commander of the Norfolk Naval Yard until 1862, when he became chief of the Bureau of Ordnance and Detail. In the summer of 1863, he became commander of the James River Squadron until the final stages of the war when he joined Johnston's Army. He was paroled at Greensboro on April 28, 1865; by June 19 he took the amnesty oath at Richmond and settled in Georgetown, near the District of Columbia.

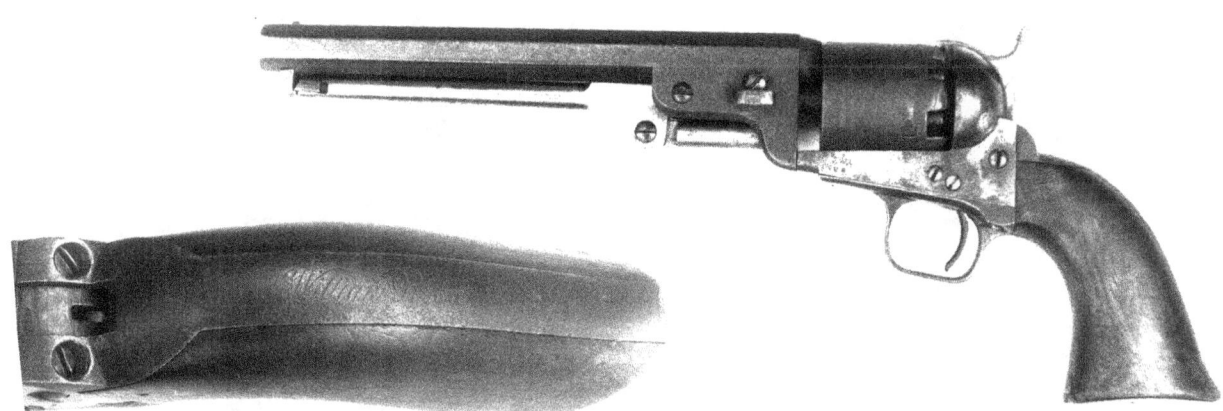

INSCRIBED 1851 COLT REVOLVER. This is a navy single action, six-shot, .36 caliber pistol. The six-sided barrel is marked on the top "Address Sam'l Colt New York City". The trigger guard is iron and the iron back strap is engraved in script "William Ryan." William R. Ryan of Baltimore joined Zarvona's Maryland Zouaves and participated in the capture of the St. Nicholas in the Chesapeake Bay. On June 15, 1861, he officially mustered in Walter's 1st Company Zarvona's Zouaves in the Provincial Army of Virginia as a corporal. With the capture of Colonel Richard Thomas this unit became Company H, 47th Virginia Infantry. They were then transferred to the 2nd Arkansas Battalion until discharged on June 15, 1862. On July 22 he re-enlisted in Company A, 3rd Virginia Cavalry, as a private. Upon the withdrawal of the Southern forces, he was captured on July 5, 1863, in his native state at Williamsport and incarcerated at Fort Delaware and Point Lookout. He took the oath of allegiance there on April 27, 1865.

ADAMS-BEAUMONT MODEL NAVAL BRITISH ADAMS REVOLVER. This five-shot, .36 caliber, double-action pistol from London Armoury belonged to Seaman George H. Pielert. This revolver was issued to him on August 8, 1863. Thirteen sailors were sent from Drewry's Bluff to Alberdin Creek to stand sentry duty on April 10-11 armed with revolvers and saber bayonets. The cylinder is stamped with the serial number ending with a B which stands for Beaumont, although the name Adams-Beaumont is no longer visible. The pistol has been abused, as the frame is cracked and a nipple is missing.

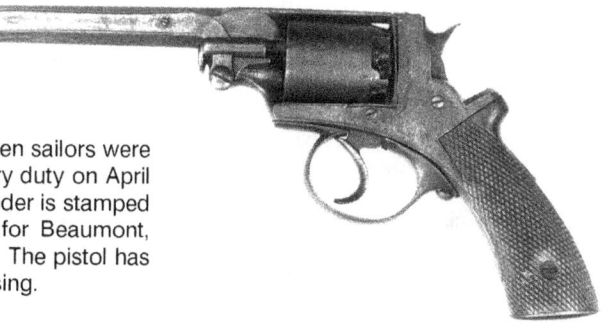

PRESENTATION ENGLISH NAVAL SWORD. This exquisite sword was given to Raphael Semmes by his English colleagues of the United Service and Junior United Service naval clubs. The superb ornate silver grip is decorated with gold and jewels in beautiful enamel work of the flag of the Southland and the flag of Great Britain entwined with "Peace and Fellowship." The silver motif work of flowers and anchors leads to the pommel of cannon balls with several missing. An exotic silver angel warrior forms the backstrap. The elegant silver guard is the main sail of a ship's rigging and is not pierced. The reverse counterguard is hinged. The gorgeous blade has an undistinguishable maker's touch mark in gold in the center of a six-pointed star. In the center of the finely etched scroll work is the following inscription "Presented to Captain Raphael Semmes C.S.N. by officers of the Royal Navy and other friends in England as a testimonial of their admiration of the gallantry with which he maintained the honor of the country's flag and the fame of the Alabama in the engagement off Cherbourg, with a chainplated ship of superior power, ornament, and crew June 19 1864" in plain, non-styled, modern spurred Gothic. The incredible scabbard is also of silver, adorned in high relief with cannon and a goddess and is still cased in the original mahogany box lined in blue velvet.

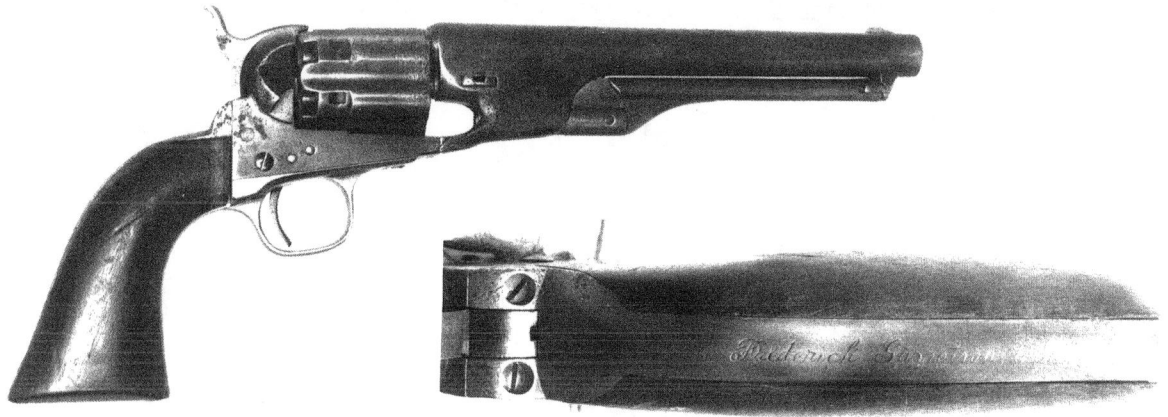

NAVAL SURGEON'S INSCRIBED 1860 COLT REVOLVER. This fluted cylinder army revolver shows pitting from salt water exposure. This revolver, carried by Dr. Frederick Garretson, is engraved on the back strap "Frederick Garretson CSN" (1837/1887) Educated at St. James College, Garretson interned under his uncle, Dr. W.C. VanBibber in Baltimore, and graduated from the University of Maryland Medical College in 1857. Appointed an assistant surgeon in the navy, he resigned to go into Confederate service, being listed as dismissed on May 6, 1861. Upon entering the Confederate navy he had his last name changed to his mother's maiden name. On September 13, 1862, he was promoted to past assistant surgeon and became medical officer on the C.S.S. Florida. Paroled on May 17, 1865, at Augusta, he returned to Baltimore and practiced medicine but never again used the VanBibber name.

The majority of Marylanders in the U.S. military, prior to the start of hostilities, resigned and threw in their lot with the new Confederacy. The Marine officers were no exception. Most continued to carry the Mameluke pattern sword specified in the 1859 Old Corps Regulations. General Charles Sidney Winder was carrying one of these when he was killed at Cedar Mountain. During the first two years of the war the Confederate Marine Corps was issuing horse artillery sabers to its officers, who had to pay for them. Newly appointed 2nd Lieutenants T. St. George Pratt and Lloyd B. Stevenson both received swords in early 1864 from the military storekeeper at the Richmond arsenal, for which they paid $35. However, no description of the swords is given. Other officers carried swords which they purchased outside of the Corps. In the capture of the C.S.S. Atlantic on June 17, 1863, it was stated that "marine officer James Thurston had a sword and a fine one it is with equipment made by Firmin & Sons, 153 Strand and 13 Conduit Street, London." Other swords are known to have been smuggled through the blockade from Maryland. Captain Reuben Thoms was given his sword by the ladies of Baltimore for his conduct on board the Merrimac.

Long arms varied according to the time, station, ship or assignment but normally were .557 Enfield rifles or .58 caliber U.S. rifles. On December 4, 1864, French Forrest, of the Gosport Naval Yard, wrote Colonel Beall about the "10,690 Enfields received from Europe on the Fingal." Captain Julius E. Meiere, commanding at Mobile, wrote on March 20, 1863, that the muskets he had were "very worthless, old flinklock muskets altered. A few will snap a cap, some with bayonets some without." He received 150 Austrian rifles on June 6, 1863, and requested suitable accoutrements be sent. The bayonets were received two weeks later but proper scabbards could not be found. Ammunition was a problem because the old rifles were .69 caliber and these new ones were not. Consequently, the cartridges were not interchangeable.

The records of Major Algernon S. Taylor, of the Richmond Quartermaster Corps, show that the common accoutrements issued were black waist belts, bayonet scabbards, cap pouches, cartridge boxes and Enfield rifles. Small arms aboard the ships were whatever type of rifles could be purchased when they were outfitted. For instance, the 35-man Marine Guard of the C.S.S. Tennessee were armed with Springfield muskets while the small arms on board the ironclad Merrimack were Enfield

192 - Weapons

rifles. In the Maryland Line Confederate Soldier's Home was an Enfield that was used on board the ironclad C.S.S. <u>City of Richmond</u>.

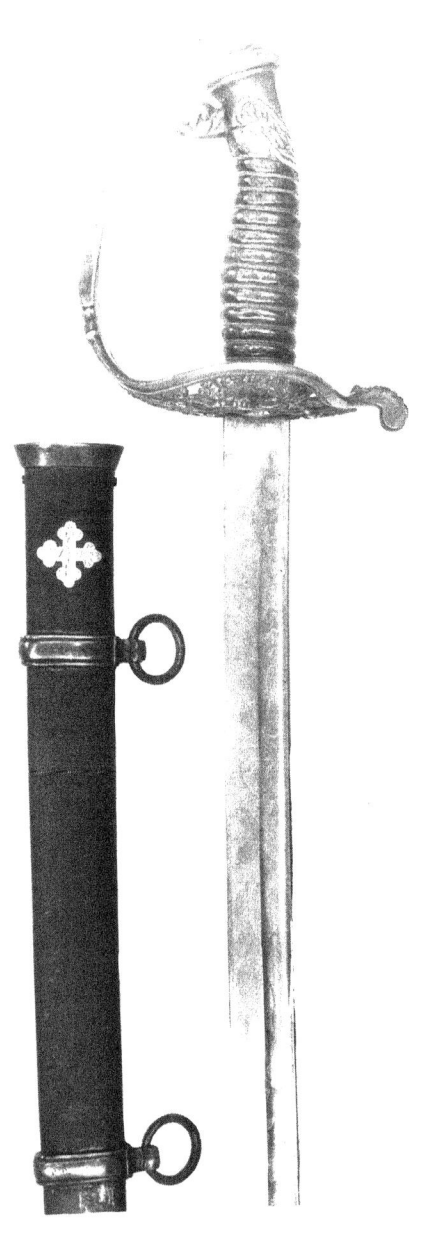
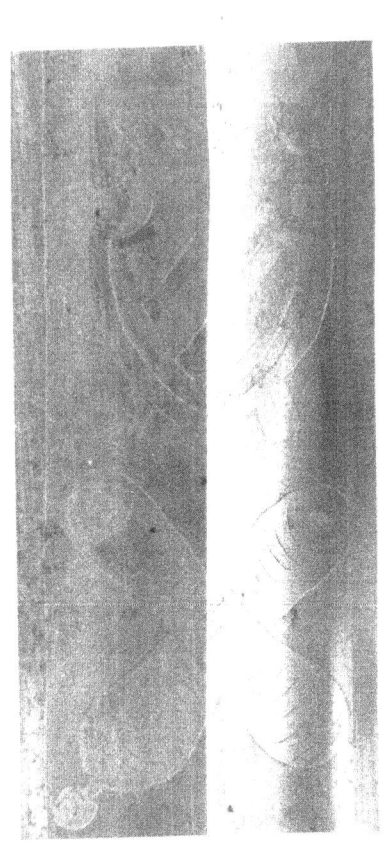

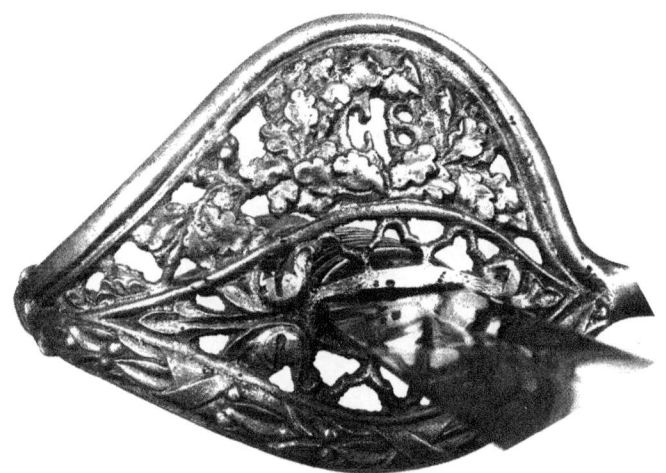

MARINE KRAFT, GOLDSMITH AND KRAFT OFFICER'S SWORD. The hilt of this staff and field officer's sword is brass. The pommel is decorated on the obverse side with laurel leaves, center indentations and berries. A parting line that was not completely polished out goes up the center, while the reverse forward edges contain relief oak leaves and acorns. An encircling ring is stamped on the reverse upper portion "33", facing in the opposite direction "22", then there is a large two-step build up, the first step being the most prevalent. The solid knuckle bow originates just below the back of the pommel in the form of a gargoyle, broadens into a ribbon and has distinctive leaves which match the head of the gargoyle. The lovely pierced counterguard bears three types of leaves. On the obverse side with the letters "CS" are oak leaves and acorns. On the reverse side are laurel leaves and berries with crossed bands of ribbons, while around the blade are the same type of leaves as on the head of the gargoyle and at the junction between the knuckle bow and counterguard, along with the Roman numerals "VII" on the reverse side. The inside of the counterguard is completely smooth. The grips have a very slanted appearance with a large brass ferrule at the bottom. They are wrapped in leather with the seam at the back towards the front. The broad, single-edged blade is straight with a slightly rounded back and has a single, unstopped fuller on each side. The blade is in superb condition, as is the rest of the piece, and shows typical Confederate manufacturing. The obverse side is etched in relief, "K. G & K.", broad maple leaves and clusters of cotton bolls which are line decorated, a shield and stand of arms, crossed cannons, long leaves, broad maple-style leaves and cotton blossoms. The reverse side is line etched, "Columbia", above that in a sun, "S.C.", while the sun rays and the rest of the blade is relief etched, with the center of the vegetation also being line etched. This side bears another style leaf which is in a long, broad fern appearance, a shell design, "C.S.", in plain, non-style, modern, spurred Gothic letters with a slight leaf decoration in the center of each, another leaf design and a long branch with alternating leaves going out each side. The silver conventional Maryland cross is engraved vertically, "Lt Marines", and horizontally, "J.C. Murdoch". The brass, bell-mouthed throat is held on by two screws on the superior and inferior side and holds two strips of wood on the inside of the scabbard. The bands are heavy brass that were line decorated and cast together with a neck and a stud, the stud being slightly smaller than the band.

Chapter 14

ACCOUTREMENTS

Confederate belts, cap boxes and cartridge boxes were to be of black leather but most were made of russet bridle leather. On August 28, 1861, Zarvona's Maryland Zouaves received black waist belts and bayonet scabbards. Later, some of the russet colored belts were blackened to conform, but conformity was not a Southern attribute. Bayonet and artillery short sword scabbards were to be brass bound, but as material became more scarce in the South they were mounted in tin. Cavalry pistol cartridge boxes were made of russet bridle leather. However, Yankee pouches were preferred over some of the Southern-made canvas flapped pouches. Canteens were universally worn by all branches of service. Metal canteens were cylindrical, convex-sided or flask type, and were made of tin. The wooden drum style, with barrel rims, was very common. Two Richmond firms, Robert Hough & Co. and Meredith Spencer & Co., formerly of Baltimore, obtained accoutrements for several Maryland companies. By 1863 knapsacks and haversacks were no longer being issued by the Confederate ordnance department because of the dire need for more important accoutrements.

George H. Steuart, commander of the 1st Maryland Infantry, was issued 10 drums and 2 bugles from the quartermaster department, which were used in the band under Bandmaster Alexander J. Hubbard, while Hosea Pitt led a drum corps. Pitt's drum in the Confederate Room of the Maryland Historical Society does not have a label. There are military drums bearing the label of William Boucher Jr. who advertised from 1845 through the war as a manufacturer and importer of musical instruments in Baltimore. In March of 1862, when they relieved the 13th Virginia on picket duty west of Sangster Station, the Marylanders were attacked by a body of enemy cavalry. One drummer tossed his instrument aside and was retreating when Colonel Steuart grabbed him from behind and demanded in an awesome tone, "Where's your drum?" Turning to Drum Major Pitts, Steuart said, "It's a good thing that I have not yet had the Maryland flag painted on the drums."

The Marine Corps prescribed black leather waist belts, British-style cartridge boxes, cap boxes and bayonet scabbards. The records of Major Algernon S. Taylor reveal that in 1864 the enlisted Marines at Richmond were being issued belts, cap pouches, canteens, haversacks and bayonet scabbards with frogs for the Enfield rifle bayonet.

The state's Billy Yanks, who referred to themselves as loyal Marylanders, had all the Federal issued accoutrements they needed, while the Johnnie Rebs, who referred to themselves as true Marylanders, endeavored to personalize their accoutrements with symbols of their origin. The exciting embellishments are found as belt buckles, cartridge box plates, identification badges and buttons. Each of the state's seal device plates have some variation according to the die engraver's interpretation. The shield is narrow and the eagle head is raised on the rectangular belt buckle pieces. The similar oval and cartridge box plates have a slightly arched ribbon and the height of the cedar trees is reversed. The shako type pieces have the state name above, a curved ribbon with motto below and a large breasted eagle. Two examples of the two-piece buckle have a convex shield. All of the Maryland plates bear the 1854 version of the state seal with an eagle, escutcheon crest of Lord Baltimore, dexter supporter of a farmer and sinister supporter of a fisherman. The scrolled motto "crescite et multiplucamini" varies in location and the state name does not always appear. The description of the seven Confederate used pieces points out the variations in the engravers' representations.

There are nine brass accoutrement plates that bear the Maryland state seal. A description, illustration and the weight of each can be found in <u>Arms Makers of Maryland</u>. The author believes two to be of post-war vintage and are not pictured in this work. They are the large seal lead-backed oval plate with M. N. G. standing perhaps for Maryland National Guard. The studs and the hook are of those of the war period and have been excavated at Gettysburg, but are considered to be of the late 1860s and probably lost at one of the many post-war re-encampments. The other possible post-war buckle is a two-piece metal cast plate having decorative inside loops with the state seal that has a flat device which appears to have been copied from the shako seal.

The rectangular solid brass Maryland belt plate has a belt loop on the right end and was made from a metal mold. The center, which bears very fine detail, has horizontal lines in the back. The device bears a straight-legged fisherman and the farmer's legs are angled to the right, with their hands on the shield. There is nice detail on the eagle's wings and on the shield with vegetation in the background. It is encircled with a raised rib which is inscribed on the upper half "cresite et multiplicamini," the state motto, meaning increase and multiply. The entire area outside of the circle device is stippled. Some are found with Roman numerals stamped on the reverse near the hook. None have been found which bear a maker or dealer's name. These are believed to have been pre-war militia plates that made their way south. Lieutenant Colonel James Breathed wore one of these examples.

RECTANGULAR STATE SEAL SOLID BRASS BUCKLE with a high degree of detail. It was worn by Henry Hollyday Sr. of the 2nd Maryland Infantry. It is 2.003" in height and 3.466" in width. The unmarked, typical Confederate-made cap box and buckle are on a russet bridle leather belt.

The second rectangular solid brass Maryland plate was directly copied from the aforementioned type by sand casting. The details of such copies are much less distinct. There are no pronounced horizontal lines in the background behind the device and the entire seal is not well defined. Repeated casting in sand also accounts for the reduction in size. This buckle is believed to have been made during the war because of the demand by the Southern army for Maryland buckles. These should not be confused with the reproductions of today. The copies that are currently being produced are over .001" larger because they were cast by the lost wax method from ones which were produced from a metal mold.

SAND-CAST COPY OF THE PRE-WAR RECTANGULAR PLATE believed to have been made in the South during the war. It does not possess the crisp detail of the former but has the same type single belt hook on the reverse. It is 1.909" in height and 3.293" in width.

RECTANGULAR STATE SEAL BUCKLE worn by an unidentified Confederate Maryland cavalryman. It cannot be determined if he is wearing one of the pre-war or war-period buckles.

The oval Maryland belt plate is double-die stamped in brass in order to produce its fine detail. The farmer and the fisherman are straight-legged and their hands are on top of the shield. The ribbon below is inscribed with the state's motto. Below the relief ribbon is a stippled area while behind the device are horizontal lines. The height of the cedar trees is reversed on the left side from that of the rectangular plates. The reverse side of this hollow brass plate was filled with lead with two oval studs, referred to as "puppy paws," and one hook. These buckles are believed to have been pre-war militia buckles that made their way south. An example of this type was worn by Warner G. Welsh who served in Company G, 7th Virginia Cavalry, Company F, 12th Virginia Cavalry and Company D, 1st Maryland Cavalry.

198 - Accoutrements

MARYLAND OVAL BELT PLATE on a bridle leather belt. The double stamped buckle is 2.125" in height and 3.326" in width. It is lead backed and contains two oval puppy paw studs and a hook.

JOHN HUDSON SNOWDEN WEARING A LARGE MARYLAND OVAL BUCKLE. He enlisted in Weston's Maryland Battalion and his Maryland guard company was transferred to the 21st Virginia Infantry as Company B. After 12 months of service, he was a lieutenant and aide-de-camp on the staff of Commissary General Lucias Bellinger Northrop. Snowden was under the Quartermaster Department providing food for its Southern armies.

The oval Maryland cartridge box plate was made from the exact same double-die stamp as the oval buckle. By using the same die stamp, the entire device is the same. The back was filled with lead and contains two iron wire shank loops for attaching it to a leather cartridge box. They are stamped in the lead in small letters, "E. Gaylord". This firm produced various state seal plates in the 1850s. The well-defined cartridge box plates that are marked would lead one to suppose that the oval buckles were probably made by the same firm. The buckle and box plate measure just slightly differently but are essentially the same. They can be found on several different styles of pre-war and war-time cartridge boxes. There are also two examples of these plates found on U.S. issue cartridge boxes. They are embossed in the leather with U.S. and bear this Maryland plate over the top, leaving one to surmise that the yankee boxes were altered for southern Maryland designation.

MARYLAND CARTRIDGE BOX AND PLATE. This .58 caliber cartridge box is probably of militia origin. The box is made of black patent leather with an inside flap stamped, "E. Gaylord Chicopee, Mass." It has an inside flap and two inside tins. The back contains two straps attached by copper rivets. There is only one roller buckle and brass stud remaining on the bottom for use with a shoulder strap. It shows both shoulder strap and belt wear. The Maryland oval cartridge box plate is stamped on the back, "E. Gaylord", and is held by a leather thong. The length is 3.376: and the breadth is 2.137".

The earliest shako-type Maryland state seal buckle was produced from .035" sheet brass. The round shako (hat) chin scale device is surrounded by an octagonal sunburst which is also of thin brass that was die stamped. Within the circle is a nicely detailed device bearing "Maryland," a large breasted eagle, a farmer with his hands on the shield, a fisherman with his elbows on the shield and a motifed ribbon. This device was the one that was copied for the two-piece buckle, which is not illustrated, and is considered to be of the post-war period. The shako plate, however, is pre-war and is secured by four brass wires that are hammered over on the reverse of the oval buckle. The concave back is not filled and there are three sheet brass hooks which are soldered on for its attachment to a belt.

EARLY OVAL MARYLAND BUCKLE with a shako device in the center. The sheet brass body is convex with three thin brass belt hooks. The double stamped seal is 2.092" at the center and 3.103" in width and is firmly held to the body by four brass wires which are bent over the open back.

200 - Accoutrements

This two-piece state seal buckle is very high quality. The loops are plain and were bent after casting to fit the wearer's body. The inferior part of the reverse side is marked with Roman numerals that are assembly marks. "Maryland" is at the top, a spread-winged eagle, the farmer and fisherman both have flexed knees, and the farmer's left hand and the fisherman's right elbow are at the top of the shield. The motto of the state is on the ribbon and is very legible. This device seal was made by a two-piece die set which created high relief on the figures. The horizontal lines from the original mold are prevalent in the background. The brass seal is hollowed and the brass tongue is soldered on both edges to the back of the seal. The wreath was sand cast in one piece and is very well done, but it does not have the great detail that the seal does, which was created by the two-piece die set. This cast portion contains four decorated crossed ribbons, oak leaves, eight acorns on the outside and four acorns on the inside. The wreath is hollow on the reverse side. The excellent casting indicates that this buckle was probably produced before the war for the militia.

SUPERB, TWO-PIECE MARYLAND BUCKLE worn by Quartermaster Captain John Eager Howard (1824/). The double die stamped state seal device is circular being 1.412". The wreath was cast in fine detail and is 2.144" in diameter. The loops on each end were bent inward when cast. He enlisted at Harpers Ferry in the 1st Maryland and was appointed quartermaster sergeant. In the spring of 1862 he received a captain's commission as the quartermaster of the battalion, and later was quartermaster of the 2nd Maryland Infantry.

Another two-piece state seal buckle is a sand cast copy of the preceding one. The reverse side has many defects and the obverse is much less distinct. The seal lacks the crisp detail because of the way it was produced. The male portion was cast in one piece and the reverse is of solid brass. The wreath, likewise, is a sand cast copy and not the quality of the aforementioned one. The back of the female wreath bears filed steps for the insertion of the tongue. The loops are not bent, but flat. This sand cast buckle is considered to have been a war period product of the South.

TWO-PIECE, SAND-CAST MARYLAND BUCKLE, believed to have been produced from the previous buckle, on a dry, flaking blackened leather belt which has the rough side out. The center seal device is 1.374" and is solid. The circular wreath is 2.112" in diameter with loops that are flat.

TWO-PIECE MARYLAND STATE SEAL BUCKLE worn by an unidentified Confederate officer. Magnification does not reveal if it is the high quality pre-war buckle or the war period sand-cast variety on his belt.

Another sand cast example of the superior quality two-piece buckle is one that is in relic condition. The back of the state motto is opened and the indentations from the original double-die stamp were copied. The wreath is of another variety with long pointed leaves and plain crossed ribbons.

EXCAVATED TWO-PIECE MARYLAND BUCKLE. The state seal device is well made and is unlike the other two. Corrosion from the elements does not allow accurate measurement of its true dimensions. The decorations of the wreath are different from the other two illustrated two-piece buckles.

The first rectangular buckle, the oval buckle, the oval cartridge box plate, the shako seal on a buckle and the first two-piece buckle are believed to be of pre-war vintage. These were probably taken into Confederate service by Free Staters who wanted to indicate their state of origin.

The crude copies of the gilded rectangular, the flat looped two-piece and the relic two-piece buckles are war period products. These were sand cast copies and thought to have been made during the war.

The collecting of C.S.A. belt buckles, with all the reproductions, is the most difficult for discernment. Only the serious, advanced student can distinguish originals from fradulent copies by examination with only his knowledgable eyes. Some honestly made plates are replicas, which are so marked on the back, but by refining and simulating patina they have been bogusly sold as geniune. The skepticism caused by counterfitting has somewhat diminished the interest of southern buckles by some collectors. These Maryland state seal pieces were analyzed by commercial Kevex x-ray equipment. The pre-war classed pieces varied in component metal percentages from genuine war period specimens. The alloy compositions provided by Marvalaud, Inc. of New Windsor, Maryland, enables accurate conclusions to be drawn. However, they will not be divulged in this writing so that they cannot be used for modern reproductions. The author had three different modern-day reproductions analyzed. Modern industrial examination of composition will be the deciding factor for future generations to distinguish originals from fakes.

There are about a dozen Maryland state seal hat pins known today, but none are complete and all are excavated and in relic condition. They were stamped from sheet brass and are .018" in thickness, .1506" in breadth and 1.414" in height. Eight of these thin brass hat pins, a number of Gardner .58 caliber minnie balls and a large Maryland state seal button were found on a ridge west of Strasburg, Virginia, overlooking the town. This was a winter camp of Companies A and D of the 1st Maryland Cavalry who were sent on pickett duty on February 23, 1863.

EXCAVATED STATE SEAL HAT EMBLEMS which were found near Strasburg at the 1863 winter camp of A and D companies of the 1st Maryland Cavalry. They are double die stamped from thin sheet brass and none are complete.

MARYLAND STATE SEAL HAT PIN worn on the kepi of Private James Clark. Leaving his Howard County home near Mathew's Store, he proceeded to Virginia where he enlisted on May 23, 1862, in A Company, Scott's Partisan Rangers. They were commanded by Captain Christopher C. Callan. They were disbanded on January 29, 1862. The Howard County draft records show him as gone South. Following his commander, he re-enlisted for the war as a private in Callan's Company of the Maryland Line, on July 27, 1863, at Richmond. They were known as Winder's Rangers, and were later attached to the 2nd Maryland Infantry as Company H.

MARYLAND STATE SEAL HAT PIN showing above the strap on the kepi worn by Lieutenant McHenry Howard (1838/1923). This picture was taken in Richmond in July, 1862. He was one of five brothers to serve in the C.S.A.

In the War Between the States, personal ID badges and corps badges of various configuations were engraved by jewelers and were worn by Union men. The most prevalent personalized emblem was the round disc, generally referred to as a dog tag, which often has a die-stamped state designation on one side and individaul letters and numbers bearing the soldier's name and unit on the other. From the great seal of Maryland, the Confederate patriots adopted the cross bottony consisting of alternating quadrants of red and white from the Crossland's coat-of-arms. The crosses are considered by the few collectors who have knowledge of these rare works of art, to be the insignia of the Maryland Line, yet it is interesting to note that they were worn by men in the infantry, cavalry, artillery, marines, navy, medical corps, and the signal corps. The surviving crosses are of seven patterns, each having enough sufficient difference from the others to indicate that they were not produced by the same jeweler. Many are inscribed with names, whereas others have never been engraved. The "finding," or pin, is the means of attachment to the uniform or hat. It is found on the reverse side of the cross and is usually one of two types. The hinge joint is either long and tubular, or small and U-shaped, with the stem or pin projecting out of it and going over to the catch which is opened at the top or the bottom and has a heavier diameter than the stem.

The big crosses are made of brass that had been silver plated. One belonging to Surgeon Charles Macgill is the biggest of the large crosses being 1.413" in breadth and 1.419" in length. Some without pedigrees vary in thickness from .039" to .031". All have on the reverse side a large trace of solder which has been filed. The big cross associated with William P. Zollinger reveals why the solder is on the lower reverse side. It bears an attached silver stamping of "2 Md". The number and letters are individually stamped out with a rope design on the obverse. The reverse is hollow and is soldered onto a bar to hold the badge in place. Across the back of the large "M" is another bar, which is soldered to the reverse of the cross. These large crosses are made of brass which have been silver plated. Zollinger enlisted on June 18, 1861, in Company H, 1st Maryland Infantry. Upon being discharged after his 12-month enlistment, he re-enlisted in Company A, 2nd Maryland Infantry, and was elected a 2nd lieutenant so it is from his later unit. The findings on the reverse side of all three crosses are identical. The stem is made from a single wire, which is twisted to form a hinge and the catches are identical.

LARGE BRASS CROSS of Lieutenant William P. Zollinger with silver plating which is worn off in most areas. The thickness is .038: and it is 1.421" in height and 1.396" in width. Attached by a wire to the reverse of the lower lobe is "2 MD" in a rope design on the obverse that is hollowed on the reverse.

Another variation, also belonging to Zollinger, is a flaring-armed cross that is engraved, "Lt. W.P. Zollinger, 2nd Md" on the obverse in large block letters and small script. On the reverse is "W.P.Z." in script, possibly the initials were done upon purchase and the obverse decorated at a later date. This solid silver, flaring-armed cross is the smallest of all crosses. The quadrants vary from .326" to .355", while each center lobe is larger than those on each side.

FLARING-ARMED SOLID SILVER CROSS of William P. Zollinger with his name and unit engraved in the inner straight lined decorations on the obverse. It is .962" in height and .927" in width. The initials on the reverse appear to be from a different hand. The findings are a large external tubular hinged joint attached to a stem.

On the basis of the author's experience, the solid silver conventional cross was evidently the most prevalent style. Although not common, there are at least eight examples known of this conventional form. Most are engraved and associated with cavalry troopers. Many of these conventional silver crosses have been finely engraved by a jeweler. The craftsmanship exhibited by these nameless artisans frequently raised their works to the level of art and, of course, they are highly prized. Others are sparsely decorated. Dr. Henry Brisco of Chaptico, a surgeon of the 26th Virginia Infantry, wore one that is only engraved in block letters "Major H. Briscoe."

No two of these conventional crosses appear to have been decorated by the same hand. William H.B. Dorsey, who was elected a 1st lieutenant in Company D, 1st Maryland Cavalry, after serving as an enlisted man in the 1st Maryland Infantry, had a very deeply engraved, fully ornamented cross. In the top quadrant is "D," in the lower "Md Cav," while in the lateral arms and quadrants "W.H.B. Dorsey" is engraved in Old English script. This cross has many curved line decorations. The cross of Private Thomas Broughton, the harness maker of the "Flying Maryland" artillery, is completely outlined in deep lines. "1st Md Arty" appears laterally and "T. Broughton" vertically in small, narrow script engraving. The outline is coarse and appears to have been done at the time of construction. This piece was apparently lost by Broughton after the war, because it was excavated in the town square at Princess Anne. The conventional cross of Corporal William Price has distinctly engraved vertical quadrants which terminate in a point and a short tubular joint attached to the stem. The most exquisitely engraved cross is that of Gresham Hough, a private in Company H, 1st Maryland Infantry, until he was discharged and re-enlisted in A Company, 1st Maryland Cavalry. After a year's enlistment, he became a member of Mosby's Rangers, 43rd Virginia Cavalry, Company D, a company composed of Marylanders.

CONVENTIONAL SILVER CROSS of Lieutenant William H.B. Dorsey. It is deeply engraved and fully ornamented. The height is 1.089", the width 1.075" and the thickness .025".

BROTHERS EACH WEARING A CONVENTIONAL MARYLAND CROSS on their chest. A. Polard Jenkins (/1882) (left) and George C. Jenkins (1836/1930) (right) went to Rees Studio together and had individual cartes de viste made which are consecutively numbered.

MODIFIED SOLID SILVER CROSS of Corporal William C. Price (1865/) with the engraver's decoration in the vertical quadrants, which terminate in a point and alters the appearance from the original state seal. It measures .035" in thickness, 1.110" in height and 1.118" in width.

MARYLAND CONFEDERATE CONVENTIONAL CROSS displayed on the left chest of Private Henry Peabody Hayward. This C.D.V. bears the imprint of Bendann and Brothers of Baltimore and was taken when Hayward was home.

The elegant Kraft, Goldsmith, and Kraft staff officer's sword carried by James Cambell Murdoch, which is pictured in the weapons chapter, bears a cross of this style soldered on the iron scabbard between the brass throat and the first band. He probably had acquired this cross while he was a trooper in Company K, 1st Virginia Cavalry prior to April 8, 1863, when he accepted a commission in the C.S.A. Marine Corps. However, it is engraved "MARINES."

The composition of two conventional silver crosses was analyzed by a metallurgist. The Gresham Hough cross and the James Cambell Murdoch cross on the scabbard underwent the "energy dispersive x-ray analysis with a scanning electron microscope indicating that the crosses themselves are a very good quality of silver with less than two percent copper and a bit more than two percent nickel and a trace of sulphur. Modern usage is that sterling silver must contain at least ninety-two and one-half percent silver, so the number just quoted would be someplace up around ninety-five or ninety-six percent, making them better than modern silver." The analysis of the findings on the reverse side of the Hough cross reveals that the metal is of the same purity as that of the cross itself. The brazing alloy that was used to fasten the hook to the cross is principally copper, silver and nickel with some zinc, iron and phosphorous. The sheath, i.e. the tube that provides a hinge for the pin, has an analysis of nominally 82% nickel, 14% iron and the balance chromium with traces of phosphorus, zinc and silver. The pin itself is a copper, nickel and zinc alloy running nominally 66% copper, 17% percent nickel, 16% zinc and about 1% of iron. The weight of the Hough cross is three grams.

208 - Accoutrements

SILVER CROSS IN CONVENTIONAL STYLE. It belonged to Private Gresham Hough and appears to be professionally ornamented by curved lines utilizing rhythm and flow with tracings and interlacing lines. The ingenuity of the engraver is reflected in the use of lines and dot-shading to highlight. It is .028" in thickness, 1.092" in height and 1.106" in width.

CONVENTIONAL CROSS on the left breast of the subject in this carte de viste by Rees while serving as a private in the Signal Corps. The back is inscribed "Geo A Henley CS Army August 1864". Taken after he returned from the Army of the West in Holbrooks Independent Maryland Artillery.

TWO BROTHERS WITH ONE CROSS. Captain James McHenry Howard (1839/1916) (left) and Private David Ridgely Howard (1844/1927) (right) are pictured here in a photo taken in Canada. For an individual pose, James used David's cross on his hat as seen in the book James McHenry Howard, A Memoir. David's straight left leg depicts the artificial limb he received while in Canada.

Among the large variety of memorabilia is a thin, silver, narrow-armed cross that belonged to Lieutenant John W. Bennett. Bennett, after graduating in the first class at the Naval Academy, and having seen 11 years in the old navy, resigned his commission, returned to his Talbot County home, and after a month, hastened to Richmond where he joined the Confederate Navy. He commanded the steamer Nashville, and the gunboat Gaines and the new sidewheeler Nashville during his gallant career. His cross is .038" in thickness, while the width and the heighth are both about the same. This asymmetrical configuration of the cross bottony has rounded edges where the arms originate and swell slightly as they go out to the quadrants. Further to accentuate its design, it is outlined by coarse engraving lines. On the reverse, the hinge joint is of tubular construction, while an identical thin, narrow-armed cross of William C. Boone of the Winder Cavalry has a U-joint hinge.

THIN, NARROW-ARMED SILVER CROSS that is coarsely outlined and lightly engraved "WC Boone" and "1st Md Ca-y" on the obverse. The reverse has a bent U hinge attached to the stem and a large diameter catch. The thickness is .028" while the height is 1.038" and the width 1.029".

Another unusual cross which does not conform to a standard pattern is the clover-tipped cross of Charles Porterfield Kahler. He enlisted as a private in May of 1863 in an independent organization of partisan rangers composed of men who were born under Maryland's black-and-gold flag. They were known as Gilmor's Battalion, and later would be designated as the 2nd Maryland Cavalry. Because of their courageous riding, the unit was dubbed "The Band." The cross is solid silver, .023" in thickness, and the width is longer than the heighth. The edges of the clover-tipped cross are beveled and the center lobes of the quadrants are longer than the ones on each side.

CLOVER-TIPPED SILVER CROSS that is engraved on the obverse "2 Md CAV GILMOR'S BATALn". The reverse is engraved "C.S.A. 1863 Chas P Kahler" with a small internal hinge attached to the hinge. The measurements are .023" in thickness, 1.109" in height and 1.039" in width.

It is evident by measuring the crosses with a dial caliper that they were not stamped out, but sawed out individually. Not only do the four quadrants in each cross vary in dimension, but each individual lobe does not correspond with the other. File marks can also be found on the edges where they were dressed. This fact has been recently substantiated by the examination of the seven recovered relic crosses and a state seal button found in Hanover County, Virginia. This site was the 1863-1864 winter encampment of the Maryland Line. Five of these crosses measured by the author are of the same initial size, but again measurements within the arms and quadrants vary. They are brass and have layout lines inscribed up the arms through the quadrants which are revealed because of deterioration of the silver plating. The reverse sides of the crosses have two large deposits of solder where apparently a pin was attached at one time. The obverse side, under magnification, shows traces of silver plating. Silver plating a brass cross would be a lot less costly for the producer because it involved laying a thin coat of the expensive material over a less valuable metal. This could be done by three means: mechanically with the use of cladding, which forcibly brings two metals together; electrically, a process developed in England in the 1830's, or chemically by dipping, which is commonly referred to as "washing." An excavated cross identical to the ones described above was found during an earlier period and until recently was considered a Federal 18th Corps Badge. However, there are distinct differences between an 18th Corps Badge and a Maryland Confederate cross.

BRASS CONVENTIONAL CROSS that was silver plated with very little silver remaining. It was excavated from an 1863-1864 winter encampment of the Maryland Line in Hanover County, Virginia. The thickness is .021", the height is 1.097" and the width is 1.073".

Such personalized insignias were eagerly sought by those from the black-and-gold state who did not serve in Maryland commands. Some of the war-period photographs of men wearing crosses are illustrated as being significantly different than those previously represented. Several photographs of Bradley T. Johnson reveal a sketched on cross. A spiral-pointed cross is on an albumin of Spencer Monroe Grayson which is believed to have been an artist's rendition of the Maryland symbol. William H. Smith appears to have been wearing an enameled cross, an appearance that might have been caused by the lighting in the studio.

SPEAR POINTED CROSS. Private Spencer Monroe Grayson (1847/) is shown in a Confederate uniform with a mustache and goatee that were painted on. The spiral-pointed cross may have also been an artist's rendition.

UNUSUAL LOOKING CROSS. A cross on the left chest of Sergeant William H. Smith, who served in Company A, 2nd Maryland Infantry, and was one of three brothers to serve in the C.S.A. The light in the photograph makes this cross appear to be enameled.

John Poole Sellman, while in Old Capitol Prison, took a small beef bone from his cup of soup and with is penknife made it into a cross. After carving his initials upon it he filled the scrimshaw letters with red wax. He used a common brass pin to make a pin and catch so he might wear the cross on his coat. At the age of 83, his wife wrote of the above and said the cross is one of her most cherished possessions.

The membership badge of the Society of the Army and Navy of the Confederate States in the State of Maryland was struck in 1871. It has a top bar for the inscription of the veteran's name, a ribbon of red and white and, incorporated on the medal, are two fond remembrances of the past: a flag of Confederate colors "1861-1865" suspended by two-thirds of a Maryland cross bottony with "A & N CSMD". Above the main entrance of the Southerners' old soldiers home in Pikesville, Maryland, was a four-foot wooden conventional cross bottony, over which was written, "Maryland Line Confederate Soldiers Home." Envelopes from this home were imprinted with the cross and it is found chiseled in the stone monuments over the graves of veterans.

The 5th Maryland National Guard Infantry was formed in 1867. It was organized by many Confederate veterans and officered by them. About the time of the Spanish-American War, the "Dandy Fifth," as they were referred to, began to wear three types of bottony crosses. They are all enameled with red and white flags on the front, and their arms and quadrants are thinner than the Confederate period crosses. The plain variety is enameled over copper. The second type bears a brass star in the center with starbursts between the arms of stamped-out brass, which were enameled on brass. The third has a super-imposed number "5." All three contain different modern-style findings.

During the colonial period, Maryland officers had worn silver gorgets. During the War of 1812 silver breast plates worn on shoulder straps were lavishly engraved for the militia rank and file. During the War Between the States, Southerners extensively used state seal buttons to adorn their uniforms. From the plain jacket of Private Henry Hollyday, to the coat of General Robert E. Lee which was made by the ladies of Carroll and Frederick counties, Maryland buttons were worn with pride. In the relic room of the Maryland Line Confederate Soldiers Home there were displayed Confederate naval

STATE SEAL CUFF BUTTON, large coat button and two wooden buttons belonging to Lewis Webb. He was born in Montgomery County. In August of 1862 he was arrested in Baltimore when he and his brother got in a fight with a Union soldier. Upon being released from jail he proceeded to Frederick where he met the Southern army and enlisted in the Maryland Line Artillery. He was paroled at Appomattox on April 9, 1865. Proceeding to Washington, he took the oath of allegiance on April 22. He returned to Baltimore and was arrested on April 26. Webb carried a letter throughout the war which had offered him a commission in the Union army, but he chose instead to become a private in the 1st Maryland Artillery in the Confederate army.

buttons from the uniform of Captain John Taylor Wood and Past Midshipman John Thompson Mason. Also displayed were Maryland buttons from the uniforms of Corporal William Henry Pope, who was superintendent of the home, and General Bradley T. Johnson. Civil War period state seal buttons were constructed in three pieces. The front, which bore the seal, the back with the shank and the band which connected the two. The front was made of a thin piece of brass that is .021" which was double die struck. It has a small .049" flange which the .015" band secures the front to the back. The back is the same thickness as the front and has a circular shank. Usually the manufacturer is found on the back.

Large Maryland buttons are found to bear 24 different dealer's names or logos. The majority of these were only retailers. There are three variations of the war period state seal large buttons leading one to suppose that there were not more than three manufacturers. The two-piece die plate and cup that were used by Scovill, Waterbury and Steele & Johnson are still in existence. The dominant feature of war period seals is a spread eagle over the crest. Button variations and biographies of the dealers may be found in the accoutrement section of <u>Arms Makers of Maryland</u>.

MARYLAND STATE SEAL BUTTONS on the left sleeve of the double-breasted medical coat of Harry Woodward Dorsey Jr. (1831/1903). The large buttons are marked "Waterbury Button Co. * Extra *" and the small sleeve buttons "Canfield Bro. & Co." Dorsey of Glenmont, near New Market, was graduated from the University of Pennsylvania as a physician in 1857. Assistant Surgeon Dorsey was with the 1st Maryland Cavalry and wore this regulation, tailor-made, medical double-breasted cadet gray frock coat with a black collar and black cuff facings.

EXCAVATED 1ST MARYLAND INFANTRY RELICS. These block-I buttons, M sheet brass letter and civilian buttons marked "Hinds Balto" and "W.O., Linthicum Balt. Md" were found at the camp of the 1st Maryland Infantry where the Richmond and Harpers Ferry companies were united on June 24, 1861. Over 50 block-I buttons were found which are believed to have been cut off their uniforms and replaced by Maryland seal buttons. This camp also yielded a U.S. box plate scratched with a large M on the reverse, snake buckles, a spoon handle engraved "Sollers" (Summerfield Sollers, 1st Maryland Infantry), and many .54 caliber round balls.

Free Staters often desired to change their Confederate issue buttons for ones bearing the state seal. However, these buttons were not easily obtained. On June 16, 1863, Joseph Trundle wrote to his sister "Ask Ma to get some nice gray cloth and some Maryland buttons and tinsel trimming and a pair of Mexican spurs for I feel I might soon get home." John D. Smith wrote on January 13, 1862, desiring a great coat "These articles are very high here and difficult to be had. A fair overcoat such as the one he has costs $40. An ordinary pair of coarse boots for army use $12. I paid $8.50 for a pair of common blankets ... Maryland buttons are greatly sought after here. I should have a set myself."

WOODEN BUTTONS on a mid-war Richmond depot jacket worn by James Waring Jr. - 1842/ - Chaptico in St. Mary's County was the place of his birth and he attended Georgetown University. On September 10, 1862, at Charlottesville, he enlisted in B Company, 1st Maryland Cavalry, for three years or the war. At Monteray Springs his horse was shot while he was helping to protect the wagon trains of General Ewell. He was captured afoot on July 3, 1863, and was confined at Fort McHenry on July 9, and later sent to Fort Delaware. Waring was exchanged on December 25, 1864, when he again returned to his company. He reported to federal authorities at Mechanicsville, Virginia, on April 28, 1865, and was paroled. Returning to his native area, he was a member of the Bradley T. Johnson United Confederate Veterans Camp No. 1110 of Leonardstown.

Many Confederate horsemen furnished their own saddles and bridles. The most common saddle used by the South before the war was the civilian English round tree model. This model was not fitted to carry much equipment and its use in military service soon lead to sore-back horses. The ordinance department's answer was the Jenifer pattern saddle. It had a curved valise, which tightly fit around and under the cantle, and had an opening in the center. It was much lighter than the English seat, and was pleasant to the rider. The Jenifer tree worked well with horses in good condition, but it came down on the horse's backbone and withers as soon as the cushion of fat and muscle dwindled. The Union McClellan saddle was easier on the horse as it's weight deteriorated. McClellan, Campbell, and Grimsley saddles were modified by Confederate producers. Southern artillery saddlery and draft harness were essentially the same as those used by the Federal Army.

ENGLISH RIGGED JENIFER SADDLE. The tree is made of oak and the seat is cotton padded. The tool work bears a sunburst and moon. It has a skirt and fender, the skirt being a double thickness of russett leather. It has small iron rivets and large copper rivets with iron staples and a ring on the back of both sides. The candle was decorated in sunburst roses and the rawhide is reinforced on the tree. Walter Hanson Jenifer (1823/1878) - St. Mary's County was the place of his birth and he obtained an appointment to the U.S. Military Academy. Although he did not graduate, he was fortunate to obtain a 2nd lieutenant's commission in 1847 and was appointed to the cavalry stationed in the west. In 1855 he was advanced to the rank of captain and, upon the secession of the "Cotton States," he resigned his commission. He was arrested by order of Governor Curtis at the Carlisle Barracks, where he was stationed, because of his resignation in order to go South. His men were outraged and forced their way into the jail and freed him. On March 16, 1861, he was appointed a captain of cavalry. Jenifer was given command of the cavalry of General N.G. Evans as a colonel on September 24, 1861. At the Battle of Ball's Bluff he was in charge of all cavalry operations. On January 16, 1862, he was assigned to the 8th Virginia Cavalry which was composed of nine companies. They were reorganized on May 15, 1862, and he was not elected. Jenifer was appointed to the staff of his old Indian-fighting commander, General E. Kirby Smith, as colonel of cavalry in the Trans-Mississippi Department. In 1863 and 1864 he was stationed in Alabama and then later in Georgia.

Accoutrements - 215

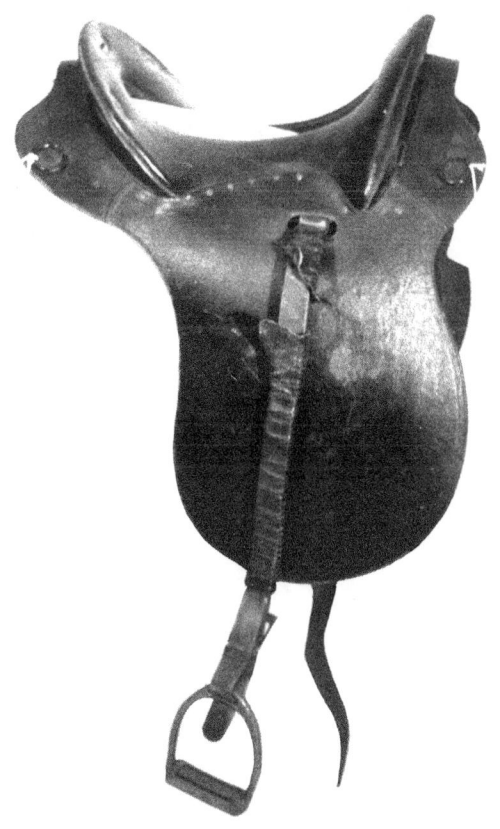
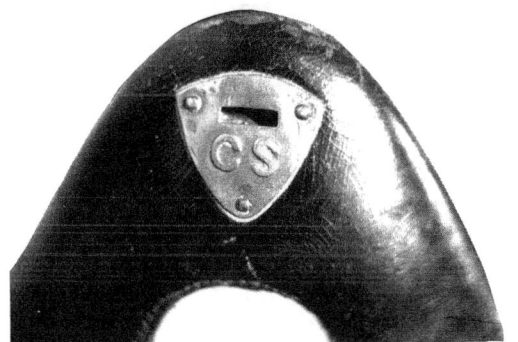

FEDERAL McCLELLAN SADDLE TRANSFORMED TO CONFEDERATE used by William Stuart Symington (1839/1912). Federal McClellan saddles were by far the most widely used in the Southern army. The saddle of General Charles Winder was a McClellan, with a custom-fitted quilted cover. Symington's saddle was a regulation McClellan and was made at the Allegheny Arsenal with a custom-fitted cover. Symington's saddle is very elaborate, of southern production, and it is made of russet leather which includes matching coverings for the stirrup straps. On the high pommel is a high reliefed, cast brass plate bearing the letters "CS". Brass brackets are mounted on the rear of the cantle and in the front and back are large brass rings. The stirrups are made of iron. The underneath side of the saddle is also lined with russet leather. Symington enlisted in Company B, 21st Virginia Infantry, and was elected 2nd lieutenant. After his enlistment had expired he re-enlisted as a private under Ridgely Brown and was detailed to Richmond in recruiting. In May of 1862 he was asked to serve on the staff of General George E. Pickett. On August 9 he was advanced to 1st lieutenant and appointed adjutant. In September of 1863 he held the rank of captain and soon became major in the Adjutant and Assistant Inspector General Department. He was paroled at Appomattox, and returned to his native Baltimore. He was arrested by Federal authorities, held for two weeks, and upon being released, went to Germany for a year before returning home. In 1867, he was captain of Company F, 5th Maryland Militia Regiment.

Chapter 15

DEVASTATIONS OF WAR

The sectional partisanship that was so strong in Maryland divided families and turned father against son, brother against brother. The glamour and glory of war soon turned into a terrible horror.

On June 15, 1863, two pieces of the 1st Maryland Artillery held a bridge over a railroad cut near Stevenson's Depot. The enemy made four successive attempts to carry the bridge, and 13 out of 15 cannoneers were killed or disabled. The official report from the Army of Northern Virginia for this battle, which listed every man in the unit, was the only one throughout the war which mentioned the individual names of privates. One of these gallant artillerymen was Private A. James Albert Jr. who lost an arm. When Robert E. Lee was in Baltimore after the war, Mr. Albert Sr. spoke to General Lee with great regret about his son having lost his arm. "My dear sir, if you knew the circumstances under which he lost it, you would feel proud of it. I regard this as the thermopyle of my campaign. It seems beyond a doubt that these two guns alone, absolutely unsupported by infantry, held the bridge and practically won the battle."

There was a multitude of mangled lives resulting from the madness of the Civil War. The sickening cost in human lives was worsened by the appalling injustice to some of the combatants. J. Gabby Duckett, a youth of 20 years and son of Dr. T.B. Duckett of Washington County, attempted to cross the Potomac in order to join the Southern army. He was ambushed and nothing was heard from him for several weeks until his body washed ashore at Shepherdstown with a bullet hole in his chest.

William K. Jenkins said, "when I left my dear mother, her last words to me were sooner should she see me dead on the field of battle than to know that I had shirked my duty to the cause so dear to our hearts. Yes, had I seven sons to give to the cause gladly would I do than that you should be false to the colors you now go to defend."

Many of the soldiers and sailors from the Land of Sanctuary, as Maryland was called in colonial days, secretly travelled home to see their families during the war. They would wear civilian clothing to hide their identity and when captured were held as spies under the penalty of death. Hamilton Lefevre, on a two-week furlough, returned to Harford County, was captured and held as a spy. Only the wearing of his Confederate belt buckle saved him from going before a firing squad.

In the spring of 1862 Jesse W. Wharton, a resident of Prince Georges County who had resigned from the Old Army, was standing in his cell in Old Capitol Prison and looking out a window. A guard of the 91st Pennsylvania called out "Get away from that window or I'll blow your damn head off." Wharton, feeling he was violating no rule, paid no further attention but stood with his arms folded and was deliberately killed.

Harry A. Steuart, of the 3rd Maryland Artillery, returned to Maryland to procure medical supplies. He was captured on December 15, 1861, in St. Mary's County and was taken to Old Capitol Prison. On Sunday, May 11, 1862, he bribed a guard from the 86th New York Volunteers, who for $50, agreed to let him escape. At 4 A.M., the guard called to him in a low tone, "Come on, it will soon be too late." As Steuart was preparing to drop from his second floor window, the guard changed his mind and shot him. A tourniquet was applied by his roommate but they could not check the flow of blood. He received no surgical treatment before 9 A.M. the next morning, and after his leg was finally amputated in the afternoon, he died soon thereafter from the loss of blood. Captain Steuart's family had difficulty in getting his remains from prison authorities and soon afterward his father, Dr. William F. Steuart, left for the South and joined the medical corps.

RETALIATION OF A BITTER FATHER. William Frederick Steuart Sr. (1815/1885) - Coming from Anne Arundel County he obtained a medical degree from the University of Maryland in 1839 and settled in Baltimore. Dr. Steuart was a medical practitioner for the 5th Maryland Militia for a number of years. On April 15, 1861, he was advanced to a line officer as a lieutenant colonel and served during the militia's resistance for the next month. His two sons were officers in the C.S.A. William F. Jr. was in ordnance and Harry A. in the 3rd Maryland Arillery. After the senseless killing of Harry, Dr. Steuart departed for the South and received an appointment in the medical department. On June 10, 1863, the star of a major was placed on the collar of Surgeon Steuart and five days later he was ordered to the medical director's office. On November 24 he was sent to the Board of Examiners of Conscription for the 5th Congressional District of Virginia. After the war he returned to Baltimore where he became a resident physician at the Physician's Quarantine or Marine Hospital in Baltimore from 1874-1876.

During the Antietam Campaign, Alexander Young received a day's furlough to visit his home near Sugarloaf Mountain. He was killed by a shot from a bushwacker's ambush just a mile from his home.

John Chapman Spencer was killed during his first charge in his first engagement. He penned, "I shall be very sorry if my departure south causes any pain to my father, and I hope he will not be vexed at my saying that I consider all other duties subordinate to the great duty of fighting for the liberties which have been handed down to us by our fathers. I have long desired to help the South, and when the opportunity presented, I embraced it."

Captain Walter Gibson Peter, of Darnestown, was an aide-de-camp to Colonel Walter H. Jenifer at the Battle of Ball's Bluff. He joined Company A of the 35th Virginia Cavalry and was elected lieutenant. While carrying dispatches to his cousin Colonel Horton Williams in Tennessee, he was captured on June 8, 1863, and was found to be wearing a Federal officer's uniform. His court martial conviction carried a sentence of death by hanging. He was executed at Franklin, Tennessee, and news of his death reached the Maryland boys of White's Comanches on the battlefield at Gettysburg.

Andrew T. Leopold and John Redmond Burke were detailed to Jeb Stuart in 1862 and operated independently as partisan rangers. They were referred to by the Federals as guerillas. They were both from Washington County and Shepherdstown was their headquarters. Burke was killed and his two sons captured during the winter of 1862. Leopold was captured in February of 1864 and confined in Fort McHenry. A Captain W.B. Compton was due to be hung but made his escape. General Lew Wallace and his staff had come down from Baltimore for the hanging but there was no one to hang. Leopold, convicted as chief of guerillas, had the sentence of hanging read to him instead the morning of May 25. He was soon ushered out to ascend the scaffold. Leopold said that he was ready to die in the defense of his country and trusted that God would yet give Her independence and liberty. He then pointed to General Morris, the commandant, and said "that that old, gray-haired man was the cause of my death, but God is the judge, not he; that I forgive General Morris, and hope that I will meet with him in Heaven." He waved his hankerchief twice to the officers, offered a prayer to God, and then told them he was ready. At 5:30 A.M. he was launched into eternity leaving his widowed mother in Washington County.

CONVICTED GUERILLA. Andrew T. Leopold (1841/1864) was born and reared in Washington County and at the beginning of hostilities enlisted in the 1st Virginia Cavalry, Company F. As a private Leopold became one of the favorites of Colonel Ashby and led squads of men on different raids. Operating as a partisan ranger in the spring of 1863 General Lew Wallace sent several expeditions to capture Leopold, who had been termed the chief of guerillas. He was captured in February of 1864 and was sent to Fort McHenry. He was tried before General Morris as a guerilla and was under the sentence of death. On May 25 he was informed at day light that the sentence would be carried out in an hour because there was no one else to hang.

In 1864, Privates Churchill Crittenden and John L. Hartigan were procuring provisions for Company C of the 1st Maryland Cavalry in Page County. They were captured, and attempting to escape, were both wounded and recaptured. After they were taken two miles to the rear, General Powell of Averill's Old Brigade ordered them shot in cold blood. They were buried by the last farmer who had given them supplies and he notified their command. When the graves were opened by the men of Company C and circumstances of the manner of their deaths verified "vows were uttered over the dead bodies of their comrades to avenge their deaths - and they were avenged, though Powell escaped."

On April 9, 1865, when Lee was about to surrender, General Mumford's Cavalry broke through the lines west of Appomattox. In the last charge Private William C. Price of Company E, 1st Maryland Cavalry, was killed. His was the last blood of the Army of Northern Virginia shed in the War Between the States.

HANGED MOSBY'S RANGER. Lucian Love (1844/1864) - Color photograph - Love enlisted on April 30, 1862, in the Border Rangers for two years. At the reorganization of the Rangers they became Company E, 8th Virginia Cavalry. After only 8 days of service he was captured in Cable County, Virginia. Love was to have been taken to Camp Chase, Ohio, but was sent instead to Jackson, Mississippi, where he was exchanged on September 29. He was pressed into infantry service but requested to be sent back to Richmond. After finally returning he joined Company D, 43rd Virginia Cavalry, as a private. On July 4, 1864, they were authorized to form a light artillery company for Mosby's Battalion. On September 23, again after just a short period of service, he was captured by the 2nd U.S. Cavalry and was taken towards Front Royal. There were six captured Rangers who were hung or shot by their captors in retaliation for the death of a Federal officer, Lieutenant McMasters, who they alleged was killed after he had surrendered. Four of the unarmed, defenseless Rangers, including Love, were taken out and barbariously shot to death while two were hanged in sight of Front Royal. Mosby ordered the execution of seven Federals in retaliation and a letter from him to Sheridan, stating this, caused Sheridan to put a stop to such further measures.

As the veterans grew older they desired to continue their fraternization with one another, and Confederate Reunion Camps, as well as Federal, were organized throughout the state. In Westminster in 1880, an attempt to organize a Union veteran's camp "was openly and bitterly opposed. Heated arguments were plenty and fist fights were common." William Henry Pope wrote in the first volume of the <u>Confederate Veteran</u> magazine in 1893 "Now a little insight into the way we do in Maryland; we have no ex-Confederate societies, but several large, strong and active Confederate societies. We have never mixed in any manner with the other side - have no joint reunions, no joint banquets, no decoration for Memorial Days in common. In fact, we do not mix, we go our own way and they go theirs, and we find that we gain more respect by doing so. We do not belong to that class of Confederates who believe that they were right. We know that we were right in 1861. We know that we were right when the war closed and we know today that we were right." By 1917 there were 629 Confederate Veteran Camps in 17 states and the District of Columbia. There were 39 camps established in Maryland along with 2 in Washington. The strength of the Confederate veterans groups varied from 30 members in Company A, 1st

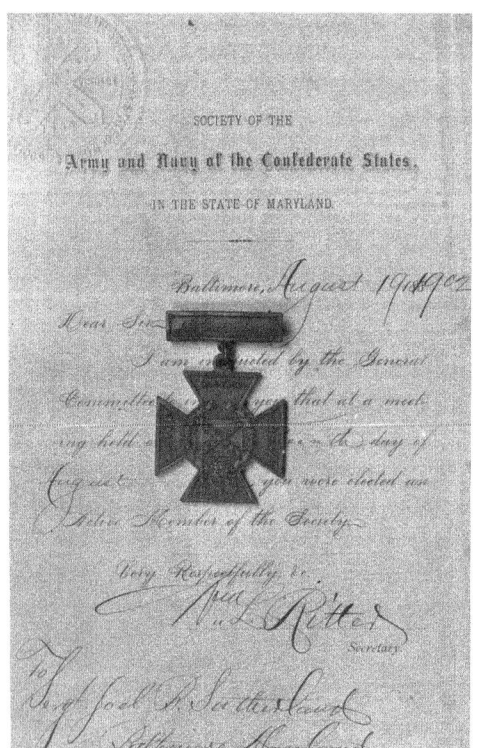

SOCIETY MEMBERSHIP CERTIFICATE AND CROSS OF HONOR. These belonged to Joel Barlow Sutherland (1845/) - He was the son of Samuel Sutherland, a gunsmith who moved from Baltimore to Richmond in 1852. As a young lad Joel apprenticed in his father's gun shop, enlisting on March 7, 1862, in Company C, 25th Virginia Infantry. He was discharged on February 28, 1863, due to being a minor. By April 20, 1864, he had re-enlisted as a private in B.L. Fairnholt's Reserves, Company C. These reserve forces were not required to perform any service outside of Virginia. Shortly after his enlistment, his unit was called to permanent duty and received the same pay and allowances as other state troops. After the war Sutherland returned to Richmond where he again assisted his father as a gunsmith until 1870 when he returned to Baltimore. He received this Southern Cross of Honor from the General Robert E. Lee Chapter No. 2043 of Baltimore, United Daughters of the Confederacy. On August 19, 1902, he was inducted into the Society of the Army and Navy of the Confederate States in the State of Maryland.

MARYLAND VETERAN'S BADGE. This is the badge of the Society of the Army and Navy of the Confederate States in the State of Maryland. The top bar was for the engraving of the veteran's name. From the bar hangs a silk red and white ribbon, blue enameled upper arms of the Maryland cross containing "A & N C.S. Md", and a battle flag containing 13 stars which is inscribed with 1861 and 1865. The society was the largest of the 31 Confederate veterans camps in this state and was organized in 1871.

FATHER AND SON IN THEIR CONFEDERATE VETERAN UNIFORMS. Levin Lake Sr. (1817/1911), seated, and Albert Crawford Lake (1844/1908) - Cabinet card - Levin Lake Sr. was born at Oxford in Dorchester County. He moved to Jackson, Tennessee, and later to Grenada, Mississippi. When the war began he received an appointment as post quartermaster for equipping state troops and was commissioned a captain. In 1863 he was ordered to Texas to handle Confederate cotton moving through Brownsville to Mexico, the profits from which he used to purchase quartermaster supplies. Returning to Mississippi, he was assigned to duty on the Mississippi River forwarding supplies to Montgomery. After the fall of Atlanta, he was ordered to Grenada where he was forced to surrender at his home. Of the nine children born to Levin Sr. and Harriet N. Crawford Lake, three sons saw service in the Confederacy: Levin Jr., in the Army of Northern Virginia; Charles Henry, who served as a bugler, and Albert Crawford, a private in Stanford's Battery, Mississippi Light Artillery. After his battery was organized at Grenada, Albert saw service with General Polk in Kentucky and Tennessee. After the Battle of Shiloh he was sent home sick but later was able to return to his unit. In front of Atlanta he received a chest wound which furloughed him for 30 days. After the fall of Mobile when Choctaw Bluffs were abandoned, the battery was moved to Meridian where Albert surrendered on May 5, 1865. He made his home in Crystal Springs, Mississippi.

Maryland Cavalry Camp, to 1,100 in the Society of the Army and the Navy of the Confederate States in the State of Maryland.

Charles Worthington Dorsey, a resident of the Maryland Line Confederate Soldiers Home at Pikesville, was missing and no one knew his whereabouts. After about a week he suddenly reappeared wearing the uniform of a Union soldier. When questioned he replied that he had impersonated a Yankee veteran and applied for orders at the Union Soldiers Home. He stayed there a short while because he said he just wanted to see how those damn old rascals lived.

James Innis Randolph, the author of "I Am a Good Old Rebel," wrote the poem in complete bitterness, but today it is taken in humor. Randolph always considered himself an unwhipped Confederate.

John R. Stonebreaker wrote "I am not one of those to half apologize by saying that we fought for what we believed to be right. I think that we fought for what was right, and I have never had a regret for the part that I took in the strife." Sydnan Bailey wrote in his last days in the Maryland Line Confederate Soldiers Home, "When I pitch my tent on the eternal campground, I can truthfully say that I am proud that I was a Confederate soldier and have no excuse to offer anyone."

MARYLAND UNITED CONFEDERATE VETERAN'S FLAG. The dark blue silk banner bears the 1854 state seal flanked by the Confederate 1st National flag and the St. Andrews flag on the reverse. The obverse contains the battle flag with "1861 TO 1865" above and "Manassas To Appomattox" below. It has gold fringe on three sides, flag tassels and is on the original pole.

Other Available Published Works by Daniel D. Hartzler
To order: P.O. Box 249, New Windsor, MD 21776
Add $3.00 per book for shipping and handling

ARMS MAKERS OF MARYLAND (Shumway Longrifle Series) $45.00

Biographical data of more than 500 arms makers from the 1600s through the 1880s. An abundance of illustrations of all types of weapons. 310 pages.

MEDICAL DOCTORS OF MARYLAND IN THE C.S.A. $25.00

Biographical data on 207 physicians along with a list of 59 Confederate veterans who became licensed practitioners after the war. It serves as a resource book about medicine during the Civil War. It contains many illustrations. 98 pages, soft-bound, 2nd edition.

MARYLANDERS IN THE CONFEDERACY $25.00

Exhaustive listing of 12,000 men giving name, unit, highest rank, residence and 1670 reference sources. 420 pages including 75 pages of narrative, soft-bound, 3rd printing.

CONFEDERATE PRESENTATION
AND INSCRIBED SWORDS AND REVOLVERS $35.00

Personal sketches; prolific photographs of swords, pistols and knives that were presented to, inscribed for, or associated with Southern patriots. 369 pages.

MARYLAND LONGRIFLES $45.00

Profusely illustrated with 784 photographs which study geographical areas and their various trends. It emphasizes 160 longrifle producers along with 278 new gunsmiths. 400 pages.

Index

A

Albaugh, Ira H.	1
Albaugh, John W.	1
Albert, A. James, Jr.	217
Aldridge, J. West	64
Allison, Richard Taylor	93, 95, 164
Anderson, Richard T.	4
Anderson, Samuel W.	4
Andrews, Richard Snowden	35, 36, 40, 152, 171, 173
Archer, James J.	3, 9
Archer, Robert H.	26
Athey, James	58
Avirett, James B.	103

B

Bailey, Sydnan	223
Bailey, William Thomas	139
Ball, Dabney	106
Barnes, George D.	129
Barnes, Jacob Smallwood	146
Barney, Joseph Nicholas	91, 163
Barry, Edmund	55, 67
Bayly, Alexander Hamilton	39
Beall, Lloyd James	93, 95, 164
Bean, W. B.	38
Beatty, Edward W.	48
Bell, Alexander T.	98
Bellinger, Lucius	97
Benedict, Howard	94
Bennett, John W.	86, 130-132, 209
Best, Emory Fiske	3
Biser, Charles Tilghman	176
Biser, William Doddridge	176
Bishop, Elijah W.	56
Bispham, Stacy B.	64
Blackford, Eugene	105
Blackistone, Thomas	67
Blakiston, Willmington	186
Blanchard, James C.	60
Blessing, John P.	8
Bond, Frank A.	23
Bond, John Thomas	138
Booker, Thomas	65
Boone, William C.	209
Booth, George Wilson	86, 144, 153, 175
Boteler, Robert H. E.	26
Bouchelt, J. M.	14
Bowie, Thomas Fielder, Jr.	28
Bowie, Walter	64
Brand, Robert	133
Brandenburg, Jesse W.	56
Breathed, James	36, 42, 54, 55, 98, 101
Breckinridge, Cary	97
Brent, Joseph Lancaster	9, 133
Briggs, Daniel	95
Briggs, William	95
Brisco, Henry	205
Briscoe, David Stone	62
Briscoe, John Hanson	150
Brockenborough, John Bowyer	37
Brogden, Harry Hale	39
Broughton, Thomas	205
Brown, John	21
Brown, John A.	20
Brown, Ridgely	46, 52, 123
Browne, Eugene H.	162, 175
Buchanan, Franklin	9, 38, 41, 62, 71, 74, 85, 91, 94, 95, 130, 162, 164, 168, 169, 188, 221
Buck, Samuel D.	79, 86, 186
Burke, John M.	104
Burke, John Redmond	219
Burke, Polk	130
Burns, Arthur P.	103
Bussey, James Thomas	68, 82, 156

C

Callan, Christopher C.	203
Cameron, Stephen J.	103
Carey, Alexander G.	60
Carlisle, Daniel G.	60
Carroll, John C.	181
Carter, William Fitzhugh	87
Cary, William Miles	116
Chambers, Robert Marion, II	35, 36, 39
Charlesworth, Joshua	94
Chestney, Theodore O.	78
Chew, Robert Bowie	64
Chew, Walter S.	172
Chisolm, Julian J.	101
Claggett, Edward L.	140
Claiborne, Charles H.	109
Clark, James	203
Clark, James Louis	63, 144, 148, 149
Clarke, J. Lyle	15, 67, 112, 115, 175
Clary, Richard C.	56
Clary, Thaddeus W.	56
Clemson, John Calhoun	2
Clendenin, Alexander	97
Colston, Frederick Morgan	8, 40, 63
Colston, William E.	63, 65, 175
Colton, Lodge	188
Conrad, Thomas Norton	105, 106
Contee, Charles Snowden	40
Contee, Richard S.	40
Cooke, George Addison	151
Cooper, J. B.	95
Corbin, John W.	60
Crane, James Parran	68, 80
Crane, William S.	80
Crittenden, Churchill	219
Cross, Alexander	15
Culver, William	172

D

Dame, William Meade	106, 107
Darden, Redmond J.	94
Davis, James W.	57
Davis, T. Sturgis	54, 56, 57, 180
Dement, William F.	25
Diggs, Eugene	70
Ditty, C. Irving	144
Dixon, John T.	60
Dobbs, Thomas	130
Dodd, George W.	187
Dorsey, Charles Worthington	223
Dorsey, Edward R.	14, 15, 67, 112, 175
Dorsey, Gustavus W.	46, 86, 130
Dorsey, Hammond	47
Dorsey, Harry Woodward, Jr.	212
Dorsey, William H. B.	5, 205, 206
Douglas, Henry Kyd	73
Doyle, Joseph T.	129
Duckett, J. Gabby	217
Duval, Henry Rieman	55
Duvall, Ferdinand C.	68

E

Earnest, J. Thomas	38
Edelin, Charles Columbus	18, 35, 67, 136, 153
Ellery, Albert	68
Ellmore, George T.	51
Ellmore, John D.	51
Elzey, Arnold	9, 40, 55, 67-69, 78, 155, 173
Emack, George Malcolm	70, 178
Emack, James W.	70
Emory, Richard	3, 97
Everett, William B.	97

F

Farrell, James	19
Favour, Charles R.	54
Fay, John B.	55
Fendall, James Robert Young	94, 164
Ferry, William	20
Figg, John Hugh	129
Foley, Richard Fleming	88
Ford, Henry	7
Ford, Stephen H.	95
Foreman, Arthur L.	97
Forrest, Douglas French	92, 106, 108, 162
Forrest, Dulany A.	92
Forrest, French	162, 189
Forrest, Joseph	35, 172
Forrest, W. S.	92
Foster, John Henry	69
Freeman, Robert J.	97

G

Gaither, George Ridgely, Jr.	27, 44
Gale, Frank	37
Gale, George Littleton	37
Gale, John	37
Gallaird, Edwin Samuel	99
Gardner, William F.	106
Garretson, Frederick	191
Gatch, Thomas Benton	57, 144
Gatelry, John Thomas	160
Geiger, George	177
Gibson, Charles Bell	97
Gill, George Murray, Jr.	45
Gill, John	45, 178
Gill, Summerville P.	83
Gilmor, Harry W.	41, 50, 53, 54, 57, 70, 103, 124, 144, 147, 148, 151, 165, 179
Gilmor, Hoffman	147
Gilmor, Richard Tilghman	130, 148
Goldsborough, Robert H.	36, 39
Goldsborough, William Worthington	67, 68, 80
Gordon, Henry	5
Grayson, Spencer Monroe	83, 210
Green, Daniel Smith	100
Green, William	100
Griffin, William Hunter	15, 37
Griswold, Elias	55, 67, 72
Grogan, Charles E.	60, 156, 184
Grove, Francis Thomas	59
Gwynn, Andrew Jackson	68

H

Hack, Henry Clay	19
Hafry, John	95
Hall, Edward Howard	49, 145
Hall, Thomas William, Jr.	23, 74, 172
Hambleton, Thomas Edward	88
Hamilton, John W.	19
Hammett, Daniel	68
Hammett, David	68
Harding, Charles R.	137
Harris, W. H.	95
Harrison, Dalney Carr	104
Harrison, William H.	141
Hartigan, John L.	219
Haslett, Robert E.	21
Hawks, Wells J.	75
Hayden, Horace Edwin, Sr.	108
Hayden, John Alexander	138
Hayden, William S.	138
Hayward, Charles Eccleston	69
Hayward, Henry Peabody	207
Heiskell, J. Monroe	60
Henley, George A.	208
Henry, John C.	137, 142
Herbert, James R.	67, 79
Hering, Frank Louis	50, 181
Higdon, Francis Leonard	137
Hitzelberger, Charles Francis	178
Hitzelberger, Stephen	178
Hobbs, Nathan Chew	45
Hoffman, Richard Curzon	15, 71, 115
Holbrook, Thomas H.	19, 35, 68, 69, 128
Hollins, George N., Sr.	9
Hollyday, Henry, Sr.	143, 196, 211
Hood, John Miffin	149
Hough, Gresham	60, 145, 205, 207, 208
Hough, William Dickinson	90
Howard, Charles, Jr.	155
Howard, David Ridgely	208
Howard, Edward Lloyd	153
Howard, George W.	159
Howard, James McHenry	208

Howard, John Eager	200
Howard, McHenry	153, 159, 166, 203
Howard, Ridgly	83
Hoxton, Lywellyn Griffith	42
Hubbard, Alexander J.	138, 195
Huddleston, William G.	95
Hurst, Edward S.	63

J

Jenifer, Walter Hanson	214, 218
Jenkins, A. Polard	206
Jenkins, E. Courtney, Jr.	135-136
Jenkins, George C.	206
Jenkins, James Wilcox, Jr.	49
Jenkins, Theodore Robert, Jr.	28
Jenkins, William K.	129, 217
Johnson, Bradley Tyler	10, 20, 26, 33, 67, 80, 110, 112, 113, 119, 123, 125, 126, 136, 144, 147, 153, 156, 175, 178, 210, 212, 213
Johnson, James Thomas, Jr.	26
Johnson, Philip Preston	36
Johnson, Richard Potts	99, 127, 140
Johnston, Elliott	153, 157, 158
Jones, Albert	26
Jones, Spencer C.	134

K

Kahler, Charles Porterfield	209
Kane, George Proctor	4, 143
Kane, James C.	4
Kane, John K.	4
Keepers, Louis	67
Kemp, William H.	24
Kennedy, Styles	99
Kennon, Beverley	91, 92
Kidd, T. O. G.	27
King, Amasa W.	175
Kline, John D.	41
Knight, Louis W.	151
Knows, W.	39

L

Laird, James Winder	83
Lake, Albert Crawford	223
Lake, John Craig	139
Lake, Levin, Sr.	223
Latimer, Thomas Sargent	99, 127
Latrobe, Henry B.	35
Latrobe, Osmun	2
Lattimer, Charles W.	129
Lee, Daniel Maury	90
Lee, Philip Henry	62
Lefevre, Hamilton	58, 217
Leopold, Andrew T.	219
Lewis, John William	129
Linthicum, Charles Frederick	104
Little, Lewis H.	10
Lloyd, Daniel, Jr.	95
Love, Lucian	219
Lovell, Mansfield	10
Lynch, James I.	130
Lynn, Sprigg S.	55
Lyon, James William	71

M

Macgill, Charles	97, 99, 100, 204
Macgill, Charles G. W.	99, 100
Mackall, William W.	10
Maddox, William J.	67
Manning, Richard I.	78
Marmaduke, Henry H.	163
Marmilstein, Adolphus F.	89
Marshall, Charles	73
Martin, James	18
Mason, Dan Murray	60
Mason, John Thompson	89, 212
Mason, John Thompson O.	89
Maxwell, John Thomas	103
McAleer, Joseph L.	68
McBlair, Charles Henry	91
McCahan, J. H.	95
McCool, Dennis	175
McCoy, Harry	67
McDonald, Daniel M.	176
McIntosh, David Gregg	35, 135, 151
McKim, Randolph Harrison	103, 104, 152
McKim, Robert Breckenridge	175
McVeigh, Richard Newton	60, 61
Meiere, Julius Ernest	94, 164, 191
Mercer, T. Douglas	1
Miles, Francis T.	133
Mitchell, James Jackson	60
Montgomery, J. Norris	35
Morfit, Mason	166, 168
Morgan, James Morris	91, 188
Murdoch, James Cambell	165, 193, 207
Murphy, Richard Davis	61
Murray, Alexander	119, 140
Murray, Clapham	81, 119, 140
Murray, Edward	75
Murray, William Henry	15, 62, 67, 68, 80, 81, 83, 140, 168, 175
Myrick, John D.	67

N

Nelson, Rawling W.	178
Nicholas, William	44
Nicholas, Wilson Carey	24, 67
Nickerson, Charles E. V.	97
Nickoles, Thomas	95
Noal, James	95
Norris, George Smith	77
Norris, William	72

P

Page, John Randolph	99
Parker, William Harwar	87, 130
Parsons, Daniel	94
Parsons, Joseph	94
Paxson, Charles	65
Pearre, Aubrey	41
Pearre, Charles Baer	41
Pearre, Charles Morgan	41
Pearre, Oliver Hazzard	41
Pearson, James F.	15, 83
Pendleton, John S.	125
Peter, Walter Gibson	218
Peters, George	13, 99

230 - Index

Phillips, William F., Jr.	94
Phipps, John S.	124
Pielert, George H.	128, 160, 161, 189
Pitt, Hosea	138, 195
Polk, William Stewart	175
Pollock, James Dickson	58
Poole, Dennis H.	77
Pope, William Henry	212
Post, John Eager Howard	144
Pratt, Thomas St. George	164, 191
Price, Frank S.	18
Price, Thomas A.	76
Price, William C.	205, 207, 219
Purnall, George Washington	53

R

Raborg, Samuel A.	97
Raleigh, William H. H.	165, 167
Ramsay, Henry Ashton	91, 92
Randolph, James Innis	77, 223
Rasin, William Independence	122, 182
Redwood, Allen C.	48
Rhett, Thomas Smith	19, 173
Rich, Edward R.	105
Richardson, William H.	125
Riddle, A. J.	7
Ridgley, Charles	24
Ridgley, John	130
Riggs, Joshua	60
Ritter, George W.	24
Ritter, William L.	5, 38, 129, 152
Robertson, Henry G.	76
Robertson, Michael Stone	67
Robertson, William Wirt	36
Robinson, Claiborne	60
Rowen, John B.	38
Rust, Charles P.	183
Ryan, William Henry	71, 119
Ryan, William R.	189

S

Schacleford, Durand	166, 167
Schacleford, Elzey D.	167
Schaeffer, Francis B.	67
Schwartz, Augustus F.	144
Scott, John Emory	166
Selby, James	19
Sellman, Alonzo	52
Sellman, John Poole	52, 211
Sellman, Wallace	52
Semmes, Raphael	10, 85, 91, 92, 130, 162, 190
Semmes, Warfield P.	78
Severe, Francis M.	180
Severe, John O.	180
Shanks, Danial	36, 55, 129
Shellman, George K.	26
Shepard, Richard H.	176
Shepherd, Henry E.	74
Sherwin, Thomas	46
Skinner, Frederick Gustavus	75
Skinner, William Dorsey	82
Slater, Henry	60
Slinghoff, Fielder C.	144
Smith, Allen P.	97
Smith, J. Henry	60
Smith, J. Louis	67, 68
Smith, James Henley	76
Smith, John Donnell	36, 154, 174, 213
Smith, William	83
Smith, William H.	210, 211
Snowden, John Hudson	198
Snowden, Nicholas	28, 33
Sollers, Summerfield	212
Sothorn, Webster H.	35
Spencer, John Chapman	218
Sprigg, Richard Lamar	79
Spurrier, Grafton D.	14
Sterett, Isaac S.	91, 94, 116
Sterett, James Samuel	91, 135
Steuart, George Hume, Jr.	10, 37, 56, 67, 69, 76, 110, 126, 127, 152, 195
Steuart, Harry A.	217, 218
Steuart, William F., Jr.	218
Steuart, William Frederick, Sr.	217, 218
Stonebreaker, John R.	223
Stump, Herman	26
Sulivane, Clement	74, 117, 221
Sullivan, John	21
Sutherland, Joel Barlow	222
Symington, Thomas Alexander	41
Symington, William Stuart	130, 215

T

Talbot, Joshua Frederick Cocky	147
Tarr, Charles T.	36
Taylor, Algernon S.	93, 95, 164, 191, 195
Taylor, I. S.	94
Taylor, John H.	129
Thelin, William T.	120
Thomas, James William	186
Thomas, Allen E.	11
Thomas, Daniel L., Jr.	6, 60
Thomas, George	166, 168
Thomas, Jacob G.	26
Thomas, James William	168
Thomas, Richard Zarvona	67, 86, 138, 165, 168
Thompson, Ignatius Davis	97
Thurston, James	191
Tilghman, Lloyd, Sr.	11
Tilghman, Ogle S.	67
Tolson, Thomas H.	154
Torsh, John W.	68
Trail, Charles M.	83
Trimble, Isaac Ridgeway	11, 19, 22, 38, 63, 64, 71, 73, 74, 162, 221
Trippe, Andrew Cross	160, 221
Trundle, Joseph	213
Trundle, William	62
Tunis, Theophalius	178
Turner, James	21
Turner, William H.	65
Tyler, Charles S.	11
Tyson, Henry H.	163

W

Waddell, James Iredall	85, 86, 92, 164
Wagner, Gustavus	95
Walker, Samuel T.	18
Walters, William C.	67

Warfield, Milton — 27
Waring, James, Jr. — 213
Warren, Edward — 97, 101
Waters, Hugh T. — 63
Watson, J. R. — 60
Webb, H. W. — 130
Webb, Lewis — 212
Welsh, Warner Griffith — 47, 107, 185
West, Nelson Grey — 166, 169
Weston, J. Alden — 13, 63, 67, 91, 112, 135, 175

Wharton, Jesse W. — 217
Wheeler, James R. — 134
White, Benjamin S. — 27
White, David G. — 59
White, Elijah Veirs — 50, 51, 57, 185, 186
White, James McKinney — 82
White, Samuel C. — 27
Williams, Bodisco — 3
Williams, John — 36
Williams, Ned — 130
Williams, Thomas H. — 97
Williams, Thomas P., Jr. — 50
Williamson, James J. — 8, 180
Williamson, John B. — 54
Wilson, Frederick S. — 146
Wilson, George — 150
Wilson, Robert — 21
Wiltshire, James Jerald — 64
Winder, Charles Sidney — 11, 112, 153, 166, 191
Winder, John Henry — 11, 67, 119, 155, 188
Wise, Charles B. — 187
Wise, Henry A. — 187
Wood, John Taylor — 91, 169
Wood, William — 19
Worthington, Eugene, Sr. — 37
Wright, Daniel Giraud — 60, 62
Wright, Robert — 95

Y

Young, Alexander — 140, 169, 218
Young, William Proby, Jr. — 98

Z

Zacharias, John Forney — 100
Zimmerson, G. H. — 21
Zollinger, Jacob E. — 83
Zollinger, William P. — 83, 204, 205

SURGICAL STAFF.

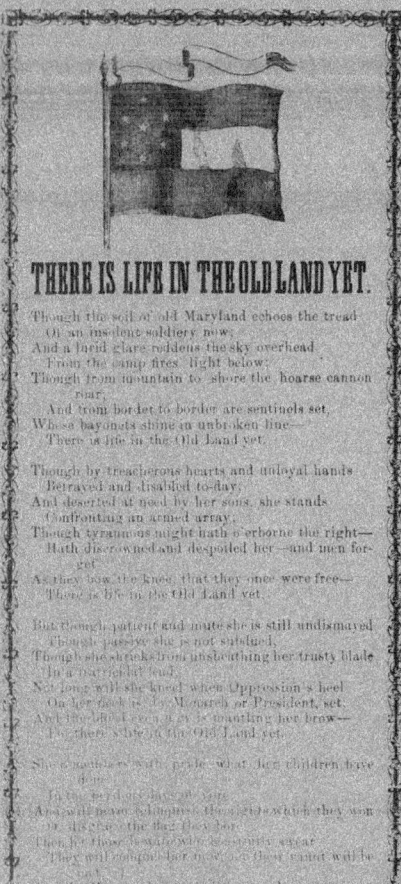

THERE IS LIFE IN THE OLD LAND YET.

Though the soil of old Maryland echoes the tread
    Of an insolent soldiery, now;
And a lurid glare reddens the sky overhead
    From the camp fires' light below;
Though from mountain to shore the hoarse cannon
        roar,
    And from border to border are sentinels set,
Whose bayonets shine in unbroken line—
    There is life in the Old Land yet.

Though by treacherous hearts and unloyal hands
    Betrayed and disabled to-day;
And deserted at need by her sons, she stands
    Confronting an armed array;
Though tyrannous might hath o'erborne the right—
    Hath discrowned and despoiled her—and men for-
        get
As they bow the knee, that they once were free—
    There is life in the Old Land yet.

But though patient and mute she is still undismayed,
    Though passive she is not subdued,
Though she shrinks from unsheathing her trusty blade
    In a fratricidal feud,
Not long will she kneel when Oppression's heel
    On her neck is by Monarch or President set,
And the nobler sons are a-mounting her brow—
    For there's life in the Old Land yet.

She'll mothers watch with pride what their children have
        done,
    In the victories they've won,
And will hoar exultingly the tale which they soon
    To their children's children will tell,
Then let those who would with security wear
    They will forgive her now, nor their taunt will be
        met

And her Maryland men shall be heard in accents—
    For there's still life in the Old Land yet.

The Exiled Soldier's
Adieu to Maryland.

Air—"Bertrand's Adieu to France."

Adieu my home! Adieu dear Maryland!
    For honor calls me now away from thee;
To end my days within my native land,
    Has ever been the sweetest hope to me,
But tyrants trample thee into the dust,
    And drive me forth to fight, but still for thee,
My sword shall not ingloriously rust;
    Exiled, I swear to die, or set thee free!

I love my home, I love its mountains blue,
    Its sea-washed shores, its vales, its pleasant fields,
And its fair cities; and the brave and true,
    Who bared unarmed their breasts as Freedom's shields
But leaving all I place in God my trust,
    And go to battle for the right and thee;
My sword shall not ingloriously rust;
    Exiled, I swear to die, or set thee free!

Adieu dear hearts! Ah! Mother, Sister, Wife!
    One tear at parting, and one heart-felt sigh
For brothers still in chains and then to strife,
    Where free we conquer, or still free we die.
Hope on, then Maryland, God still is just,
    For battle and love, and Freedom wait for thee!
My sword shall not ingloriously rust;
    Exiled, I swear to die, or set thee free.

THE BATTLE SONG
OF THE
MARYLAND LINE.

To arms! to arms! the fight's begun.
    Virginia sounds the call;
Her soil with heroes' blood is damp,
It echoes to the hirelings' tramp,
    Arouse ye, one and all!

For gold let Lincoln's legions fight,
    Or plunder's bloody gain;
Unbribed, unbought, our swords we draw,
To guard our rights, to save our law,
    Nor shall we strike in vain.

We leave awhile our native shores,
    A band of brothers true,
The Southern cause we will defend,
And battle for it to the end,
    Against the tyrant's crew.

To arms! to arms! the battle waits,
    Shall vengeance call in vain?
The foe is master in our home,
Our brethren wait until we come,
    To break their galling chain.

Shall we, too, bend the stubborn head,
    In Freedom's temple born?
No! rather famine, wounds and death,
No we can draw untainted breath,
    And hurl back force with scorn.

To arms! the cause is ours to win;
    Our homes are still to save!
To arms! our brethren are in chains,
The tyrant's hirelings tread our plains,
    Arm! Freedom or the grave!

Farewell awhile to home and friends!
    Adieu each tender tie!
Resolved, we mingle in the tide,
Where charging squadrons furious ride.
    To conquer or to die.

To arms! to arms! "Old Maryland!"
    High sounds the battle call!
Combined by Honor's sacred tie,
Our word is LAW AND LIBERTY!
    March forward, one and all!

THE FLAG.

The Stars and Stripes! is that the flag the Northern
        army waves,
To make ignoble races free, and noble nations
        slaves?
The Stars and Stripes! and shall they dare to quell
        us with a name
That we ourselves have proudly placed upon the
        heights of Fame?
Oh! constant rather to the deeds than to the flag are
        we,
Of Virginia's glorious rebels, her Washington and
        Lee.
Yet, by that flag which Lawrence loved (New Jer-
        sey's gallant son)
I charge you think how by his side, our Shubrick
        fought and won.
McDonough's, Henly's courage, the Stars and
        Stripes maintained,
When the English struck their colors, and the broad
        Champlain was gained.
By Southern valor guarded, by Southern heroes
        led,
Those Stars shone bright in Mexico, o'er hosts of
        vanquished dead.
And generous Tatnall, Ingraham brave, have made
        that flag a sign
Of refuge for oppression, though born and sheer
        combine.
Yes—prize that flag, New England! our glory cling-
        eth yet,
But the nobler one, I swear, if you the heritage
        forget.
It is strong to crush oppression, but I will sunder
        the band,
Which bears it 'gainst a Brother, defending home
        and land
Reclaim the shame, brave Maryland of glory in thy
        folds;
No longer the true Southern stand its honor now
        upholds;
So fail it, like the flower, apace the unreborn
        name
The blessing of the free, o'er them the southern
        Flag shall claim.